REGARDING
LIFE

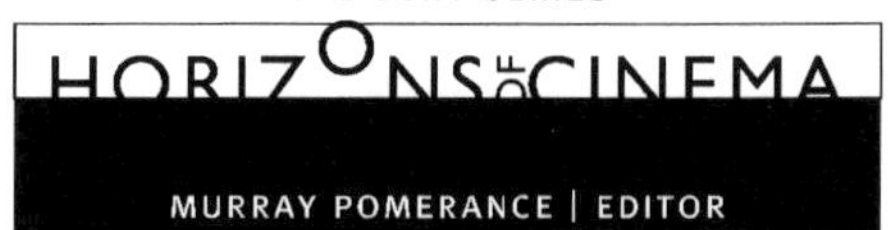

Also in the series

William Rothman, editor, *Cavell on Film*

J. David Slocum, editor, *Rebel Without a Cause*

Joe McElhaney, *The Death of Classical Cinema*

Kirsten Moana Thompson, *Apocalyptic Dread*

Frances Gateward, editor, *Seoul Searching*

Michael Atkinson, editor, *Exile Cinema*

Paul S. Moore, *Now Playing*

Robin L. Murray and Joseph K. Heumann, *Ecology and Popular Film*

William Rothman, editor, *Three Documentary Filmmakers*

Sean Griffin, editor, *Hetero*

Jean-Michel Frodon, editor, *Cinema and the Shoah*

Carolyn Jess-Cooke and Constantine Verevis, editors, *Second Takes*

Matthew Solomon, editor, *Fantastic Voyages of the Cinematic Imagination*

R. Barton Palmer and David Boyd, editors, *Hitchcock at the Source*

William Rothman, *Hitchcock: The Murderous Gaze, Second Edition*

Joanna Hearne, *Native Recognition*

Marc Raymond, *Hollywood's New Yorker*

Steven Rybin and Will Scheibel, editors, *Lonely Places, Dangerous Ground*

Claire Perkins and Constantine Verevis, editors, *B Is for Bad Cinema*

Dominic Lennard, *Bad Seeds and Holy Terrors*

Rosie Thomas, *Bombay before Bollywood*

Scott M. MacDonald, *Binghamton Babylon*

Sudhir Mahadevan, *A Very Old Machine*

David Greven, *Ghost Faces*

James S. Williams, *Encounters with Godard*

William H. Epstein and R. Barton Palmer, editors,
Invented Lives, Imagined Communities

Lee Carruthers, *Doing Time*

Rebecca Meyers, William Rothman and Charles Warren, editors,
Looking with Robert Gardner

REGARDING LIFE

ANIMALS AND THE DOCUMENTARY MOVING IMAGE

BELINDA SMAILL

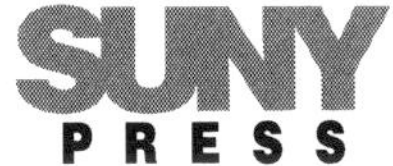

Cover Image: *Sweetgrass* (2009), directed by Ilsa Barbash and Lucien Castaing-Taylor. Courtesy of Harvard Sensory Ethnography Lab/The Kobal Collection

Published by
STATE UNIVERSITY OF NEW YORK PRESS, ALBANY

© 2016 State University of New York

For information, contact
STATE UNIVERSITY OF NEW YORK PRESS, ALBANY, NY
www.sunypress.edu

Production, Laurie D. Searl
Marketing, Anne M. Valentine

Library of Congress Cataloging-in-Publication Data

Names: Smaill, Belinda. author.
Title: Regarding life : animals and the documentary moving image / Belinda Smaill.
Description: Albany : State University of New York Press, [2016] | Series: SUNY series, horizons of cinema | Includes bibliographical references and index.
Identifiers: LCCN 2016007286 (print) | LCCN 2016015188 (ebook) | ISBN 9781438462493 (hardcover : alk. paper) | ISBN 978-1-4384-6248-6 (pbk. : alk. paper) | ISBN 9781438462509 (e-book)
Subjects: LCSH: Documentary films—History and criticism. | Animals in motion pictures.
Classification: LCC PN1995.9.D6 S555 2016 (print) | LCC PN1995.9.D6 (ebook) | DDC 070.1/8--dc23
LC record available at https://lccn.loc.gov/2016007286

10 9 8 7 6 5 4 3 2 1

Contents

List of Illustrations

Acknowledgments

A number of people have contributed to the writing of this book in a number of different ways. Portions of the book have benefited from specific feedback and on this count my heartfelt thanks go to André Dias, E.J. Cartledge, Guinevere Narraway, Scott Richmond (in his capacity as the editor of a special issue of *Film Criticism*) and special thanks to Kelly Donati. Others have offered support, encouragement, and time at crucial moments during the development of the project and for this I thank Therese Davis, Julia Vassilieva, Con Verevis, Rebecca Hill, Lesley Stern, Tania Lewis, and Patrick Smaill. Over the course of writing a number of research assistants have given their time and energy, especially Kirsten Stevens and Rob Letizi. My colleagues in Film and Screen Studies at Monash University have been consistent in offering the intellectual community that is vital for any scholarship to flourish in the present day academy.

The three anonymous reviewers for State University of New York Press read the manuscript with great care and generosity and I greatly appreciate their feedback. Their insights have been vital in bringing the project to its fullest fruition. I would also like to thank Murray Pomerance for his encouragement and careful reading. I thank Alexa Weik von Mossner for organizing the "Moving Environments: Affect, Emotion and Ecocinema" workshop at the Rachel Carson Center for Environment and Society in Munich in 2011. This event planted the seed of an idea from which the book grew. It has been an undertaking close to my heart for the past three years and over difficult times.

A version of chapter 3, titled "New Food Documentary: Animals, Identification and the Citizen Consumer," has been published in *Film Criticism* 39.2 (2015): 79–102. Portions of chapter 1 and chapter 2 have been published in an essay, titled "Documentary Film and Animal Modernity in *Raw Herring* and *Sweetgrass*," in *Australian Humanities Review 57* (2014).

Belinda Smaill
November 2015

Chapter 1

Introduction

Released in 2005, *March of the Penguins* (*La Marche de l'empereur*), a French film about the cyclical mating habits of Antarctica's emperor penguins, became the second highest grossing documentary in cinema history. *Grizzly Man* was also released in 2005 and it became a breakthrough film of a different kind—it brought the work of German auteur, Werner Herzog, to a wide audience and became one of the most discussed and critically acclaimed documentaries of the decade. While employing very different approaches, the two films share a fascination with nature as an arena for storytelling with animals playing a central role. Herzog began his next documentary, the Oscar winning *Encounters at the End of the World* (2007) set in Antarctica, with the proclamation that he was not going to "come up with another film about penguins." The reference to the French documentary was clear to most—penguins had become draw cards of the big (and small) screen.

Although penguins have achieved particular star status, the allure of documentaries focused on animals has extended well beyond this single species. *March of the Penguins* and *Grizzly Man* represent two high-profile examples that punctuate a much broader terrain of television and film. Referring to wildlife and nature onscreen, Gregg Mitman makes the case that there is a contemporary "green wave" of film and television, enabled by the popular penchant for "eco-chic" (214), underpinned by not only commercial, but also ethical and environmental concerns. He cites that of the "$631 million in gross revenues earned by 275 documentaries released between 2002 and 2006, $163.1 came from eight wildlife documentaries" (216). Another term that has gained momentum in the popular press is "eco-doc" or "eco-documentary," which describes a broader body of films tasked with critiquing corporate dominance and investigating and advocating on issues concerning the decimation of the environment and its natural resources.[1] Bringing a critical perspective to this body of films, Helen

Hughes identifies its iconography and principle characters, posing the environmental documentary as a distinct subgenre (*Green Documentary*, 7–9). These developments in the documentary representation of environment and animals dovetail with the increased popularity and circulation of feature-length documentaries more broadly over the past two decades.

The period Mitman describes, 2002–2006, was a particularly important phase for the genre, labeled by scholars and the popular press as a "boom" or "renaissance" in documentary.[2] A cluster of documentaries achieved unprecedented box office success over this time; however, beyond a small number of French and British films this group was overwhelmingly American.[3] While commentators are still, albeit with less regularity, proclaiming a new era for documentary, *Fahrenheit 9/11* (2004) and *March of the Penguins* have maintained their position as the most commercially successful documentaries produced in decades. Nevertheless, nature documentaries, especially those produced under the Disneynature brand, are following closely behind.[4] Further, while other examples of "animal-led" documentaries such as *Blackfish* (2013) and *Darwin's Nightmare* (2004) may not rank in lists of high-grossing films, they have found sizable audiences on the festival circuit and DVD distribution.

While the documentary boom and the subsequent decade have proven to be a significant time for animals onscreen, to focus on the growing (commercial) prestige and high circulation won by a small group of feature-length documentaries is to recognize only a fraction of a wider phenomenon. This book demarcates the contours of a rapidly expanding documentary terrain in which the representation of animals is becoming markedly more complex and multilayered. There is a new tide of ecologically inspired film work that expands beyond blue chip nature documentaries and beyond the auteurist vision of Werner Herzog. It includes a range of wildlife natural history film and television, advocacy documentary, avant-garde nonfiction and developments in new media. Observing this breadth, I am less concerned with proposing a new subgenre than exploring a certain momentum that exists across a range of nonfiction modes and approaches.

The energy of this impulse to represent the nonhuman[5] is also genre-specific—documentary is increasingly the preeminent format for rendering nature, especially animals, onscreen. Moreover, one of the most striking features of these films is the growing emphasis on paradigmatic debates about anthropogenic knowledge or use of animal life, whether it concerns food, agriculture, science, exploration, or species loss. The growing awareness in the twenty-first century of the human impact on the nonhuman world has influenced this contemporary archive of documentary. Films and filmmakers have become centrally concerned with the intersection between the institutions and practices of modernity and the life and death of nonhuman animals.

This book elucidates how the momentum of film and media I have described works to structure knowledge of animals and the relations between humans and animals in the contemporary epoch. It begins with the question of how particular films instantiate humans and animals and to what ends—do they center the human in familiar ways, supporting anthropocentrism, or do they offer examples of animal difference, suggesting avenues for the recognition of the distinctiveness of animal being in ways that question the privileging of human identity? Cinema functions across multiple and intertwined registers, engaging both the cerebral/political and the intimate/corporeal. I propose an approach to this question of anthropocentrism that perceives cinema as an aesthetic practice, a social artifact that trades in ideology and cultural norms and a medium that inheres with sensuous meaning, sustaining a sensory and epistemological relation with the viewer. By the end of this book it should be clear how nonfiction examples appeal to the horizon of experience of viewers in ways that reference the history and conventions of documentary film, the desire and expectation it evokes. An inquiry that explores how animals are recognized or disavowed, how nonhuman life is regarded, observed, or acknowledged and, crucially, how it is respected in its otherness, is pivotal to an understanding of the contemporary role of the moving image.

Rather than simply examining how animals onscreen are visualized, this approach coalesces around the proposition that the systems of knowledge that produce debates about life and its uses subjectify humans and animals. This notion dovetails with the idea that both humans and animals are positioned and made sense of by the apparatus of cinema, and other media, and the conditions of reception. Fully grasping this concept relies on identifying the human subject-centric or anthropomorphic conventions of film and documentary in particular. For Adrian Ivakhiv, cinema is anthropomorphic "because film shows us human or human-like subjects, beings we understand to be thrown into a world of circumstance and possibility like us" (9). Building on Ivakhiv's formulation, I argue that the task for cinema and media studies, in thinking beyond the human, is to consider anew how the properties and economies of documentary center the human, relying on its form and subjectivity for identification and social purchase. Only through interrogating this powerful anthropocentric impulse is it possible to theorize the fissures in this representational order and ascertain documentary cinema's capacity to show and express all life, not only the human.

Film Studies and the Nonhuman

Growing constellations of scholarship are wrestling with how to understand the nexus of film or media and the nonhuman environment. One of the most influential studies has been Sean Cubitt's *EcoMedia* (2005), a book that follows multiple theoretical pathways in order to explore the problem of technology and mediation in relation to ecological thought and environmental politics. Cubitt identifies developments across media forms media since the 1980s. This work poses new interdisciplinary conceptual tools with which to consider the mutually constitutive relation between nature, technology, and the human, largely through examining popular cultural texts, including blue chip natural history film.[6] I take inspiration from Cubitt's interdisciplinarity, but argue for the value of considering a more specific field of production and circulation, elucidating the documentary as a discreet form with particular histories (intellectual and industrial) and modes of audience address. There are specific pleasures and expectations associated with nonfiction that warrant a close examination of the documentary form in its different guises.

John Blewitt's *Media, Ecology and Conservation: Using the Media to Protect the World's Wildlife and Ecosystems* (2010) addresses the media as an even broader phenomena, attending to photography, advertising, the Internet, and television. Within this he focuses on a number of important documentary examples, again including blue chip wildlife films. Blewitt is chiefly concerned with the potential for media to operate pedagogically, examining media literacy and the role of communication in the conservation movement across international sites. With its concentration on politics and animals, Blewitt shares with my study a sense of responsibility to our "nonhuman others" (11). He elaborates on this responsibility by determining how conservation movements gain purchase in the public sphere. Helen Hughes offers the first book-length study of environmental documentary, bringing much needed attention to the genre. Like Blewitt, she takes up the problem of communication, couching her work in debates about environmental education and psychology. The concise body of documentary she discusses is assessed in relation to questions of rhetoric and argumentation, rather than the narrative and aesthetic work of genre.

This book is not only more concerned with animals, but also more attuned to documentary aesthetics than the work of Cubitt, Blewitt, or Hughes. It draws on film studies and documentary studies with a view to considering the properties, circulation, and history of the form, while also extending the boundaries of the genre as they are normatively understood.

Scott MacDonald has been one scholar to consistently address the aesthetics of the moving image in shaping our perception of place and nonhuman nature. His book, *The Garden in the Machine: A Field Guide to Independent Films About Place* (2001), might be seen as an early example of eco-film criticism, one that takes historical American avant-garde cinema as its object. His recent *American Ethnographic Film and Personal Documentary: The Cambridge Turn* (2013) continues this focus, exploring pioneering approaches to ethnographic-inspired documentaries and many of the filmmakers he discusses turn their cameras to the nonhuman as much as the human world. Moreover, MacDonald explicitly advocates for an eco-cinema, an aesthetic and industrial alternative to the mainstream that might offer an "Edenic respite" ("Toward," 109) from the contemporary media apparatus. I take a cue from MacDonald in observing the importance of a film historical perspective, one that values traditions and conventions of filmmaking and what can be gained by understanding the changing form and circulation of images. Unlike MacDonald's work, however, this study encompasses both the alternative and the mainstream, making a case for the importance of popular culture in the field of documentary culture.

I use the conditional phrasing "documentary moving image" not to isolate a single (visual) dimension, but to indicate that many of the examples I discuss fall outside documentary proper. They either predate the invention of the term in the 1920s or sit as much in categories of new media, television, or avant-garde and essay film. The following chapters explore an array of forms of nonfiction, both valued and devalued, in order to find productive sites where the canon can be put in dialogue with popular commercial cinema (or consumer-generated content). The most relevant of these "devalued" forms, for my purposes, is wildlife film and television, particularly in its "Disneyfied" expression. In a 1998 essay Derek Bousé makes a case that while the film industry and television schedules nominate "documentary" as the preferred category for wildlife film, in accounts of film history and in film and media studies more widely this mode, beyond some notable exceptions, has been excluded because it occupies an ambiguous location ("Are Wildlife Films," 116). Bousé discusses this ambiguity in terms of the assumed disparities between wildlife film and that of documentary, most notably the perceived lack of social relevance of "nature films" and their associations with entertainment, artifice, and fictionalized storytelling ("Are Wildlife Films," 118–132). Since the time Bousé made these observations a number of scholars have critically engaged with wildlife and natural history film and television, instituting it as a subfield of film and media studies and distinguishing the diverse makeup of this category.[7] Despite this attention, the form continues to sit outside the field of documentary studies, attracting little interest from documentary scholars.

Jan-Christopher Horak's article, "Wildlife Documentaries: From Classical Forms to Reality TV," crucially intervenes in the erasure of wildlife film from the canon of documentary film studies. Horak brings the weight of archival research to his survey, bringing early cinema, television documentary, and reality television under the umbrella of documentary. In charting the transformation of the narratives that structure wildlife film, Horak identifies and critiques strategies of anthropomorphism that are a feature of increasingly entertainment-oriented wildlife film and media. In a different way, Cynthia Chris's influential book, *Watching Wildlife* (2006), maps the development of wildlife as a distinct moving image form, firmly establishing the significance of wildlife film and television as "a prism through which we can examine investments in dominant ideologies of humanity and animality, nature and culture, sex, and race" (xiv). This book builds both on Chris's assertion and the attention to documentary traditions in Horak's work while taking in a broader notion of the animal in documentary, including and moving beyond animals in the wild.

While I explore examples from an array of moving image contexts, all confront the intricacies and challenges posed by anthropocentrism and its manifestation in cultural artifacts. Chapters thus contribute to a groundswell of critical approaches in animal studies, a body of interdisciplinary scholarship that has been referred to as the "animal turn."[8] The most influential pockets of this work emerge from Continental philosophy and are occupied with the being of animal life, the distinctions between humans and animals and the status of animals in (human) society and culture. Anat Pick has been a decisive figure in bringing a consideration of critical animal studies to bear on film studies analysis. In her groundbreaking work, *Creaturely Poetics: Animality and Vulnerability in Literature and Film* (2011),[9] Pick formulates an account that is founded in extensionism (extending moral considerations to animals), and the recognition of the corporeality and vulnerability of animal existence (*Creaturely*, 2–3). *Creaturely Poetics* establishes a mode of scholarship that this study is indebted to—it brings the question of the animal to cinema by foregrounding poetics and acknowledging the central role of aesthetics and form in unmasking the anthropocentrism of cinema. This poetics is one that recognizes the significance of embodiment and vulnerable animal materiality. For Pick, "notions of embodiment—the material, the anonymous, and the elemental—provide a powerful antidote to anthropocentrism" (*Creaturely*, 6). Moreover, she examines key documentary examples, such as the work of Fredric Wiseman and Werner Herzog, testifying to the importance of the genre in this context. This book orients the emphasis on aesthetic considerations established in *Creaturely Poetics* toward the sociohistorical positioning of animals while mapping a contemporary body of film work.

Finally, I wish to address Jonathan Burt's considerable contribution to the field. His 2002 book, *Animals in Film*, was the first to outline how animals might feature as a disciplinary concern in film studies and the related arena of visual culture. Elaborating on a history of moving images across a range of genres, Burt brings a cogent analysis, rich with examples, to the relationship between film, animal imagery and ethics. His book is a forerunner in a field that is still young. Nevertheless, recent analysis in film and media studies has profoundly extended how we think about animals and the environment. In turn, this book argues that we must consider the specificity and importance of the documentary form, how it powerfully shapes audience expectation and produces knowledge of the (nonhuman) world. I extend this intervention with a double-edged approach, one that asks how the materiality and immediacy of the documentary moving image *and* histories of documentary representation that work to organize and subjectify life impinge on one another to structure an address to the viewer.

From Muybridge to the Green Wave

From his perspective as an archivist and film historian, Horak describes how little attention documentary filmmakers have historically paid to animals:

> As a casual subject of moving images, animals have been present ever since Eadweard Muybridge photographed his animal locomotion series, yet within classical documentary forms, animals have seemingly remained ghettoised in the scientific and educational sphere, only intermittently the subject of mainstream theatrical experience. (460)

While animals may not be the focal point of classical documentary, their presence and meaning is understated in Horak's characterization. A focus on the cannon of historical theatrical documentary, often defined by the Griersonian tradition, Soviet cinema, and the influence of Robert Flaherty, only tells one story of documentary and its nonfiction precursors in early cinema. Science and education, more to the point, both align with what Bill Nichols, in his cardinal documentary text *Representing Reality* (1991), refers to as the "discourses of sobriety" (3). They have underpinned much documentary or nonfiction practice and were closely tied to the capacity for drama and entertainment in early cinema. These discourses informed, and made use of, representations of animals in important ways. A broader appraisal of the form must take science and education films out of the ghetto and measure their influence on dominant contemporary modes. In this respect, they sit alongside and intersect with other cinematic traditions that represent animals, such as ethnographic or travel and exploration film, the representation of labor and film surrealism, the essay film and observational cinema.

It is possible to trace a significant epistemological relationship between the nonfiction image and animals even if, at times, animals are in the margins of the frame. As Horak notes, this relationship extends back to Eadweard Muybridge's iconic and much-cited precinema proto-animations in the 1870s that captured the movement of a galloping horse, birds, and other animals. From this point, early cinema and film theory consistently drew attention to the affinities between biological life and the vitalist potential of the new form. As Chris Tedjasukmana notes, proto-cinema apparatuses were named in a manner that invoked the energy of biodiscourses: the Bioskop, Biograph, and Vitascope. He also observes "the film-theoretical fascination with cinematic vitality in the context of the history of modernity," exploring how scientific, cultural, and aesthetic exploration of the time labored under the expectation that the technology of cinema would produce a form of vitality and life. From a different perspective, in Muybridge's experiments the movement of human *and* animal bodies offered an avenue to test the capacity of the moving image to convey the dynamism of life. Moreover, these proto-cinematic devices were not only, as Elizabeth Cowie writes, "prostheses for human sight" (13), they verified the detail of the movement of living bodies to the degree that the human eye could not. They functioned as a knowledge and truth-telling instrument in a way that was tied to the phenomenon and sensation of life.

After Muybridge, animals' screen roles expand and proliferate. Thomas Edison consistently featured animals in his early actualities: *Feeding the Doves* (1896), *The Burning Stable* (1896), *Electrocuting an Elephant* (1903). Films that pose animals as vital to the exoticism of travel and adventure include the renowned *Nanook of the North* (1922) as well as a wealth of safari films (some titles include *Native Lion Hunt* [1909] and *African Animals* [1909] through to *Heia Safari* [1928], *Simba: The King of Beasts, a Saga of the African Veldt* [1928]). Animals were invariably extras in scenes depicting the vibrancy of the modern city with horses playing a starring role—this is seen most famously in *Man with a Movie Camera* (1929). Grierson's expressive depiction of the labor of fishermen, *Drifters* (1929) is aesthetically devised through the interaction between the movement of men and the movement of schools of herring. Other pivotal films include the nature experiments of prolific filmmakers Percy Smith (*The Acrobatic Fly* [1910]) and Jean Painlevé (*The Seahorse* [1934]), the formal innovations of the Oscar-winning *The Private Life of the Gannets* (1934) and the essayist surrealism of Georges Franju's *Le Sang des bêtes* (1949). In each of these examples the capacity for cinema to observe the materiality of its animal subject in space and time is crucial.

With the advent of "direct cinema" the works of Fredric Wiseman become defining works in the representation of animals in documentary with four films devoted to animals in human institutional settings: *Primate* (1974), *Meat* (1976), *Racetrack* (1984), and *Zoo* (1993). The most discussed documentary in this group is undoubtedly *Primate* and this attention is well deserved—the film offers complex and carefully crafted insight into both human and animal actions and responses. The film was shot at Yerkes Primate Research Center in Atlanta and follows the interactions between scientists and their primate subjects as they undergo testing. The experiments on the animals are largely shown without explanation or rationale. While the film is highly confronting, Wiseman's aim was not to mount a case against vivisection.[10] The film is much more engaged with telling a story, through documentary sound and image, about human *and* animal beings.[11] While portions of *Primate* work to anthropomorphize animals, it asks the viewer to regard animals by offering sustained attention to different species of primates, in particular their faces and gestures, in a way that is unparalleled in the history of nonfiction film. The documentary, and Wiseman's animal *oeuvre* more broadly, constitutes incisive work that explores social institutions in order to redraw perceptions of how animals are co-opted into human enterprise, while defamiliarizing human sociality (and perhaps even human existence) in the process.

Audiovisual representations of animals in the (nonhuman) environment appear in much greater numbers, offering a counterpoint to the representation of animals inhabiting the realm of science and industry. In his study of early wildlife photography, Matthew Brower identifies a "discursive regime of wildlife photography" (xvii) that positions animals in the wild (as distinct from domestic animals) as "real animals" (xvii) due to their function in supporting the extremes of the nature/culture divide and sustaining the assumed existential separation between humans and pristine wildlife. This separation, and the attribution of a "real" animal, denies the connectivity between all life, that humans exist on a continuum with all other animal species and inhabit a mutual planetary ecology. The wildlife genre frequently appeals to audiences precisely due to its disavowal of this connectivity. To a degree, the promise of narrative pleasure involves maintaining an emphasis on a picture of resilient and harmonious nature, insulated from the human world of sociality and progress. This promise is tied into the reasons mainstream wildlife and natural history film and television (typically constituted by high-cost productions) has been slow to take up the problem and reality of climate change. These reasons are largely industrial. Until recently "bad news" stories of environmental decline have damaged ratings.[12] Additionally, climate issues have been separated out from the core concern of zoology in the wildlife mode in order to increase its market longevity. Blewitt describes this when he notes "films that deal with current issues and problems soon date and become unsaleable" (100).[13] Nonetheless, this should be considered against the fact that mainstream programming exists as one component of an expanding market for wildlife imagery. In the current media landscape diverse forms of niche programming have also burgeoned.

Since the 1970s, subscription television has provided increasing avenues for viewing wildlife with Animal Planet, the National Geographic Channel, and the Discovery Channel broadcasting twenty-four hours a day. Discovery Communications International, the parent company for Animal Planet and the Discovery Channel, boasts a total of 2.9 billion subscribers, across 189 countries for its stable of channels.[14] There is clear evidence that both the production and popularity of this niche programming is substantial.[15] Further, more recent developments, such as specialist and nonspecialist film festivals, and online distribution mechanisms such as *Netflix*, *Amazon Studios*, and YouTube, have taken not only documentary, but also the portrayal of nature and environmental politics, into a new territory of production and distribution. Film and television representations of nature, and animals specifically, have secured valuable currency in the contemporary media sphere—they are both ubiquitous and diverse.

This book explores the green wave while also rethinking its parameters, taking a wide view of the documentary genre and attending to varied styles employed to represent the real. It also considers, as I have noted, how cultural narratives and practices work to structure our idea of animals. The examples under discussion do not all necessarily offer explicit messages of environmental or ecological consciousness, rather they provide differing avenues for understanding how nonfiction forms play to and enable recognition of changing human impact on the nonhuman.

My approach is one that focuses the histories, practices, and uses of the documentary moving image in ways that chart how particular examples trouble, revise, or reiterate the humanism of this history. Chapters pinpoint dominant concerns in the tide of filmmaking I describe—they focus on the themes of food, agriculture, species loss, science, and digital technology. Case studies exploring food, agricultural labor, and technology delineate bodies of film and media examples dealing with institutions and practices. Those examining species loss and science/exploration focus on environment and wildlife, attending to films set in defined geographical regions. This structure is designed to pose three contingencies for understanding the figure of the animal in modernity: the subjection of industrial livestock to formal institutions, the wild animal other positioned historically by narratives of science and the Anthropocene, and the negotiation with subjection and objectification where digital modes of vision allow for a rethinking of point of view and animal agency.

The question of subjection is a decisive reference point—conceived as a process for organizing and interpellating human identity, subjection (and its correlation in subjectification[16]) is a term that refers to regimes of power that take life as their object. While usually understood in relation to human subjectivity, the three contingencies I have proposed provide a pivotal taxonomy—they bring into view the notion that subjection should crucially be understood as a process that acts upon or defines all life, not only human life. Yet I want to be careful to emphasize that subjection to human systems of power (which are by definition anthropocentric) only tells part of the story of what cinema can accomplish—as I discuss later, it can also conceive of animal life and embodiment in ways that challenge the anthropocentric web spun to capture the meaning of the animal.

Representation, Biopower, and Modernity:
"Producing a History of Animals"

The primary reference for those theorizing animals in the epoch of capitalist modernity has, without doubt, become John Berger's "Why Look at Animals?" Encompassing a wide range of examples and contexts, Berger's 1980 long-form essay asserts that since the precapitalist, preindustrial era, animals have become marginalized. With the decline of feudal agrarianism and the rise of the machine age we have less proximity with animals. For Berger, they have lost their autonomy figuratively as they have been demystified in nature and physically, as they have become domestic pets. Berger articulates this in his famous maxim that in modernity "animals disappear." Berger's story is one of transforming metaphors. For him, the fading figure of the animal is replaced by the spectacle and the sign. While Berger oscillates between discussing the treatment of *actual* animals in history and changing *metaphors* of animality, Akira Mizuta Lippit is almost wholly concerned with the animal as an epistemological category. In his study of the animal in modernity, Lippit examines sites of mediation, technologies of knowledge, and metaphors of modernity. He is interested in how animals have transformed over the past two centuries, principally through changing conceptualizations in Western thought, but also through the technologies of photography and cinema: "modernity can be defined by the disappearance of wildlife from humanity's habitat and by the reappearance of the same in humanity's reflections on itself: in philosophy, psychoanalysis, and technological media such as the telephone, film and radio" (3). Again, changing proximity with animals produces an altered paradigm for posing animals, one that is spectral, with animals reduced to a haunting referentiality.

The approaches offered by Berger and Lippit are pioneering and serve as a foundation for considering the social and epistemological status of animals in the human world, particularly as it is constituted in practices of representation. Such practices, where cinema is concerned, are themselves tied to the technologies and aspirations of modernity. Indeed, cinema poses animals as objects of vision and knowledge, potentially supporting Berger's claim that "animals are always the observed. The fact that they can observe us has lost all significance. They are the objects of our ever-extending knowledge. What we know about them is an index of our power, and thus an index of what separates us from them" (16). Cinema, on this measure, is another technology of human mastery that increases animals' separation and distance from humans. An explanatory frame, however, that views cinema only as a distancing device, minimizing or failing to recognize its impressionistic or expressive power, is limiting.[17] Moreover, both Lippit and Berger emphasize the animal as metaphor (albeit with a critique of this status) or epistemological object, and similarly, such a frame is not sufficient for understanding the range of approaches in the documentary culture I refer to, or the way cinema grapples with the materiality of animal life and animal embodiment.

The concept of "biopower" provides an important supplement to Lippit and Berger, offering an avenue to discern how life of all kinds becomes an object of power against the changing logics of technology, capital, and cultural value. Describing human subjectification, Michel Foucault identifies a historical shift in the seventeenth century that took the foundation of Western culture from sovereign power over life (the power to take a life) to biological modernity (the regulation and optimization of life). The power over death that was once held by the sovereign, the king, "now presents itself as the counterpart of a power that exerts a positive influence on life, that endeavors to administer, optimise and multiply it, subjecting it to precise controls and comprehensive regulations" (137). Further, Foucault refers to the "anatomo-politics," or machine-like productive capacity of humans under capitalism. Biopower is both productive and deductive—it is concerned with the productive capacity of life and the power to destroy or degrade biological life. The notion that institutions and discourses are centrally concerned with shaping, using, or optimizing life takes on a different tenor where animal life is considered the object of human knowledge.

Human history has been founded on the labor of animals and the use of their bodies as food.[18] The use of animals has transformed under capitalist modernity. Jacques Derrida describes the increasing manipulation and use of animals in his essay, "The Animal That Therefore I Am (More to Follow)," when he writes that the subjection of the animal has become unprecedented in type and scale:

> In the course of the last two centuries . . . traditional forms of treatment of the animal have been turned upside down by the joint developments of zoological, ethological, biological, and genetic *forms of knowledge* and the always inseparable *techniques* of intervention with respect to their object, the transformation of the actual object, its milieu, its world, namely, the living animal. (Emphasis in original 394)

Recent scholarship has taken up biopolitical approaches to rethink the human "bios" in political terms and through its continuities with nonhuman life. Matthew Chrulew reconceives the work of Giorgio Agamben and Michael Hardt in ways that "bring closer together the lives of humans and animals (. . .) who, notwithstanding their ontological differences, are nonetheless exploited in common by the workings of capitalist biopower and the anthropological machine" ("Animals in Biopolitical," 63). Nicole Shukin, in her book *Animal Capital: Rendering Life in Biopolitical Times* (2009), offers a perceptive study of the biopolitical uses of animal bodies under different instances of capitalism, critiquing entanglements across species, race, and labor.

Alongside the productive capacity of animal labor and animals as food, understandings of the biologization of power also offer a way to reframe institutions and practices of care and protection. Modern animals have not only been exploited in unparalleled ways, they have also benefited from the ethos of liberal humanism. In the nineteenth-century romanticism's respect for nature and a forward-looking modernity jointly contributed to the institutionalization of the humane treatment of animals. Burt charts this development in Britain, noting government legislation on animal welfare and numerous societies that were founded in the nineteenth century.[19] For Burt, the advent of animal welfare coincides with the growing concern with display and surveillance: "the mark of a more civilized society—a common trope of animal welfare literature generally—is the way in which a society displays its humanity. The appearance and treatment of the animal body became a barometer for the moral health of the nation" (*Animals*, 36). Practices involving the slaughter of animals became less apparent in the public domain, particularly in cities. Burt adds more specificity to Berger's hypothesis in this respect, proposing that it was animal *death* that became obscured at this time, rather than animals disappearing per se ("John Berger's," 213). He goes on to note "the interplay between visibility and invisibility, or imagery and the animal body, are therefore much more problematically aligned in relation to welfare and killing" ("John Berger's," 213). In part Burt attributes the promotion of the ethical treatment of animals to a fear that the mistreatment of animals would trigger disorder, particularly among the underclasses ("John Berger's," 212). While the sensibilities of animal welfare emerged through a concern for the animal other, they were founded on an anxiety about maintaining the civilizing progression of the body politic.

These insights and approaches point to histories characterized by loss or disappearance, by spectral animals, and by forms of knowledge that enable care and responsibility as well as the unprecedented transformation of animals and their worlds. Putting the biopolitical aside for the moment, I turn to the stakes of representation and how it functions at the nexus of animals and history—what does it mean to produce a history of animals in modernity? Necessarily modernity is a term that indicates and draws on the history of human enterprise since the enlightenment. Significantly, Lippit and Berger are not concerned with the modernity of animals, but rather with history as a form of knowledge produced by humans and concerning human actions and perspectives. Erica Fudge confronts the spirit of this erasure, addressing the problem of writing a "history of animals" as a methodological one and in doing so brings to the fore the anthropocentrism of understandings of history and modernity, in which animals are accessed only through the proliferation of human texts about them.

Focusing on the written archive, Fudge notes that such texts more consistently signify the problem of the human rather than the existential reality of animals, nullifying and subordinating the material body of the

animal (7). She argues for the conditional utility of the rhetorical: "Material
and rhetorical are linked in their context, and the history that recognises this
can, in turn, force a reassessment of the material through its analysis of the
written record" (11). At stake for Fudge, then, is a rethinking of modernity
through a focus on the nonhuman. This is a project that entails the possibility of refiguring the status of the human: "history should reinterpret the
documents of the past in order to offer a new idea of the human" (Fudge
15). Such a claim brings into relief the question of how history has been
rendered in humanist terms, shaping and constructing perceptions of the
nonhuman. However, I wish to pursue the potential of the visual in such a
history. Following Fudge's lead, I recognize a history of animals in modernity by attending to the processes through which they have been perceived.
But this must be specified on cinematic terms. Film realism manifests life
for the viewer (an embodied animal, and a sensory experience of this), in
a manner the written word cannot. More to this, while I pose three contingencies for rendering animals within regimes of biopower, within this I
wish to acknowledge film's capacity to bring forth elements of indeterminacy. How might films shape our seeing and sensing of animals, in ways
that allow perception of their difference, irreducibility, ephemerality—their
material otherness?

Film and Animal Life

Suggesting a special place for what they refer to as the performativity of
animals when regarded as spectacle, Lorraine Daston and Gregg Mitman
argue that there is an element that escapes the anthropocentrism of rhetorical or textual deployment. They refer to this as "magnetism" and "the active
reality of animals" (12). Lesley Stern's work on "things" in narrative fiction
film provides an avenue to consider this indeterminacy more precisely in
relation to indexicality and the moving image in ways that, I suggest, include
documentary. Stern moves beyond simply proposing a taxonomy of objects
in order to examine the way *things* take on a weight of meaning, via both
their affective and signifying power:

> I assume that while things are never without signifying power
> (taking signification to entail more than the semantic) nevertheless
> they carry affect and an indeterminacy that frequently derives at
> least in part from their indexical relationship to the real world.
> I pose this indeterminacy as simultaneously a resistance and an

allure; at the very least it is an opportunity to shift the emphasis from the signifying potential of things to the sensuous, to the affect produced through tactility, the generation of a sense of touch. (334)

Stern's notion of indeterminacy is tied to affect and the senses and interpreting the experience encouraged by cinema in this way offers one avenue for rethinking the anthropocentric power of systems of representation. Her film theoretical approach also anticipates scholarship in "new materialism," a field in which approaches such as Jane Bennett's "highlight the active role of nonhuman materials in public life," giving "voice to a thing-power" (2). However, another maneuver is needed here to distinguish "the active reality of animals," to borrow Daston and Mitman's phrase, and the distinctiveness of animal *life* as it might be produced by the moving image.

Elizabeth Grosz, in her book *Becoming Undone: Darwinian Reflections on Life, Politics, and Art*, couples matter and life, understanding both in terms of their "temporal and durational entwinements [. . .]. They transform and are transformed. This is less a new kind of materialism than it is a new understanding of the forces, both material and immaterial, that direct us to the future" (5). The material qualities of life are also realized in temporal terms by Stern's point that "in cinema, it is the mutability of things that matters" (354). Encounters with the animal in cinema and encounters onscreen between life forms are produced in ways that rely on different modalities of time—the time of the narrative unfolding in shots, audio, and edits; reception and the instant of bodily response to bodies onscreen; and the interval between capturing the image of life with the camera and projecting it on screen. Because it brings together the impermanence of life and the mutability of the moving image, a discussion of the audiovisual representation and perception of life is inevitably underpinned by considerations of temporality.[20] For this reason the productive capacities of time is a recurring theme in individual chapters. This includes exploring how the length of a shot might allow for the contemplation of animal bodies, the montage of manufacturing in which animals become meat, or the archiving of images of wildlife that anticipate a future of species loss. In each case, moreover, perception and the senses are activated through temporality, whether it is the experience of cinematic time or the evocation of the relation between time and life.

Siegfried Kracauer's conception of realism recognizes the importance of a film's temporal progression. Further, it navigates the viewer's experience of modernity and cinema's ability to address the viewer in ways that engage the senses, the ephemeral, and the gestural in order to open a space for an experience of reality. Kracauer's realism of the everyday is interested in how cinema might harness "the flow of life" or "nature in the raw." His theory of film is motivated in part by his desire to seek out how some forms of cinema provide relief from the alienating experience of modernity. He describes the viewer's "susceptibility to the transient real-life phenomena that crowd the screen. [. . .] Along with the fragmentary happenings incidental to them, these phenomena—taxi cabs, buildings, passers-by, inanimate objects, faces—presumably stimulate the senses and provide him with the stuff of dreaming" (170). While Kracauer was not concerned with the natural environment per se and was more likely to describe city scenes such as this, the way he captures the material sensibility of the image remains relevant. Because his realism is shaped by material phenomena and its otherness rather than simply human subjectivity, it offers distinct avenues for moving beyond an anthropocentric approach to the medium. Film profoundly engages the material reality and the physiology of the spectator, embracing the human and nonhuman world.[21] It does so because it has the facility for "shocks" or "eruptions" of physical reality. There are clear references here to film phenomenology, a suggestion that is borne out in Kracauer's interest in Edmund Husserl's notion of lifeworld or *lebenswelt* and the way the indeterminacy and openness of lifeworld aligns with the indeterminacy of the film image,[22] a quality that also lends itself to engaging the viewer in material phenomena, life and its otherness.

The sensual work of cinema theorized by Stern and Kracauer before her has more recently been explored in a growing body of work in film studies that attends both to the audiovisual materiality and spectatorial corporeal experience. The scholar most associated with this turn is Laura U. Marks, with her book, *The Skin of the Film: Intercultural Cinema, Embodiment, and the Senses* (2000), proposing a theory for how a mode of cinema might provoke memories of the senses for intercultural subjects. Subsequent work[23] has expanded the utility of the sensual as a conceptual tool. Thomas Elsaesser and Malte Hagener's *Film Theory: An Introduction Through the Senses* (2010), is one such work. Indeed, Elsaesser and Hagener argue that the "idea of the body as a sensory envelope, as a perceptual membrane and material-mental interface [. . .] is the ontological, epistemological 'ground'" (11) for the broad film theoretical history they elaborate. Elsaesser and Hagener's work as well as studies by Vivian Sobchack (2004), Malin Walberg (2008), and Steven Shaviro (1993) inspire discussions in this book. My contribution to this scholarly landscape is the proposition that film analysis must avow, and be oriented away from, a frequently implicit anthropocentrism. The stakes of this endeavor are significant. Attending to the body of the animal is a pursuit that can push understandings of cinema and the senses into a domain that rethinks not only the rendering of animal life, but also human narratives, perception, and corporeality as they are posed in relation to the cinematic image.

As I have noted, chapters are organized to address three different (interrelated) alternatives for structuring our understanding of animals, possibilities that are driven by the evident preoccupations of contemporary documentary culture. The first two chapters identify clusters of films that explore institutions and practices related to food and agriculture. They are concerned with the subjection and representation of industrial livestock. Chapter 2 observes the work of agriculture though identifying a stylistically coherent corpus of film. The examples in question turn the camera to humans working the earth and laboring over or alongside animals. This is an international grouping and I focus principally on three films, *Sweetgrass* (2009), *Raw Herring* (2013), and *Los Herederos* (2008), produced in the United States, The Netherlands, and Mexico, respectively. All are concerned with a certain style evolved from documentary and ethnography, preferring long takes that capture action uninterrupted by edits. I examine how these films deploy the long take and Bazinian realism to both confront questions about precarious social existence and bring a new awareness to the materiality of animals. Chapter 3 is again interested in a new concern in the feature-length documentary and looks at a contemporary cycle that confronts the food system and a crisis of industrialization. It focuses on a selection of films including *Food, Inc.* (2008), *King Corn* (2007), *Darwin's Nightmare* (2004), *Our Daily Bread* (2005), and *The Moo Man* (2012), exploring how the relationship between meat and animals is rendered, melding sensory and social modes of viewer identification. I consider Vivian Sobchack's approach to identification to unlock the ways in which the power of animal death and materiality structure the embodied knowledge of the viewer, disturbing the separation of animal and human corporeality.

Chapters 4 and 5 focus on the putatively nonhuman environment and the conventions that frame our understanding of the "wild" animal other, examining two dominant themes in this sphere of filmmaking, species loss, and science. I focus on environment and wildlife by choosing films set in defined geographical regions. I concede that there is a range of possible case studies that might address this aspect of contemporary documentary culture. I chose the polar regions as twin studies because they hold a significant place in documentary history—they are the site of technological and narrative innovations (both of which, as I show, are tied to the representation of animals) and continue to offer compelling nonhuman spectacle and fascination for filmmakers.

Chapter 4 concentrates on the Arctic, examining how animals in this fragile polar region function as potent symbols for environmental movements. It wrestles with the problem of rendering life by investigating species loss and the notion of the archive. *Nanook of the North* (1922) provides an important antecedent for contemporary films set in the Arctic, rendering Arctic life in the face of potential (human) species loss and binding animals and humans together in film history. Flaherty's film provides a foundation to consider the more recent examples *Being Caribou* (2008) and *Arctic Tale* (2007) in terms of the problem of the archive; these films offer an avenue to investigate how documentary might convey endangered life in ways that either anticipate extinction by perceiving images as an archive of animals about to disappear, cohering with humanist narratives of species loss, or gesture to a more open set of possibilities for the future. Chapter 5, in turn, examines Antarctica, recognizing its status as a continent unlike any other, a preeminent site that is consistently located outside modernity and reason. This chapter explores how different nonfiction filmic modes have worked to recuperate the continent into rational cultural paradigms such as exploration and science. Focusing on three key examples, the films of the "Heroic Age of Polar Exploration," principally Herbert Ponting's *The Great White Silence* (1924), David Attenborough's television series *Frozen Planet* (2011), and Werner Herzog's *Encounters at the End of the World* (2007), I scrutinize the roles animals have played in this recuperation. Charles Darwin's work on the genealogy of the species not only inspires the scientism of wildlife film and television, but also provides a platform for evaluating how these films pose animal life and its relation to the human in radical ways.

Returning to the question of human practices and institutions, chapter 6 is informed by a reflection on technology and the ontological status of documentary. Here I pose *Grizzly Man* as a film that sits at the cusp of a new epoch in documentary that is influenced by changing manifestations of agency, digital technology, and ecological interconnectedness. This epoch exists against the background of both the "green wave" of film and television and Deborah Bird Rose's notion of ecological existentialism. I expand on this new era by considering online examples YouTube clips in which animals stage direct encounters with technology ("Hawk vs. Drone! [Hawk Attacks Quadcopter]," "Marmot Licks *GoPro*") and nature cams, such as *Africam*. These examples inhere with the potential to disturb traditions of anthropocentrism in moving image culture and contribute to a rethinking of human *and* animal agency, one that both generates the destabilization of familiar codes of humanist vision and accentuates the corporeality of animal life. A brief conclusion thinks further about the ontology of the documentary moving image, experimenting with how vision might be rethought from a nonhuman perspective, through Jacob von Uexküll's notion of *umwelt* or lifeworld.

Complicating the anthropocentric assumptions of cinema is an endeavor that must also acknowledge the biopolitical function of the camera—its ability to define and organize life for and with the viewer. In Berger's terms, one prospect here is for animals to "disappear," with animal specificity replaced by human knowledge and power. To perceive the productive capacities of biopower, in contrast, is to allow for the possibility that cinema might yield multiple manifestations of animal embodiment. An analysis of the moving image and the expression of life must seek out the material continuities between human and animal *and* the way each is distinct, equally regarded, even if such a cinematic image or utterance is momentary and ephemeral. This is because the recognition of nonhuman difference has the potential to bring with it the realization that we inhabit a world shared by a multitude of distinct autonomous beings. Cinema and media can activate this realization, encouraging human responsibility beyond the frame without perpetuating the illusion of totalizing human mastery over nature.

Chapter 2

Labor, Agriculture, and Long Take Cinema

Working on the Surface of the Earth

Sweetgrass (2009) has become one of the most discussed examples of observational filmmaking produced in recent years. This is a singular accomplishment, especially given this is a documentary about cowboys, sheep, and other service animals that make their way across the mountains of the U.S. state of Montana. As I explore in this chapter, however, Lucien Castaing-Taylor and Ilisa Barbash's film should be considered alongside a group of lesser known films that share similar stylistic qualities and a thematic focus on humans working with and over animals in the natural environment. *Sweetgrass* is nevertheless a striking example within this group. It seeks to tell the story of traditional farming practices and human hardship, inviting the viewer into a world that is both infused with the embodied materiality of sheep and with the significance of an agricultural tradition and its demise.

Anna Grimshaw celebrates the film's attention to "an expansive web of relationships that is made and remade through the ongoing, active engagement between diverse species and their environments" (256). Grimshaw's approach to this remarkable film is informed, in part, by Donna Haraway's influential work, *When Species Meet*. Haraway's work has inspired many approaches in the humanities that reflect on ethical and existential encounters with the animal world, with her notion of "companion species" establishing a paradigm in which animals are "world sharing" partners. Her characterization of a web of relations is one that explores the possibility of an "ongoing 'becoming with'" (16) companion species, entailing the destabilization of species categories. While Grimshaw elaborates on *Sweetgrass* as an ethnography that expresses relations across species and their environments, she is little concerned with the object of this ethnography, the labor of humans with and over animals.

The films discussed in the next two chapters only intermittently attend to animal well-being, an aspect that underlies Haraway's ethical approach. They are more attuned to the tensions between the utility of animals in the human lifeworld, as objects of human endeavor and industry, and animal embodiment. I suggest that these significant clusters of documentary cannot be aligned with a multispecies "becoming with" on simple terms and require approaches that can account for the diverse ways that animals are positioned and subjectified in human worlds.

The films that are the focus of this chapter are concerned with a certain style evolved from documentary and ethnography and I suggest that this style is tied, in specific ways, to the project of recording labor and animals in human lifeworlds. This chapter proposes that these distinct worlds are conveyed aesthetically in ways that ask the viewer to think anew about the circuit of relations across humans and animals, acknowledging the ways such relationships are embedded in sites of precarious existence, and ecological and social change. *Sweetgrass*, for my purposes, can be located alongside an international group of examples that includes feature length films such as *Raw Herring* (2013), *Elsewhere* (2000), *The Moo Man* (2012), *Leviathan* (2013), *Our Daily Bread* (2005), *La Libertad* (2001), *Sleep Furiously* (2007), and *Los Herederos* (2008). I focus in particular on *Sweetgrass*, *Raw Herring*, and *Los Herederos*, exploring how these three examples communicate a visual and auditory exploration of labor and life with animals.

Directed by Dutch filmmakers Leonard Retel Helmrich and his sister Hetty Naaijkens-Retel Helmrich, *Raw Herring* follows the drama and challenges that face the community of fishermen who work the two last remaining herring ships to operate under the Dutch flag in the North Sea. It conveys the labor, hardship, and textures of life *at* sea as well as *in* the sea. This observational account is underpinned by the reality facing the fishermen and their families (and to a lesser extent the fish): their way of life is under threat as fish stocks become increasingly low. In comparison, *Sweetgrass* follows events on land and the filmmakers accompany a handful of sheep herders, or cowboys, as they shepherd approximately 3,000 sheep through the mountains for summer grazing. The expedition is arduous and the conditions the men live in are basic. At its conclusion the viewer learns that the film documents the last such journey of sheep, horses, and men through the mountains of Montana. Eugenio Polgovsky's *Los Herederos* (*The Inheritors*) also depicts an agrarian existence, but rather than a vanishing tradition, it explores the experiences of Mexico's rural poor. Focusing on the stasis of inherited poverty, the film observes the labor of children as they work alongside service animals such as donkeys and goats in the villages, fields, and mountains of Mexico.

All of these documentaries privilege an observational style of filmmaking, following events as they occur in front of the camera and preferring long takes that capture action uninterrupted by edits.

Some films in this group have already been identified as offering new directions in documentary and/or nonfiction film. Unsurprisingly, *Sweetgrass* is frequently at the heart of these pronouncements of the new. Robert Koehler identifies a contemporary movement in nonfiction that coincides with the rise of slow cinema, inaugurating a new stylistic agenda. This new nonfiction is dominated by "agricultural activities" and populated by "humans working on the surface of the earth" ("Agrarian," 13). Alternatively, Grimshaw poses *Sweetgrass* in relation to "the emergence of a new agenda in ethnographic filmmaking" (249) and she elaborates on observational and expressive aesthetics, noting how the film confuses the categories of "art" and "anthropology." Also referencing an ethnographic frame, Anat Pick identifies a new avant-garde, one defined by "cinema's potential for shaping another optical reality, one not centered strictly on human form, perception and identity" ("Ecovisions"). The trend Pick identifies is one in which examples offer explicit attention to animals and while she does not mention *Sweetgrass*, this is no doubt only because her comments predate the release of the film. When taken together these observations suggest a body of films emerging at the intersection of anthropology, innovative cinematic endeavor, and conceptualizations of animal ontology. I am interested, however, in locating the examples cited by these scholars within a broader film historical frame, one that accounts for both the visualization of labor in documentary in relation to narratives of progress and industrialization *and* the role of animals at the intersection of observational cinema and the ethnographic project.

Work, Ethnography, and Animals in Documentary

The association between observation and documentary, as I noted in chapter 1, evokes different points of reference. It is tied to the historical schools of direct cinema and *cinéma vérité*. Beyond this, the capacity of the camera to observe has a privileged place in documentary epistemology, facilitating the expectation that seeing equates with knowing. In this chapter I explore observation and observational cinema in terms of their function within ethnographic film traditions. Ethnographic filmmaking, with its ties to anthropology, has a particular interest in observing and, thus, extracting meaning from the social structures in which individuals exist. Animals have consistently been interlopers in the ethnographic endeavor, appearing alongside or as part of the human lifeworld.

In early cinema's manifestations of ethnography, it is popular adventure films that provide the most prevalent images of animals. These feature films documented the expeditions of mostly American and British adventurers in the colonized territories of Africa and the Pacific and became more and more sensationalized as time went on. The spectacle of wildlife was frequently posed in ways that aligned it with ethnographic images of indigenous peoples.[1] One of the last adventure films of this period, *Simba: The King of Beasts, a Saga of the African Veldt* (1928), purports to be a film about lions. However, Martin and Osa Johnson's film is equally about the filmmakers' experiences, which include capturing images of local peoples on camera as their safari expedition unfolds. As Catherine Russell observes, *Simba* "incorporates the crudest form of American racism, which it awkwardly maps onto 'ethnographic' footage" (142). Key attributes that underpinned the popularity and scientism of early adventure films drew on the discourses of ethnography and synthesized them with gender, the colonial gaze, and the spectacle of exotic animals.

On the cusp of the categorization of documentary as a distinct form in the 1920s, these popular "factual films" married drama, often heroic drama, and the veracity of nonfiction. Merian C. Cooper and Ernest Schoedsack, the famous producer/director team for *King Kong* (1933), were responsible for a number of prominent silent films that drew on the narrative potential of animals. These include *Chang: A Drama of the Wilderness* (1927) in Thailand and *Grass: A Nation's Battle for Life* (1925), a nomadic film about droving livestock in Iran. Both films work at the intersection of fiction and nonfiction, with events often staged for the camera. These are surpassed, however, by Robert Flaherty's *Nanook of the North* (1922), a film that brought Arctic animals into focus alongside the dramatization of Inuit life. *Nanook*, as I discuss in chapter 4, has come to exemplify the ethnographic endeavor in the early twentieth century.

Beyond the silent period, ethnographic filmmaking develops in ways that constantly blur the boundaries of empiricism and art practice and filmmakers that have consciously pushed the limits of this boundary include David and Judith MacDougall, John Marshall, and Robert Gardner.[2] The McDougall's 1972 film, *To Live with Herds*, offers an important example in this tradition, viewing pastoral practices, and animals as constituents of traditional lifeworlds, through the lens of ethnographic innovation. In the adjacent tradition of observational or direct cinema, extreme manifestations of the observational style always produce excursions into the avant-garde.

In this context I understand the avant-garde as form of expression that might ask us to think anew, or retrain perception,[3] particularly in relation to the nonhuman. One avenue for achieving this is to focus on the visible. Bill Viola's *I Do Not Know What It Is I Am Like* (1986) is notable in this respect. However, Fredric Wiseman's animal *oeuvre*, composed of *Primate* (1974), *Meat* (1976), *Racetrack* (1984), and *Zoo* (1993), offers the most sustained attention to the animal in the observational avant-garde. These four documentaries focus on institutions in which animals and humans are bound together in the activities of everyday life. Through the careful structuring and ordering of footage, they present, by way of Wiseman's situated perspective, notional ethnographies. They inhere with an expressiveness that moves beyond factual meaning to provoke an unsettling existential awareness by exploring human conduct and animals.

Also exploring human worlds that are populated with animals, *Sweetgrass* and *Leviathan*, both produced by Harvard University's Sensory Ethnography Lab, indicate a new project within traditions of observational cinema. Both films self-consciously appeal to the senses of the viewer and play to phenomenological understandings of cinema. Akin to Wiseman's films, knowledge of humans and animals is conveyed predominantly through image and sound, rather than language. Yet, while Wiseman uses editing and framing to create emphasis through juxtaposition and gesture, this focus on the audiovisual is more concerned with how bodies and texture move and linger in the frame. This emphasis on somatic experience (emerging out of the empiricism of traditional anthropology) offers a distinct approach that has been theorized more widely as a new modality in the discipline,[4] extending beyond the work of filmmakers in the Harvard group. This approach has developed alongside the species turn, often associated with Haraway's approach noted earlier.[5]

Grimshaw describes the new ethnographic approach from the perspective of the researcher or filmmaker in the field as illustrating "a growing interest in the senses, embodied practice, and ways of knowing that have been variously described as sensuous, existential, or phenomenological anthropology" (256). The notion of lifeworld that is the focus of Grimshaw's approach has origins in phenomenology. Invoked here is the *Lebenswelt* or lifeworld theorized by Edmund Husserl. Following Husserl, the lifeworld is a way of apprehending the objective, mutually held interpretation of the world that is also perceptual and sensory.[6] Notably, Husserl's lifeworld represents an attempt to bring together subjective experience and the shared social structures in which we live, opening the way for understanding the subjective senses through ethnographic practice. The documentary examples

I am concerned with place emphasis on anthropocentric perspective and experience. Beyond select scenes, it is this perspective that is foregrounded in a way that mirrors the viewer's positioning as the addressee of the film.[7]

In these films the observational camera lingers on the environment, the bodies of humans at work and the animals who exist alongside them, echoing Fatimah Tobing Rony's determination that "ethnographic cinema is above all a cinema of the body: the focus is on the anatomy of gestures [. . .] and on the body of the land they inhabit" (111). Offering a different set of concerns, films interested in the function of labor contribute another dimension to the ethnographic imagination. Even though they are seldom referred to as ethnography, they nevertheless often present investigations into the subjects, bodies, and meaning of working life. The activity of work and the identity of the worker offer powerful iconographic and rhetorical material for documentary and nonfiction across the twentieth century.

In early cinema a subgenre of "actualities" (short nonfiction film that circulated in cinemas before the term documentary was used in the 1920s) emerged, termed "industrials," depicting work and workers (Cowie 64). The beginnings of cinema occurred in an historical moment that also saw the reinvention of work with the systemization that came with theories of Taylorism and later Fordism. Charting this period of radical redefinition, Elizabeth Cowie explores how labor became a subject for nonfiction in British cinema as workers were framed in multiple ways: as a threat to democracy and the nation in light of the rise of unionism, through the idealization of physical activity or as skilled and ennobled labor. Indeed, the documentary interest in labor does not constitute a single history or problem but is rather composed around a number of threads with differing concerns, from the pastoral rhetoric of the New Deal documentary in the United States, early Soviet documentary through to the works of Barbara Kopple. I return to the British documentary movement of the 1930s, however, because it offers one of the most strikingly visual explorations of the activity of work with landmark films that include *Drifters* (1929), *Industrial Britain* (1931), and *Night Mail* (1936).

Industrial Britain provides an important example not only within the history of documentary, but also as a reference point for examining the construction of labor in ways that address a broader context of modernization and change. This film was conceived by John Grierson with the production initially directed by Flaherty who was unable to complete the project after exhausting all the funds provided by the sponsor, the Empire Marketing Board (EMB). Grierson and Edgar Anstey finished the film. The final documentary reflects this hybrid authorship and synthesizes the popular appeal favored by Grierson and the expressiveness of Flaherty. It presents different working men in their environments, from coal mining to manufacturing. Through close shots of worker's hands and bodies, it proclaims the craft and skill of Britain's masculine workforce. Almost paradoxically, the film addresses industrial progress and changing labor conditions by presenting a world in which "workers are a part of a human army of craftsmen who maintain their grace and humanity in the face of the mechanisation of industry, at the same time as they become machine-like" (Williams 623). The film is concerned primarily with the heroism and humanism of the workers, rather than the machinery of industry, challenging a preoccupation with the iconography of mechanized industry of the time. For my purposes it is helpful to consider how films about the activity of labor frequently fix on the gesture, movement, and energy of the worker, accentuating this dynamism through editing and music.

In what follows in this chapter I investigate how the long take functions as a particular documentary mechanism for framing life and labor. The agrarian visions in these films should be considered not only in relation to documentary conventions and historics, but also on more specific terms that recognize their interpretation of the tradition of observational cinema. Rendering a sphere of work that poses humans in proximity with animals, these films are distinctive in their consistent use of long unedited shots. In the following section I draw on the insights offered by André Bazin to explore how the long take is deployed to formally engage the viewer in the vitality of the lifeworld onscreen.[8] Well suited to this task, Bazin's approach (like that of Kracauer described in the previous chapter) are influenced by theories associated with existentialism and phenomenology. In this respect, lifeworld is experienced as a mode of spectatorship with the viewer asked to share in the structures of life and environments perceived by those working the oceans and the land.

Men and Fish: *Raw Herring*

Raw Herring focuses on the two remaining vessels in a once strong Dutch fleet that fished the North Sea for the traditional delicacy, the *Hollandse Nieuwe* (Dutch New Herring). The opening frame shows the boat set against the horizon with a title that states: "For centuries the Dutch fishermen are the best herring fishers of Europe. They pass their skills on from father to son. But times are changing." This is the only point at which the filmmakers convey an informing social narrative beyond that which is articulated in conversation by the on-screen actors. The nature of these "changing times" becomes clear as the film unfolds, revealing the problem of declining fish stocks and the potential demise of the herring industry. The title also indicates another issue in the film—the attention to the masculine endeavor of fishing, life on board ships, and the patriarchal lineage of this traditional labor, which is passed from father to son.

The structure of *Raw Herring* demonstrates a three-part narrative that consists of the search for herring, the vigorous scene of fishing and processing the fish on the ship, and the marketing of the fish on shore. The cyclical nature of this endeavor is indicated in the closing scenes as a boy tearfully farewells his father when he must return to the boat for another stint on the ocean. The first half of the film also establishes the importance of the herring fleet for the community on shore, including the families of fishermen. Both the seascapes and the lives and work of the men who fish the seas is conveyed through long takes, often in close proximity with the subject and with a camera that moves fluidly around the action. This exemplifies a hallmark of the filmmakers, Retel Helmrich and Naaijkens-Retel Helmrich, who refer to this as "single shot cinema" (Ponsoldt).[9] The search for schools of herring occupies the first half of the film and the long takes of the camera accentuate this duration.

As the vessels move though different areas of the ocean, the location name and the coordinates appear to the side of the screen—the film begins with the ship at Devils Hole in the North Sea, 56 N/0.14 E. These indicate a particular relationship between space, time, and the subjectivity of the fishermen who presumably have precise knowledge of locations in the seemingly indistinguishable expanse of ocean. The two Dutch boats (*Wiron 5* and *Wiron 6*) work in unison, and the captain speaks to his nearby equivalent, describing the search and the movements of a nearby Norwegian ship, also looking for herring. The camera hovers on the bridge, capturing the consistent conversations over the radio. At one point the captain speaks into the radio: "A few years ago there was still plenty of fish at 57 and 58 degrees but the last few years we've had to search higher up north." His reference to the latitude location gives particular significance to the coordinates shown on the screen.

Challenging the notion that montage is the essence of cinema, Bazin emphasizes the importance of lived time and its relationship to duration. This relationship is demonstrated in *Raw Herring*, which draws attention to the waiting involved in the search for the herring. Bazin celebrates the seal hunt in *Nanook of the North* as one of the earliest examples of his views about duration:

> The camera cannot see everything at once but it makes sure
> not to lose any part of what it chooses to see. What matters
> to Flaherty, confronted with Nanook hunting the seal, is the
> relation between Nanook and the animal; the actual length of
> the waiting period. Montage could suggest the time involved.
> Flaherty however confines himself to showing the actual wait-
> ing period; the length of the hunt is the very substance of the
> image, its true object. (27)

While it is notable that Bazin's example is one that includes animals and hunting, more crucial is the way he describes the length of hunt as the substance of the image.

Time passes and the time of the image aligns with the time of viewing to produce the experience of waiting. Malin Wahlberg describes how Bazin "accounts for the measure of a take and the experience of gestures unfolding in real time, which is accomplished through the creative variation of change and stasis within a single *plan-séquence*" (33). Representing days on the ocean, the search for herring extends well beyond the time of the seal hunt. Multiple long takes convey this duration and while this is a compromise of Bazin's notion of temporality and objectivity within a single take, it nevertheless compellingly renders waiting and its frustrations through the detailed observation of life. It is an ethnography that places the accent on bodies, gestures, and seascape, exemplifying Rony's characterization. Time on the sea is drawn out with the slow rhythm of the movements of boats and the stasis of the captain at the radio. Shot with the sea out the window in the background he speaks into the radio: "What shall we do, Wim? Follow those Norwegian boats? I don't know, we've got nowhere else to go. Yesterday he caught some fish to the North, at 59 degree West." The conversation continues with a discussion about the inclement wind as the image cuts to a long shot outside, looking down on the boat from high above the bow, the horizon line a pronounced curve across the frame behind. There is movement in the frame with the boat slowly pulling up alongside its sister ship. This shot is held for almost a minute.

At the midpoint of the film the inertia of the expedition transforms. The pace of the film changes to convey the accelerated activity of fishing. With the appearance of the fish *Raw Herring* becomes more firmly realized as a story of labor organized around the textures and life of the nonhuman world. The duration of waiting has already established a tension between the fish and the men. This adds to the tension between life on board boat and that on shore. The close-up images of the movements of the men with

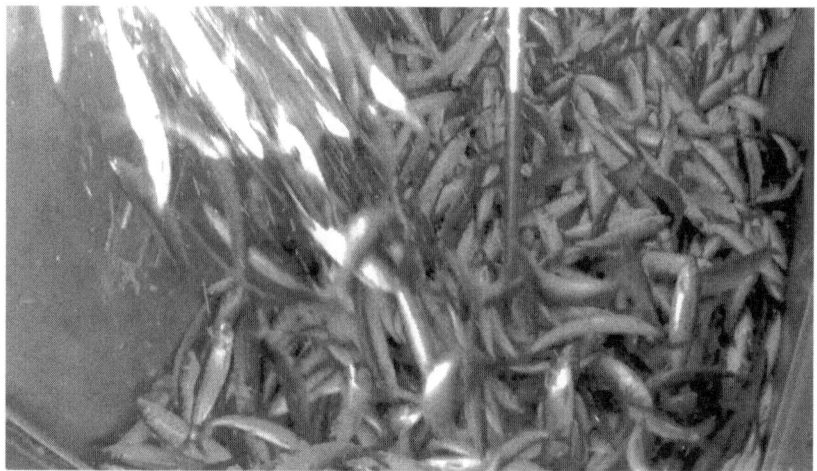

Figure 2.1. Fish flood into the hold in a slivery flow in *Raw Herring* (2013).

ropes and pulleys, wearing bright blue and orange wet weather gear have a surreal quality. The wide-angle lens skews proportion and adds to this quality. When the fish come on board in the bulging net, the camera goes beneath the waves, showing the texture of the mass of fish in the blue green water. It also looks down the line of the net as it is reeled in, offering extreme close-ups of fish caught in the net, mouths gaping. The fish flood into the hold in a slivery flow.

Once the fishing begins, it is not only men and machinery that are instilled with dynamism. Human labor and animal productivity (the herring producing fish for human consumption) are part of the same sphere in which energy and life are emphasized. The wide-angle shot that captures the net full of fish being pulled on board the boat utilizes what is also referred to as a fish-eye lens. It is possible to read this as a convention that references the perspective of the fish (even if it does not actually realize the reality of this perspective). The world of the fishermen is posed visually in a symbiotic relationship with the world of the fish. *Raw Herring* opens with images of birds above and below the water, at times diving into the ocean and plunging through the depths.[10] The fish, the birds, and the sea are highly stylized with extreme close-ups of the animals offering remarkable texture and clarity. This kind of imagery is repeated at intervals in the film, coupling the energy of the worker and the energy of the nonhuman world.

Grierson's silent film of 1929, *Drifters*, presents a conspicuously apt point of comparison for *Raw Herring* and an important antecedent in the representation of fish and fishing. Both documentaries are set in the North Sea, depicting a single fishing expedition and the search for herring. Both emphasize the iconography of fishing and experiences that distinguish the life of men working the sea. Made with the remit to present the working class and their experience in the context of industrializing modernity, *Drifters* was funded by the EMB as part of a package of promotional material. *Raw Herring* offers a slower observational style compared with the pacing of *Drifters*, which is more poetic in structure than observational. In comparison with the later documentary, *Industrial Britain*, the poetic qualities of *Drifters* surpass the social commentary present in the intertitles. Instead, the expressive approach in the film (for which Grierson has been much criticized[11]), enhance the vitalist aesthetic that shapes the presentation of fish and fishermen. The frame is filled with the physical world of the fisherman: fishing nets, the rigging of the boat, the sea, birds, fish, and the men's daily life on board the boat. Men and fish are set alongside one another, both constituent parts in the rhythm and movement of the film and both idealized as part of an ecology, one that marries the natural world with industry.

Raw Herring differs from the earlier documentary in that human labor is not triumphant. Despite the lively music that accompanies images of fishing, the broader film communicates that labor and livelihood is under threat because the fish are under threat. The Dutch compete with the Norwegian fleet for precious catch and herring stocks have collapsed a number of times in the North Sea due to large-scale industrial fishing and other contributing factors such as changes in the ocean environs.[12] *Raw Herring* does not, however, explicitly address this much-documented fact, leaving it beyond the frame. Nevertheless, it provides an underlying rationale for the film. Rather than offer causal explanations, it shows the paradox of the situation, exploring the expressive potential of the labor of fishing (and of the corporeality of fish) as this same activity drives fish stocks lower still. The Bazinian ideals of observation that maintain continuity and cinematic unity are presented in a manner that corresponds with the way of life represented in *Raw Herring*—one that is characterized by tradition and a cyclical harmony. Importantly, this dynamic is subtended by the multiple suggestions in the film that this world is disappearing in the face of over-industrialization. If the film progresses from fish and men in contestation (a dynamic that underlies *Drifters*) toward a visual emphasis on the texture and energy of fish in the worlds of the fishermen, ultimately this is a human/animal relation organized around a teleology of environmental decline.

Sheep and Men: *Sweetgrass*

Unlike the Dutch film, *Sweetgrass* features no music and the speech captured in the sound track does less to guide the viewer through an unfolding narrative. This is not to say that sound in the film is a secondary concern. Sound is carefully designed to convey the circuit of exchanges between the sheep, the cowboys (who sing and converse with one another as well as the animals), and the rest of the environment. Lucien Castaing-Taylor, who is credited as "recordist" rather than director, and producer, Ilisa Barbash, shot footage for the film over a period of three years. There is no explicit rationale announced in the film until the closing credits when two intertitles explain, "Since the late nineteenth century, Western ranchers and their hired hands have ranged animals on public lands for summer pasture. In 2003, over three months and one hundred and fifty miles, the last band of sheep trailed through Montana's Absaroka-Beartooth mountains." This final note retrospectively offers the film compelling significance—it has documented not simply a specific agrarian practice, but a vanishing tradition.

Barbash is a curator of visual anthropology at Harvard University's Peabody Museum, and Castaing-Taylor is director of Harvard's Sensory Ethnography Lab.[13] There has been substantial critical interest in *Sweetgrass* and Castaing-Taylor's later film, *Leviathan* (made in collaboration with Véréna Paravel). Scholars have aligned *Sweetgrass* with different disciplines and genre categories, referring to it as eco-cinema, sensory ethnography, avant-garde film, nonfiction, and documentary.[14] Discussions of the film have focused on the style of filmmaking, the demise of the sheep run, and the methods Castaing-Taylor used to capture this exceptional footage and audio. These factors all contribute to the film's uniqueness.[15] Within this, it is perhaps the subtly rendered personalities of the cowboys and their relationship with the animals in this extreme environment that draws the viewer's attention into the film most effectively.

Sweetgrass begins with images of sheep in the snow and in sheds in Big Timber, a family owned ranch. Scenes here include lambing, docking, and shearing. The sheep are eventually taken out into the hills. The story progresses through the events of the journey including pitching tents, managing the sheep in the dark, documenting a bear attack on a sheep, and retrieving sheep that have strayed out on a ridge. All is set against the sublime and remote landscape. The film also captures the emotional worlds of the men—anger, humor, and failing spirit are all apparent as the three-month journey grinds on. Animals in the film are not limited to sheep but include dogs, horses, and bears. Throughout, the camera is used in the service of the close contemplation of the sheep and their materiality, but this is particularly so in the early part of the film. *Sweetgrass* foregrounds animals more than any of the long take films that I focus on. While it remains focused on humanist concerns, its consistent interest in the embodiment of animals surpasses that of *Raw Herring* and *Los Herederos*.

Indeed, *Sweetgrass* exhibits a range of interconnecting concerns that constitute it as an exemplary object for the Bazinan project. These include not only phenomenology and observation, but also a particular interest in the expressive potential of animals.[16] Animals populate a number of his essays and as Serge Daney writes, for Bazin "the essence of cinema becomes a story about animals" (32). Most notably they feature as core examples of his concept of the "ontology of the cinematographic."[17] Furthering his interest in the potential of the single take and depth of field, Bazin proposed that whenever it was possible to include two heterogeneous elements in the shot, editing should be avoided. He proclaims, for example, that in Flaherty's *Louisiana Story* the scene "of an alligator catching a heron, photographed in a single panning shot, is admirable"(51). His repeated references to animals draw relationships between film ontologies and animal ontologics. For Bazin, what is represented onscreen may engage the viewer's imagination but "what is imaginary on the screen must have the spatial density of some-

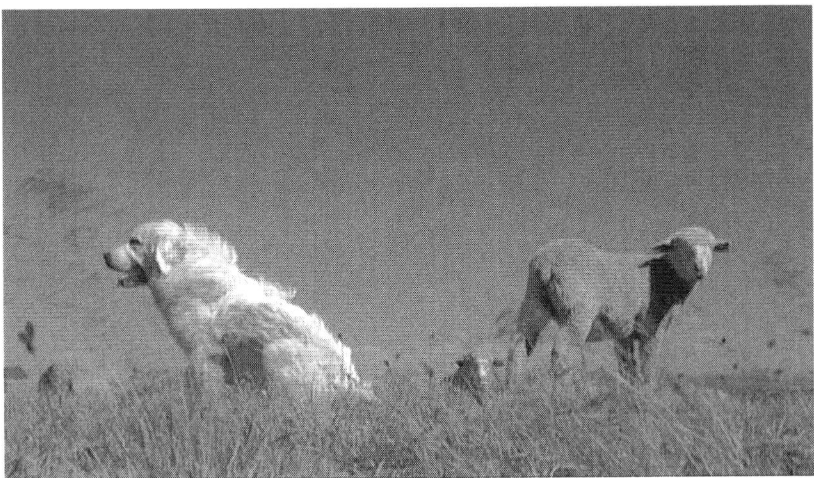

Figure 2.2. Shots in *Sweetgrass* (2009) are composed to draw the eye to the placement of different species in the frame.

thing real" (48) and encompassing humans and animals in the frame or in the shot achieves this realism because it maintains a photographic respect for the unity of space.

As *Sweetgrass* progresses, the long takes consistently capture multiple species—static shots in particular are composed in ways that draw the eye to the placement of animals and humans in the frame in the way advocated by Bazin. *Sweetgrass* also augments Bazin's orthodoxy by punctuating and unifying space with the differences between animal species. In one striking shot the figures of a dog and a sheep are outlined against the horizon, both in profile and turned away from one another. Other shots dwell on animal movement. Once the sheep are on the road the camera often takes in groups of sheep, up to 30–40, standing closely together among trees or on a hill, the frame brimming with their shape. Other times they move as a group, streaming down roads. In these instances the film seems concerned only with the duration of movement, either incremental or flowing, the embodiment of the animals and the harmony of their form in space. More than spatial unity, these images convey the compelling sensory qualities of the environment, drawing attention to nonhuman sound and image in the viewing experience. Moreover, these are not only long takes, they are *long shots* with the vista of mountains and landscape encompassed in the frame. As Helen Hughes notes, the long shot, as opposed to the medium shot, "reflects a change in narrative position in which the story of place is included in the individual story" (*Green Documentary*, 49). Elaborating on this point, the long shot enables greater attention to that which is beyond the human (given that the human figure is usually the defining feature of the shot and the way it is measured), not only place but also the constituents of the film world, including animal life.

One morning as the sun comes up a series of static shots establishes that the day is beginning. A long shot of a ridge is just close enough to discern a bear ambling up across the frame, the only movement visible. The next shot is a slightly closer long shot with a large group of sheep spread diagonally across the frame, some moving and others still, the gray of their bodies against the grayish green of the grass. It is accompanied by the sound of birds and sheep. In the next shot John Ahern, one of two central cowboys in the film, stands next to his tent with his horse. As he saddles the horse, he is speaking. Some of his words are inaudible but he distinctly addresses the horse: "you got away from those sheep all night didn't you? Yeah, that's it. You got away from those damn sheep for a night. Probably a relief isn't it? Yeah?" A dog walks into shot and sits at the edge of the frame. After almost three minutes suspended in this one frame, the shot cuts to another image of sheep. The long duration of these images provides time to study the detail of bodies and motion, aspects that attest to "livingness" of human and animals, while hinting at the long-standing role of animals in the human world of agriculture.[18]

Sometimes referred to as an example of salvage ethnography, *Sweetgrass* captures a specific way of laboring with animals that had already disappeared by the time the film reached audiences. The agrarian life presented seems to predate the industrial revolution; rather than machines, dogs, horses, and men perform almost all the labor required and the mountains show no trace of civilization. In comparison, *Raw Herring*, while conveying a strong sense of tradition, includes the capacities of modern technologies, with sonar for detecting schools of herring. In *Sweetgrass* moments that suggest the presence of modernity surprise the viewer. As in other long take agrarian films (*Los Herederos, La Libertad,* and *Elsewhere*), in *Sweetgrass* its seemingly preindustrial world is thrown into relief by the world the viewer inhabits, one dominated by the imagery of agricultural technology specific to the twenty-first century. This imagery includes the struggle over the genetic information of seeds, technologies of genetic modification and the scientism of massive industrial factory farming (images offered by films discussed in the next chapter such as *Food, Inc.* or *King Corn*). In this respect, *Sweetgrass* sits at the edge of the industrializing imagination. The agrarian vista is disrupted at points when men communicate with walkie-talkies. One cowboy stands atop a hill and talks to his mother on a mobile phone, lamenting the work and conditions that have injured his knee and worn out his dog and horse.[19] Perhaps the most significant revelation is the proclamation of the end of the sheep grazing that is revealed at the conclusion and that comes to retrospectively define onscreen events. It cements, for the viewer, the tension between cyclical custom and radical change.

Sweetgrass has a tone of melancholia. It also avoids idealizing the lifeworld it represents. Nevertheless, the negative sentiments expressed at a number points by the cowboys are juxtaposed with the carefully composed images of animals and landscape. This interaction between the aesthetic and the words of the onscreen actors produces an ambivalence, one that engages the viewer without explicit commentary. While it is not until the end of the film that the viewer realizes that it is a story of transition, it is clear that the camera is capturing a practice that is exceptional. As in the case of *Raw Herring*, the act of recording and attending to this lifeworld and labor through documentary communicates a certain respect for the men and endows the traditions with added significance. Both *Sweetgrass* and *Raw Herring* are concerned with worlds in which animals and humans are tied together in mutual industrial and environmental teleologies. Sitting beyond the worlds presented in the films is the reason for change. While in *Raw Herring* it is the collapse of fishing due to industrialization and environmental decline, the reason for the end of grazing on public land in *Sweetgrass* is equally complex and relates to a combination of factors including the rise of corporate agribusiness, the shrinking market for lamb and wool, and pressure from environmentalists.[20] More concerned with the existentialism of the worlds represented, they do not convey the detail of these multifaceted ecological situations.

The long take aesthetic and the construction of a lifeworld that accompanies it in these films offer a Bazinian unity of spatio-temporal form, signaling harmony in a way that mirrors the exploration of stability and the persistence of traditional fishing and agricultural practices. However, by the closing credits of the films, historical persistence has come into conflict with the change and progression of modernity. In this respect these films offer a counterpoint to the rendering of labor in the context of modernity in *Industrial Britain*. The 1931 film responds to changing labor demands, given increased automation, by highlighting the centrality and skill of the worker in ways that rival machines. In these later two films workers labor alongside animals, almost as they have for centuries, but without a sense of or strategy for the future. While they demonstrate Flaherty's humanist expressiveness, the films lack the purposiveness of the more socially oriented Griersonian elements of *Industrial Britain*, if not *Drifters*. Although *Los Herederos* is another film to eschew commentary and dialogue, it achieves a clearer critique of labor in its exploration of the experience of workers.

Children, Donkeys, Chickens, and Goats: *Los Herederos*

Again following a minimalist style, *Los Herederos* only features location sound and there is almost no overheard dialogue in the film. It shows the life and living environment of a handful of families working in rural Mexico and engaged in various kinds of agricultural labor. Attention to recording quotidian detail accentuates the ethnographic dimensions of this film. The director, Eugenio Polgovsky,[21] collected footage over the course of two years as he followed different families in the states of Guerrero, Nayarit, Oaxaca, Sinaloa, Puebla, and Veracruz. The families and locations, however, remain unnamed, leaving the viewer to discern different places and faces as the camera moves between low-lying villages and mountain passes. The opening frames of *Los Herederos* follow children's feet and backs as they run through dense forest. A long shot of a misty mountain orients the viewer to the scene. The next shot presents the feet of a boy whose running shoes have worn through and become open at the toes. They cross a stream and reach a donkey tethered to a tree. The donkey is untied and follows, its hooves framed in close up clicking on the stones alongside the boy's shoes. The opening scene announces a set of concerns for the film: the activities of children, poverty, and rural environments that include life lived with animals. As the film unfolds and images accumulate, the movement and activity of children takes on greater meaning and is more accurately rendered as labor as they work in fields, carry wood and water, weave yarn, and tend to animals.

The lifeworld experienced by these children is one in which animals work alongside humans, and also produce food (goats and chickens feature in many shots). While *Sweetgrass* and *Raw Herring* focus on the act of labor *over* animals, conveying the harvesting of and processing fish or rearing and shepherding of sheep, there is greater attention in *Los Herederos* to laboring *with* animals. In particular, there are repeated sequences that highlight movement and transportation. At a number of points donkeys have loads strapped to their backs, the camera showing in close-up hands tying the donkey's harness. Mirroring this, children as young as five carry water bottles across fields, balanced across their shoulders. Boys of perhaps seven

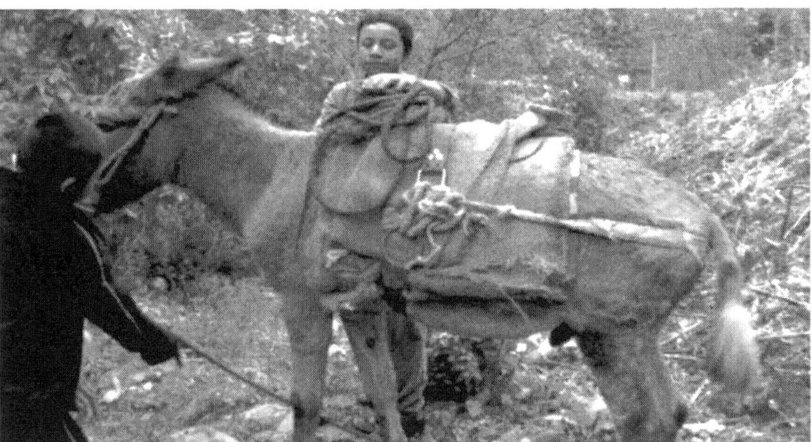

Figure 2.3. Two boys prepare a donkey to carry a load across a mountain path in *Los Herederos* (2008).

or eight run through mountain paths with bundles of wood balanced on their backs. Through repetition, emphasis is placed on the act of carrying weight, whether it is the work of human or animal bodies. The long takes of the camera follow this action, sometimes with the camera operator keeping pace on foot from behind and sometimes in front. Life here is rendered as pulse and movement. This film does not present the close contemplation or measured framing of animals and humans in the way *Sweetgrass* does. However, it is no less Bazinian in its approach. *Los Herederos* frequently combines animals and children together in the frame in ways that show this relationship as incidental and the movement of both, and the interaction between them, draws the eye across the frame. The framing achieves a harmony that suggests the correspondence between the labor of humans and animals.

Despite the potential for sentimentalizing child workers, *Los Herederos* avoids posing a clear emotional engagement with the viewer. Without voiceover, dialogue, or fast-paced editing, meaning is conveyed only through the information conveyed in the frame and the camera does not linger on faces, but prefers long shots of people (and animals) moving or close-ups of body parts in action. Once the camera has registered the essence of the activity it wishes to convey, it cuts away to another. The facial expressions that are captured are usually impassive, although children sometimes seem joyful as they look into the camera, presumably a response to the novel presence of the filmmaker. Yet, the style employed is not one that encourages particular empathy with the many individuals that populate the film.

As the images of work repeat and accrue meaning, it becomes clear not only that the film is about child labor, but also that aspects usually associated with childhood, dedicated time to play and learn, are not part of the lifeworld represented. Nevertheless, these young children, who are more often than not unaccompanied by adults, find ways to turn work into play. This occurs at a number of points in the film, and in a closing scene a group of three young boys muster a small group of animals (goats, donkeys, and dogs), down the road. Their T-shirts have been taken off and they wave them at the animals. Soon they are shouting and waving them at each other in a kind of jumping dance. The scene that follows is the last, shot at night with a weaving loom working, music playing, and children and adults dancing in a festive atmosphere. This points to a tonality in the film that references the experiences of both hardship and joy. Crucially, these moments bring a humanism to the film that otherwise objectifies the children within the focus on activity and process. Even more so than the previous films discussed, an emphasis is placed on *showing* in *Los Herederos*, and asking the viewer to deduce meaning about the physicality of this life, rather than explaining cause and effect or constructing the inner life of these subjects. I argue that what is shown affects a more political address to the viewer than *Raw Herring* and *Sweetgrass*. It politicizes the representation of life in a way that the other two, despite their greater authorial commentary (even if only in the closing titles in *Sweetgrass*) do not.

While *Los Herederos* again largely depicts an existence seemingly removed from technologized industry, without machinery or even electricity, there are aspects that hint at the contemporaneity of the film, such as the cars and trucks that pass by on the road as families work in a nearby field picking vegetables. The viewer is alerted to the fact that they inhabit the same era of industrial modernity as these families. And yet those in the film have been left behind and are precariously situated in a subsistence economy and as part of Mexico's rural poor. While it cannot be known for certain, most likely the families own the animals but not the land they work. The reliance on small numbers of animals, moreover, further suggests that this is a subsistence economy. The multiple tasks performed by animals and children are captured by the camera and accrue over the ninety-minute duration of the film, reinforcing the rhythms and persistence of this life. When viewed alongside *Raw Herring* and *Sweetgrass*, however, *Los Herederos* throws the almost completely masculinized sphere of work in the two films into stark relief. In *Los Herederos* everyone works, including children, women with babies, and the elderly woman that the camera follows as she tends to the chickens.

The ongoing and extended toil of the children, working with the concentration of adults, is discordant with modern day conceptions of both childhood and labor. Koehler refers to both *Sweetgrass* and *Los Herederos* when he writes, "the guiding force behind these representations" is "an overwhelming sadness at the process of collapse and the end of things, alongside the unspoken drama of human beings stuck in a cycle with no escape" ("Agrarian," 13). However, *Los Herederos*, I suggest, achieves a singular critique through observation alone.[22] This is because it is concerned not with change and the demise of traditional lifeworlds, but rather with the life and environments of the astonishingly poor. Images of children in visual culture are often presented in ways that signify hope and futurity. The film's title, *The Inheritors* in English, gives the greatest indication of Polgovsky's message: well before adulthood and while their parents are alive and working, these children inherit working lives at the very edge of global modernity. This is not a traditional world that is moving toward an end or a decline; there is a different correspondence between animals and humans as both labor together in a seemingly endless cycle of subsistence as both are subjected to social and cultural forces.

Sweetgrass and *Raw Herring* are concerned with worlds in which animals and humans are tied together in mutual economic and environmental ecologies that, the films inform us, cannot continue to thrive in the contemporary world. *Los Herederos*, in a slightly different fashion, shows the viewer a world in which people are caught in a cycle in which they can only subsist, left behind by capitalist modernity. In different ways each expresses a life of precarious labor and in this life animals and humans are wrought together. The broader group of observational documentaries is interesting because, as my discussion of the representation of the materiality of life and lifeworld has shown, they highlight the relative play of power across species. While agency is constituted in very different ways, nonhuman animals and humans both have negligible control over the outcome of their toil or productivity. Yet, although animal and human subjection is cast in the same frame the films do not present them as equivalent by any means. The fishermen, cowboys, and child workers are presented in a distinctly humanist manner.

Life as an Object of Power: The Problem of Humanism

Considering the aim of this chapter—to explore aesthetic and ideological questions about laboring over and with animals—I wish to elaborate on the question of life as an object of power. As I have described, *Sweetgrass*, *Raw Herring*, and *Los Herederos* present quotidian human worlds effected by the forces of modernity that are, in many instances, gestured to beyond the frame. Within these representations of life and lifeworlds such forces shape the lives of workers, threatening or exploiting their labor and marginalizing them in systems of capital; however, they also position animals, albeit in different ways, as objects of power. There are grounds for investigating how the expression of life in the three films, enhanced by the long take style, is deployed in ways that might attend to this question of power.

Foucault's notion of biological modernity situates life as the object of power, to be optimized and utilized in ways that reproduce systems of capital. While almost exclusively concerned with human subjectivity, biopolitical thought nevertheless offers methods that have the potential to theorize not only on the regulation of human life, but all species, populations, crops, and ecosystems. Understanding the external forces gestured to in the films as biopolitical forces enables a consideration of the mutually productive capacities of *both* humans and animals. This brings to the fore an awareness of the management of the bios, of life, in ways that may facilitate a critique of the informing narrative of modernity. Most scholarship exploring the biological dimensions of power has assumed, as Matthew Chrulew writes, "while nature may be worked, it does not work" ("Animals in Biopolitical," 62). Referencing Michael Hardt and Antonio Negri's approach to the biopolitcal, he goes on to argue that "in the current post-natural era dubbed the Anthropocene, it is no longer possible to maintain an absolute distinction between human and animal, social and natural, at least if one truly wants 'finally to recognise the full generality of the concept of proletariat'" ("Animals in Biopolitical," 62).[23] This should not encourage a move to equate human with nonhuman labor and productivity—rather it supports an exploration of how they are both rendered in and subjected to systems of power. If these films share an aesthetic concern with rendering life through the long take, they do so in ways that facilitate a strong focus on labor and the productive capacity of bodies, both human and nonhuman.

The films I have discussed forgo a biopolitical critique of this kind and focus on the *humanism* of labor instead—work is shown only in reference to the quotidian, both its ills and the joys of its camaraderie. The effects of disciplining forces of control and regulation are implicit in the narrative but remain largely beyond the frame where human bodies are concerned (the laments of the cowboy speaking with his mother notwithstanding). The effects of power on animal bodies are more apparent as they are reared by humans or consumed as food. In *Sweetgrass* and *Raw Herring* animals produce biomatter (food or wool) for consumption. They work with and for humans in *Los Herederos* and *Sweetgrass*, films that pose the productive capacities of animals for human gain, often encompassing both in the same frame. If consideration is given to the Anthropocene, and the anthropogenic impact on the nonhuman world, only *Raw Herring*, with its suggestion of declining fish numbers, gestures to a problem in environmental dimensions. Instead of life as an object of power, the films of the long take bring their formal emphasis on life, instead, to an alternative awareness. These films serve to alert viewers anew to the materiality of animals and lifeworlds in which humans and animals exist in close proximity.

Equally concerned with animal bodies in the sphere of agriculture and fishing are the much-discussed examples, *Leviathan* and *Our Daily Bread*. It is instructive to mention, at least briefly, how these films contribute to the cluster I have identified. They offer a counterpoint to the humanism of the three films examined so far, expressing raw productivity and flattening human labor into an affectless and machinic function. As I discuss more fully in the next chapter, *Our Daily Bread* documents different sites that contribute to a landscape of agribusiness. It stages a theater of factories, farms, abattoirs, and greenhouses, which are inhabited by workers and animals. In *Leviathan* the cold lyricism present in *Our Daily Bread* becomes a dark vision that documents life on a commercial fishing boat. In comparison with *Sweetgrass*, *Leviathan's* expressive coloring, framing, and editing construct this film in ways that require the viewer to grapple more significantly with discerning the referent of the film, which is rendered in a much more dreamlike, subjective manner.

The flatness of these examples exploits the potential for surrealism that Russell observes in traditions of ethnographic spectacle. These films highlight, as the others do not, Foucault's "anatomo-politics," or machine-like productive capacity of humans under capitalism. Moreover, while the humans here are not slaughtered or filleted, and so clearly not subjected to the same processes as the animals, the retreat from dialogue, affect, and other humanizing qualities contributes to the heightened portrayal of life as one that is systemized and optimized in the interests of productivity. There is little to discern the fishermen from the fish—both appear without agency or hope, taking the documentaries much further toward critiquing industrial systems that situate life, animal, and human, as an object of power. This moves even further from Haraway's notion of "becoming with" and "becoming worldly" (37) that structures her reciprocal encounters with animals. In *Leviathan* and *Our Daily Bread*, humans and animals are posed as companions, but in a much less affirmative way than features in Haraway's formulation.

Animals Appear

I have explored how animals are cast in worlds of modernity, as objects of the labor of fishing and agriculture, often figuring prominently in the tension between change and tradition. At the outset of this chapter I contended that this grouping of films offers a site within film culture that necessitates a departure from Haraway's concept of multispecies relations, with its emphasis on heterogeneity and contestation of human privilege. While these documentaries, for the most part, do not displace human exceptionalism in the way advocated by Haraway, they nevertheless bring a new awareness to the materiality of animals by employing the long take style. These films ask us to attend to animals, and animal productivity, by rendering them conspicuously in human lifeworlds. They overlap with a broader movement toward experimental ethnography that Pick describes as featuring "humanity's relationship to its nonhuman surroundings" in ways that involve "the redrawing of the conditions of vision that currently determine not simply how we see animals onscreen, but whether we see them at all" ("Ecovisions"). The different examples I have described achieve this through avantgarde observation and by echoing and extending histories of documentary representation featuring the activity of labor and the animal interlopers of ethnographic tradition.

The films might be viewed in relation to a frequent criticism leveled at intensely observational cinema: that observation without overt explication eschews a politicizing social narrative and offers, instead, only images open to multiple interpretation, decontextualized from the forces that produce the situations represented. But as many scholars have argued, observation is never simply objective but rather always subject to the crafting of selection and editing, which itself produces an implicit point of view. *Los Herederos* offers an example of the possibilities for more explicitly narrating the operation of power. The exposition and explication of the social structures that dictate the terms and/or failure of progress, change and the commerce of precarious labor are, in most cases, rendered implicitly through suggestion and implication.

The three documentaries present the viewer with the nonfiction representation of environments and structures of life as the outcome of an ethnographic investigation, but are attentive to an expressive practice that explores textuality and offers pleasure in the possibilities of gesture and form. In this respect, the films are attuned to the exploration of cinema's essence, in the Bazinian sense. Through the long take and the demand that the viewers give themselves over to the duration of the shot, they bring to the fore the importance of time. The experience of labor is conveyed through the movement of the body and the gesture of the worker, whether it is waiting, gathering, carrying, and herding. Persistence is thrown into relief in *Sweetgrass* and *Raw Herring* by the narrative markers that point to a cultural tradition drawing to a close. In *Los Herederos* the unceasing activity of labor is simply accentuated by the long take.

In an era of factory farming, genetic manipulation of the biotic world and mass feedlots, this contemporary grouping of films returns the viewer to questions about living with animals. Documentaries about labor are almost defined by their relationship to humanism, their potential to embrace the affective physicality of the worker or dehumanize it. These films are no different. In the case of these three long take films, the problem of precarious labor is confronted by underscoring human qualities and characteristics— these are human stories. The films do not challenge the anthropomorphism of cinema, but do, within their focus on humans, cast light on the unique lifeworld of people living and working with animals in the current epoch. Animals exist alongside humans, inhabiting the documentary long take as it asks us to stay with animals, to be with them in their distinctiveness and mutability. With the duration of the shot, *Raw Herring*, *Los Herederos*, and *Sweetgrass* enable the viewer to linger on the embodied, visual qualities of fish, birds, sheep, donkeys, dogs, and horses. They may be subordinated to human stories and identity (and be the source of human food), but they are far from invisible, and nor are they eclipsed by metaphor or anthropomorphism. The precarious lifeworlds that are the object of representation are populated with animals, with their texture and with their energy.

Chapter 3

Meat, Animals, and Paradigms
of Embodiment

Documentary Identification
and the Problem of Food

Human enterprise in late modernity has transformed the material basis of animal existence, using and manipulating animals on an increasingly massive scale. This is most clearly visible in the sphere of industrial agriculture, a setting that provides some of the most powerful and controversial imagery of animal exploitation. Such images reveal automated slaughterhouses, mass feedlots and factories that characterize large-scale industrial farming. In this chapter I investigate documentaries that reference this material transformation, focusing on animals and food production. I attend to the manner in which films speak specifically to the shared experience of eating meat in order to present arguments about the food system, melding sensory and epistemological identification in their address to viewer. The past decade or more has seen the resurgent popularity of feature-length documentaries, and a cluster of films about food production, often posed in relation to a crisis of industrialization, has emerged as part of this documentary renaissance. Frequently, animals, animal slaughter, and meat feature in these films in ways that endow them with a special status in imagery and arguments concerning food-related issues. In the previous chapter I identified an aesthetically and thematically cohesive group of examples concerned with a lifeworld specific to agriculture and fishing. Here I am again interested in exploring a consistent body of films, but one unified by an emphasis on animal life as a part of the process of producing beef, poultry, and pork.

The cluster of films I am concerned with depicts animals in agriculture, fishing and/or industry and includes films such as *Maharajah Burger* (1997), *A Cow at My Table* (1998), *Beef, Inc.* (1999), *Bacon, The Film* (2002),

45

Animals (2003), *Darwin's Nightmare* (2004), *We Feed the World* (2005), *Our Daily Bread* (2005), *End of the Line* (2009), *King Corn* (2007), *Milk In The Land: Ballad of An American Drink* (2007), *Meat the Truth* (2008), *Food, Inc.* (2008), *Pig Business* (2009), *Fresh* (2009), *Farmageddon: The Truth About the Food and Dairy Industry* (2012), *The Moo Man* (2012), *The Last Ocean* (2012), *Leviathan* (2013), *Raw Herring* (2013),[1] *American Meat* (2013), and *The Animal Condition* (2014). Many of these films identify problems with large-scale fishing or agricultural practices and "agribusiness," critiquing the interests of commerce, the activities of the state and/or the effects on the consumer and, to a lesser extent, the environment.

While offering politicized arguments about the food industry, these films are, for the most part, not concerned with the question of animal rights, ethics, or promoting vegetarianism per se. They share much with the films discussed in the last chapter; they do not lend themselves to the multispecies critiques that are prevalent in film studies and the humanities more widely. Animals are not partners in "world sharing," in this instance. They are, instead, largely framed by notions of ethical consumption and a critique of the evils of mass production, rather than the practice of the eating of meat. This presents a new figuration of the animal, inaugurated by the ethical demand to reflect on consumer practices, a development that also, I suggest, offers the possibility of rethinking documentary identification. I begin by locating these films not only in relation to the historical representation of food production and industry, but also by considering the slaughterhouse as a resonant site for understanding the sensory qualities and impact of cinema more broadly.

Slaughterhouses, Film Histories, and the Senses

Many of the aforementioned food documentaries are allied with the resurgent popularity of feature-length documentaries described in the first chapter. Although beyond *Food Inc.* few have achieved significant box office success, food documentaries have developed and circulated alongside the handful of highly visible films that have exemplified the documentary renaissance. They can be associated particularly with the significant body of films that critique corporate dominance particularly in a North American context.[2] Often food documentaries also follow arguments based in social responsibility, overlapping with films that investigate the demise of the environment and natural resources, which are often classified as "eco-documentaries." Robin Murray and Joseph Heumann usefully adapt this category, identifying a body of contemporary documentary as "eco-food films."[3] I pursue an understanding of documentary and animals as food (and the necessary precursor to this, animal death) by looking not only at the documentary renaissance but also at longer traditions of documentary film, ones that include not only representation but also the mechanical and ontological qualities of cinema.

With many examples of food documentaries seeking to persuade the viewer about a problem in the historical world, frequently arguing against the interests of industry and capital, the contemporary films reference traditions of leftist and labor documentary.[4] Especially salient in this respect is *The Hour of the Furnaces* (*La Hora de Los Hornos*) (1968), one of the most influential political films of the twentieth century. The first part of Fernando E. Solanas and Octavio Getino's monumental document of neocolonialism in Latin America juxtaposes scenes filmed in an abattoir with still images from advertising, conveying both horror and exploitation. *American Dream* (1990), Barbara Kopple's *cinéma vérité* account of striking meatworkers in Minnesota, is also notable. It is a film that opens with workers cutting up hog carcasses in the plant. While neither of these films is concerned with the problem of food, they make use of images of animal death and the production line to comment on human labor and the barbarity/artifice of capitalism.

With consistent attention to the mechanics of the factory line and other food production technologies, a number of these films find precursors in postwar food education films.[5] Another point of reference can be found in the more recent subgenre of animal rights films, such as films by PETA, including *A Day in the Life of a Massachusetts Slaughterhouse* (1998) and *Meet Your Meat* (2003). These three different modes of filmmaking all seek to educate the viewer in either a public service mode (the food education films) or to reveal a problem in the social world, as in the case of the animal rights films and labor documentaries. For Jonathan Burt, animal rights films are exceptional because they confound evaluation or, as he describes, are "at the extreme end of an identifiable, cinematic language, which—although highly manipulative of the audience's sensibilities—has very uncertain effects" ("Review: *A Day in the Life*," 350). In her study of animals, biopolitics, and capital, Nicole Shukin offers a new relevance to the connection between slaughterhouses and cinema, especially early cinema, observing that both of these technologies are bound up in the same logic of time-motion.

For Shukin, both the Fordist machinery of mass slaughter and the mechanics of precinema devices have a preoccupation with animals and movement. She refers to the correspondences between the spectacle of

Muybridge's horses and birds and the tours of slaughterhouses that were designed to show the public the astonishing new technology of the production line.[6] These tours followed "the same insistent sequential sense as the cinematic reel, a logic that frames impassive stages of deanimating animal life as an inexorable progression" (101). Both technologies are concerned with the transformation of animal life and the efficiency and spectacle of the technologies of modernity. The correspondences Shukin identifies encourage, for my purposes, a way of understanding the historical threads connecting the subgenres of education films, animal rights films, and labor films featuring animals by underlining the spectacle of industrial slaughter and its conceptual/historical ties to cinema.

The on-screen transformation of animal bodies, and its corporeal dimensions, draw attention to time-motion connections between cinema and slaughterhouses. The temporal quality of cinema, its ability to convey events and motion across time, also heightens its capacity to engage the viewers' senses. In this instance I refer especially to the sensory experience in response to animal life and death. Early and proto-cinematic apparatuses, as I explored in chapter 1, relied on not only human, but also animal vitalism to communicate the potential of moving image technology. From this time, the sensory dimensions of cinema have found an affiliation with the possibility of manipulating and observing animal bodies. Shukin extends this into the symbolic origins of cutting and editing, noting that "Vertov and Eisenstein envisaged a 'biology of the cinema,'" founded in "an affective immediacy achieved by the filmic ability to cut and paste parts into a montage whose startling juxtapositions would strike differently on viewer's senses" (102). She draws on the resonances between the cutting of cinema and the intensity of animal death on the "disassembly" line, both of which build sensory impact. Across these rich circuits of representation identified by Shukin, biological life and death is manifest as metaphor and, perhaps more importantly, materially embodied in animals.

Animal death onscreen and the momentary transition from life to matter or "thing" offers an exceptional form of visual assault on the viewer. Such transformations are central to the affective force of examples as diverse as *Electrocuting an Elephant* (1903) by Thomas Edison, Georges Franju's *Le Sang des bêtes* (1949), and *Meat* (1976) by Fredric Wiseman. Gualtiero Jacopetti, Franco Prosperi, and Paolo Cavara's *Mondo Cane* (1962) is the most infamous documentary to depict the killing of animals. Animal death also has a particular ontological relevance in cinema. At the heart of the difficulty of animal death is the knowledge that animal slaughter, unlike human death onscreen, is almost always unsimulated.

The animal death I refer to is not the slow death of illness but the abruptness of violent death—this manner of animal death is more frequently represented in film. Abruptness and violence, Vivian Sobchack argues in her discussion of the representation of death in documentary, "best articulate death" ("Inscribing Ethical," 290), activating a visceral response to the demarcation between existence and inanimate life. More than this, she outlines a special relationship between documentary and animal death. Inspired by the example of Jean Renoir's *Rules of the Game*, Sobchack notes that even in fiction film animal death is recognized by the viewer as the documentary presentation of death. The killing of a rabbit in *Rules of the Game* "violently, abruptly punctuates narrative space with documentary space" ("Inscribing Ethical," 293) because the viewer knows it's easier to kill a rabbit than have it "play dead" or perform death while the inverse is true of human death. Animal death in fiction extends off-screen, defying containment by the narrative and, I suggest, this knowledge of the ease and permissibility of animal death means that the killing of animals is often used in order to evoke horror. The actuality of such representations decisively exacerbates this horror. The sensory magnitude evoked by the representation of animal death and the disarticulation of animal bodies continues to be relevant to more recent examples that gesture to the social, ideological, and technological dimensions of the relationship between animals and food production.

The Problem of Food

If recent food documentaries often exploit the specific and powerful intensity of animal death, they do so in the service of presenting the "problem" of food (rather than disputing the necessity of animal death) and its multiple implications.[7] The problem is not singular, but rather encompasses both the troubling source of food and the negative impact of food on the physicality of the consumer.[8] Sites of crisis or difficulty in the food system, moreover, are foregrounded in the address to the viewer across these divergent examples, rather than particular concrete aesthetic or narrative consistencies. Identification necessitates that viewers recognize themselves in the address of the text. At the level of the social, documentaries that seek to have impact on the public sphere address a specific demography that can be understood as a subject-citizen. Documentary, when working for a political concern, inevitably addresses the subject of politics, the citizen, in ways that recognize civic, political, and social rights and responsibilities. Employing the discourses of science and education, food documentaries provide modes of visible evidence to inform a constituency of viewers about the process of food production. This evokes not simply a citizen, but the "food citizen" described by Jennifer Wilkins:

> In relation to our food choices, we have certain rights associated with living in a particular place—the right to safe unadulterated food or truthful product information, for example, but that there are also responsibilities that go along with this kind of citizenship [. . .] people can "eat responsibly" to help stem the decline of American farming and rural life. (269)

Wilkins is referring not only to the food consumer, but, more precisely, to the citizen food consumer.

The notion of a consumer citizen points to a potential tension between the individualism of consumerism and the shared civic values of citizenship. The two have been framed historically in political and popular discourse as mutually exclusive (Barnett et al. 33). With the rise of consumer activism over the past two decades, however, advocates have responded to this opposition by harnessing the narratives of individualism *and* responsibility to foster and normalize a common ground between these two modes of selfhood. Matthew Hilton historicizes the marriage of morality and consumerism by charting the (often negative) moralizing impulses that informed consumption and consumers from Victorian times through to the mid-twentieth century. He describes a number of contemporary examples that constitute "a discernible trend to remoralise the market through issues of ethical consumerism and globalisation" (119). The relationship between food, civic responsibility, and consumer agency provides a background for understanding how the public sphere informs many of these films and their arguments concerning food and animals.

I accentuate the dual implication of the term "consumer" as referring to one who engages in modes of capitalist exchange to acquire food commodities but also, in a more sensory register, one who must participate in the intimate process of eating. Food and eating is tied powerfully to affective and social meaning. This is especially the case where the eating of animals is concerned. With the phrase "citizen food consumer," I reference this paradigm of social and affective selfhood that describes the putative subject viewer for these documentaries. If the citizen food consumer is the intended viewer for these films, the embodied *and* social dimensions of this subjectivity must be accounted for when explicating the engagement between documentary and viewer.

Documentaries invite the spectator to understand themselves as the subject of knowledge, one who desires or comes to take the place of the other of knowledge (the one who knows), in response to the codes and conventions through which the genre "asserts itself as real" (Cowie 86). Elizabeth Cowie brings this discussion of the desire for the certainty of the knowable to an understanding of the identities onscreen: "documentary informs us of the world, offering us identities in the images and stories of other lives that it presents that become fixed as known and knowable through its account and explanation of the world it shows" (88). Documentary identification, in this respect, reinforces approaches to fiction film that pose humans as the subject and object of vision and affect. Yet, a documentary's address does not plainly or necessarily isolate semantic and epistemological concerns from the somatic and the experiential. As I have demonstrated, early cinema techniques played to the vitalist and affective potential of cinema. Attending to more recent traditions of documentary film, scholars have argued that the assertion of the real often encourages an embodied connection to the world presented. For Jane Gaines, documentary film is a mimetic technology that has the power to "reproduce the world before us as well as to reproduce its intensities onscreen, and to reproduce them most strategically in the bodies and hearts and minds of viewers" (40). Similarly, Bill Nichols writes that "the affective engagement of the viewer with social tensions and pleasures, conflicts and values—move the viewer away from the status of observer to that of participant" (194). More than a narrowly conceived notion of epistephilia, a desire for knowledge based simply in observation, these approaches point to the genre's capacity to foreground sensorial meaning as a way of accessing the world of the film.

This group of films requires an approach to documentary identification that accounts not only for the affective social participation encouraged by documentaries, but also the embodied appeal to the consumer. Thomas Csordas refers to "paradigms of embodiment" to discuss the interrelationship between knowledge and embodied experience, opening space for the possibility of a cultural phenomenology. Through this phrase it is possible to elaborate on how documentaries might initiate ways of *knowing* in conjunction with "somatic modes of attention" (151). In her well-known work on film phenomenology, Sobchack extends her earlier work on documentary film and death and focuses on the somatic in her call for recognition of the *"carnal foundations of cinematic intelligibility"*:

> [. . .] we might wish to think again about processes of identification in the film experience, relating them not to our secondary

> engagement with and recognition of either "subject positions"
> or characters but rather to our primary engagement (and the
> film's) with the sense and sensibility of materiality itself. We,
> ourselves, are subjective matter: our lived bodies sensually relate
> to "things" that "matter" on the screen and find them sensible in
> a primary, prepersonal, and global way that grounds those later
> secondary identifications that are more discrete and localised.
> (*Carnal Thoughts*, 65)

Sobchack's call for a rethinking of cinematic intelligibility, while largely posed in relation to narrative fiction cinema, is well suited to a consideration of food documentary. This is due to the way it reflects on the relationship between identification with human subjectivity (and potentially the documentary viewer as the subject of knowledge *and* the consumer) and identification with materiality and matter, which invokes food and the activity of eating. The two are figured together and with recourse to established notions of secondary and primary identification.

Locating the citizen food consumer as the privileged subject of knowledge presents an opportunity to explore how documentaries might engage sensual registers to move beyond the participation described by Nichols and Gaines, possibly in ways that evoke the sensory immediacy sought by early cinema. Moreover, the emphasis on the problem of food and its ties to meat and animals in these films facilitates an investigation into how food documentaries might either reiterate or newly revise established understandings of the human onscreen as the privileged site of cinematic identification. Moreover, what are the ramifications of accentuating identification with the corporeality of animal bodies, particularly when it involves a recognition of the intercorporeal process by which meat is consumed as food? In the sections that follow I explore these contingencies and do so by attending to particularly potent moments of spectatorial engagement. I am informed by Adrian Ivakhiv's notion that "condensed 'hyper-singaletic' or 'resonant moments'—moments in which spectacle, narrative and meaning are brought together, compactly synthesised in sound/image bits" are those that are "retained most powerfully in viewers affective memories" (64–65). Not only do particular moments stay with us as a residue after viewing, they can create sites for heightened identification due to the way they condense and sharpen meaning within the broader address of the film. I identify three sites of identification, exploring how the viewer is asked to engage with the intimate sensory process by which "things" become edible or inedible; empathize with the human body of the consumer; and identify anthropomorphically with animals. A handful of prominent documentary examples offer particularly useful ways of exploring this dimension of documentary poetics: *Food, Inc.*, *King Corn*, *Darwin's Nightmare*, *Our Daily Bread*, and *The Moo Man*.

Transformation, Animals, and Meat: Edible and Inedible Food

Many food documentaries present images of poultry, beef, fish, or pork in different stages of life and death in factories, abattoirs, and farms. Films frequently utilize stock footage of factory production lines or footage filmed during slaughter and processing, with or without the consent of factory or farm owners. Whole chicken carcasses moving through factory lines constitute a reoccurring motif, their visual form a recognizable reference to living chickens. Films concerned with fishing, such as *Leviathan* and *Raw Herring*, provide a different interpretation of this theme by showing workers harvesting and filleting fish on an industrial scale onboard ship. The first examples I consider demonstrate a direct aesthetic manifestation of the material relation between meat and animals. This aspect of the food documentary dwells on and frequently disrupts the epistemological and visual process by which animals attain the status of food by depicting the animals as, in some way, unfit for consumption.

The scenes in question draw attention to the context, primarily the industrial context, in which animals are subjected to breeding, rearing, and slaughter regimes in order to call into question some aspect of instrumentalist rationality in food production. That is to say, this emphasis on visual corporeality offers a way to question and destabilize assumptions about the merit of unfettered commercial efficiency in the different locales the films present. Most powerfully, the temporal sensory process by which "things" become food in these contexts is disrupted by images of inedible meat or fish. Also relevant here are the images and stories that present sickly animals (on factory farms particularly), rendered in ways that diverge greatly from the pastoral ideal of healthy livestock. Resonant sites of identification address the citizen food consumer by amplifying the boundary between animal and meat and meat and the human consumer.

Hubert Sauper's *Darwin's Nightmare*, a film that focuses only in part on industrial food production, offers one of the most sustained examples of the way food is visually presented to encourage the viewer to classify it as inedible. While the Nile perch is ostensibly the focus of the film, it soon becomes clear that the fish is made to embody and signify a complex network of human interaction and exploitation. The huge fish carcass consistently dominates the frame as the viewer learns about how the growth in commerce around the fish, which is harvested from Lake Victoria and transported for sale in Europe, has triggered ecological and social catastrophe at a local level.[9] The fish is not only shown in the sanitized processing plant, but the remains that are discarded by the plant are retrieved by local people and hung out on racks to dry for consumption in the impoverished local community. Sequences that depict this activity in the documentary show fish carcasses strewn in heaps on the ground and covered by maggots in racks. The fish remains offer a visual metaphor for the unfolding horror of the situation in the local community and, thus, seek a sensory *and* ideological response of repulsion from the viewer.

The documentary clearly disrupts the process by which the fish becomes recognized as edible for the citizen food consumer. These images play to the particular intimacy involved in eating, especially eating meat. There is a strong visual component to the process by which we come to recognize objects as food, and good food especially. Ocular and other sensory processes can facilitate acceptance or rejection, often in the form of disgust. Emma Roe poses an account of the process by which things become food. She examines "how a thing (an animal or plant) passes through a set of human practices and material processes that *do* the translating from food production to food consumption" (109). Consumers accept and trust that the process that the "thing" (animal and animal flesh) has undergone constitute it as edible. This is a pervasively corporeal set of connections in the respect that it invites the consumer to acknowledge their embodiment and the potential encounter with nonhuman foodstuffs that might be ingested. *Darwin's Nightmare* explicitly frames the fish in ways that accentuate its status as food but it is repeatedly presented aesthetically as unclean, abject, and therefore inedible food. It seeks to persuade the viewer, as I have noted, that this is due to the unethical priorities and commercial efficiencies of industry.

Unsettling the function of animals as food in a slightly different manner, examples such as *Food, Inc.*, *King Corn*, *A Cow at My Table*, and *Maharajah Burger* (a film that takes a cross-cultural perspective on the food industry), feature livestock that are ailing in some way. These include cattle with bovine spongiform encephalopathy (BSE), chickens given hormones to artificially accelerate their growth, or cows with stomach problems as a consequence of being grain-fed. Conveyed in images and in the narration, these ailing animals serve to support the proposition that the industrial food system is in crisis and, because of this, these animals are not attaining the status of edible food.

In her discussion of *Food, Inc.* Jennifer Barker specifically addresses the question of disgust. For Barker, while *Food, Inc.* may not explicitly depict disgusting images it "performs the very attitude it seeks in its viewers, comporting itself in ways that reflect 'disgust' and encouraging viewers to empathise with its bodily movements" ("Chew On This," 73). Barker focuses in particular on the chicken houses in *Food, Inc.* that, managed by Purdue Farms and run by farmers financially beholden to the company, are overcrowded, dark, and underventilated. Chickens are often unable to walk because their bones and internal organs cannot keep pace with the bioengineered rapid growth dictated by the company. The full impact of this scene is relayed in the narration as the camera (and viewer) is denied access to the houses. For Barker the film encourages disgust responses through strategies of delay and absence. While narration is important, I argue that the meanings pertaining to animals, the explicit and the inferred, are most powerfully rendered by what is seen, how identification is aligned with the animal as object of vision, and how the film orchestrates this.

The film presents images that specifically discourage an association with edible food. One disgruntled farmer does allow the camera access and the resulting images depict chickens at close range, dwelling on the corporeality of their bodies. One scene focuses on a chicken breathing heavily, according to the voiceover, apparently unable to stand because its skeletal

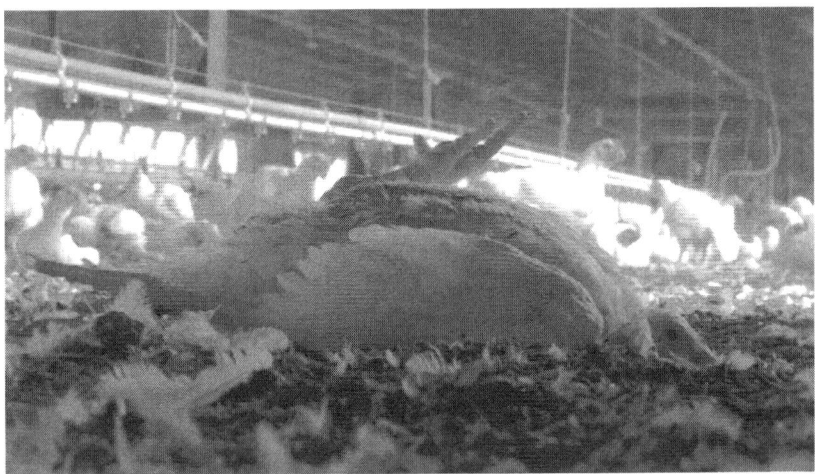

Figure 3.1. A chicken lies on its back, breathing heavily, unable to stand because its frame cannot support its accelerated growth in *Food, Inc.* (2008).

frame cannot support its weight. Another scene uses a night vision camera to show dead chickens thrown into trucks. The depiction of animal sickness and animal corpses outside the sanitized conditions of processing plants unhinges any link between the living chicken and the chicken as food.

Our Daily Bread, by director and cinematographer Nikolaus Geyrhalter, is a film that experiments with the visual as factual knowledge.[10] As I describe in chapter 2, it accentuates the work of framing and editing by eschewing any music, dialogue, or voiceover. Recording different sites of high-tech food production in Europe, the camera lingers on its object, frequently offering a tableau of factory or farm, including workers and animals in the frame. In each sequence there is a sense that the camera has caught an extended moment that continues before and after the recorded scene, thus inferring continuity and repetition. Many instances present scenes of conversion or metamorphosis in the food system, from a worker eating lunch in a tea room (consuming and ingesting food is a form of conversion), to a cow being inseminated or a series of chicks being debeaked. Notably, the film includes chickens, cows, fish, and pigs in various stages of transformation from living animal to packaged meat product (including slaughter).

The documentary deploys duration, rhythm, and image in a manner that opens a space of interpretation for the viewer to draw conclusions about contemporary European agribusiness and the alienating relations of mass

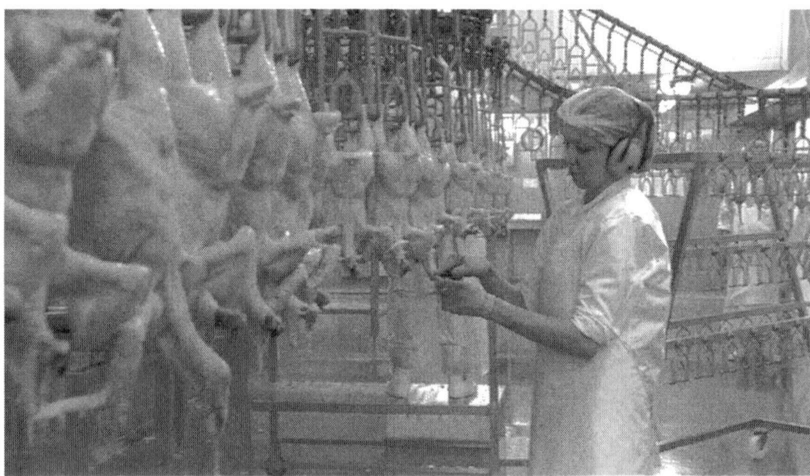

Figure 3.2. A worker trims chicken necks and the visceral is juxtaposed with the hard surfaces of the production line in *Our Daily Bread* (2005).

food production. Pick identifies a particular poetry of the mechanical in the film. She writes that the film's "aestheticism is the effect of rational excess, the point at which reason no longer pertains to or addresses the world" (*Creaturely*, 140). Animals transform into food through a banal process that is enacted by humans and machines and both are equivalent in the frame.

The rhythm of gestures and movement the film depicts revolves around repetition. A female worker trims turkey carcasses with a knife as they move past, suspended on a seemingly endless production line. Slaughter is shown most decisively in the film when a cow that is held in a rolling metal frame is shot through the head with an automated bolt, killing the animal only shortly before the camera moves on to observe another scene. The only sound is the background noise of machines in operation as they hum and clunk. It is not only the visible, audible, and visceral transition from living animal to foodstuff, but also the scale of mass repetition and automation that unsettles the status of meat as edible food in this case. In *Our Daily Bread* animal flesh becomes bland organic matter that is associated with the hard tones and surfaces of machines and automated processes. To this extent, the documentary visually evacuates a meaningful relationship between the production of meat, as it is shown in the film, and edible food.

The scenes I have attended to in *Our Daily Bread*, *Food, Inc.*, and *Darwin's Nightmare* charge the viewer's perceptions of the source and composition of meat with the materiality of the audiovisual. They contribute to an argument about the food system not by building meaning through testimony and other cultural artifacts, but rather through an evacuation of representational meaning. As the camera offers visual access to the world and the details of places and objects, it juxtaposes machine and animal, dirt ground and fish carcass, and human and animal in ways that produce abjection or alienation. The moments I have described in these films draw attention to the viewer's own corporeality and the boundary confusion that can result from eating animals. For Cowie identity arises, in part, in relation to an imaginative, cognitive and sensory "recognition of the self as entity, a bodily differentiation between what is me and what is not me, and thus other" (88). This recognition of identity is discouraged for the spectator and they are confronted with intercorporeality as the (inedible) animal other potentially becomes part of the self.

Identification, in one sense, is located in an epistemological awareness of the food system. However, in another sense, the film experience is composed most powerfully through a phenomenological register as the status of food within this industrial system is conveyed in ways that demand somatic attention to the materiality of animals, or in Sobchack's words, "the sense and sensibility of materiality itself" (*Carnal Thoughts*, 65). This dimension of identification is a sensible recognition of embodiment as intercorporeality and is testament to Gail Weiss's notion that "the experience of being embodied is never a private affair, but is always mediated by our continual interactions with other human and nonhuman bodies" (5). More than a psychoanalytic fracturing of the self, these films work to institute a mode of recognition that is specific to the relation between the human food consumer and the nonhuman animal other. The chickens, fish, and other animals and meat become abject as a breakdown of meaning characterizes the process that is needed for them to be perceived as food. The documentaries, in different ways, address the citizen food consumer's right to know about the origins of food on supermarket shelves but do so by employing indexical images and the realist style of documentary to depict the actuality of animals in ways that unsettle the boundaries of the self.

The Embodied Consumer

At pivotal moments, the documentaries ask the viewer to recognize and empathize with their mirror image, the food (specifically meat) consumer. *Food, Inc.* and *King Corn* both focus on the body of the consumer in ways that refer to food production and its potential consequences. These scenes again offer a lens through which to understand the broader rhetorical position of the film as it seeks to call into question commercial interests in the food system. In this case there is a clear critique of the impact of the industrial process on the food consumer. The feature of the food documentary that I explore in this section forgoes the visible evidence that ties animal and meat, instead inferring the animal through a focus on the human consumer.

The focus on the consumer's face and voice reinforces a history of social documentary in which the speaking (human) subject conveys the "political." John Corner identifies speech and visual material as fundamental in the portrayal of the political in documentary. As Corner notes, "more than most other topics, the political requires specific identifications to be made, articulations of relationships to be offered and arguments to be put" (119). The interview, testimony, and spoken interactions, or narration, are crucial to the way the political is articulated, given Corner's formulation. There are key moments in *Food, Inc.* and *King Corn* in which the image and voice of the human subject provide a powerful conduit for arguments about the status of the animal as food. In these instances identification is with the body of the consumer.

King Corn is directed by Aaron Woolf and features the first-person narratives of Ian Cheney and Curtis Ellis as they grow and farm an acre of corn after moving from Boston to Iowa. This activity offers a vehicle to examine the intensification of corn production in the United States and the incidence of corn in processed foodstuffs, tying both to commercial interests. The embodied address of the two narrators as they tell their story provides the locus of identification to which Corner refers. *King Corn* begins with Cheney and Ellis visiting a scientist at the University of Virginia, Steve Macko, who they recruit to test a sample of their hair based on the understanding that hair is a "recorder" of diet. Following scenes in a laboratory and images of Macko logging their samples on a computer, Macko informs the pair that the carbon in their bodies largely "originates from corn." This revelation functions as the trigger for the film's investigation into the prevalence of corn in the food system. Corn is posed as a problem for grain-fed livestock, principally cows, but also chickens and pigs, which are made to consume corn for commercial expediency. The film not only describes how a corn diet has detrimental effects on cows' digestive systems, it also leads to health problems for human consumers of beef.

Animals here are visualized variously through archival footage of processing plants or feedlots. Beef is depicted in the film in ways that encourage the connection to human consumption: one scene features Cheney and Ellis at a hamburger restaurant and the camera lingers on the frying meat and the visceral images of the pair eating burgers dripping with condiments. The voiceover discusses the high percentage of fat in grain-fed beef. The diet of the featured animals is linked throughout the film to the diets and bodies of humans, specifically Cheney and Curtis. This aspect of *King Corn* resembles another important food documentary (albeit one less concerned with animals), *Supersize Me.* This earlier documentary places an even greater emphasis on the body of the consumer as Morgan Spurlock, the filmmaker and onscreen narrator, undertakes to eat nothing but McDonald's for a month, testing the health claims of the corporation. In both films the bodies of the narrators are not only central to the onscreen events, they reflect the body of the viewer, particularly the American viewer, who is exposed to the same food system and foodstuffs.

In *King Corn* the opening scenes are crucial in mobilizing the legitimizing discourse of biomedical science to herald an address to the viewer that invokes an empathy with the human body onscreen. This is a form of empathy that aligns the viewer, ideologically, with the filmmakers' opposition to the food industry. The decisive evidence in this argument is not the meat or the animal, but rather the human body. In her discussion of

Supersize Me, Lynn Higgins argues that the body offers the most affecting evidence in the film:

> Despite all the medical and scientific evidence displayed, however, the primary document deployed in *Supersize Me* is the director's body. Nothing is more real than the body: its vomit, its flab, its impotence, its shortness of breath, its blood, with the quantifiable information it contains. [. . .] He has put himself "in harm's way," as they say, in a war against consumer culture. He thus literally "embodies" both personal and social excess, and his voluntary physical disintegration constitutes a kind of spectacularised martyrdom. (30)

It is instructive that the opening scene of *King Corn* also presents conclusive evidence by way of the body, in the form of hair samples. This later documentary does not, however, visualize the disintegration of the bodies of the narrators. It remains concerned with scientific evidence and the narrators' voicing their concerns about their long-term health in the opening scenes.

In contrast, *Food, Inc.*, directed by Robert Kenner, forgoes an onscreen narrator and yet produces more emotionally charged moments for the viewer than *King Corn*. *Food, Inc.* has become one of the most visible and commercially successful documentaries to critique the commercial interests of the food industry.[11] The film is composed of a number of "chapters," each of which advances a broader case against intensified commercial interests in the food system in the United States. Formally, the film is composed of a collage that includes stock images, animated sequences, footage of food and food production sites and interviews, many with farmers on their land. Within this collage, animals, principally cows, pigs, and chickens, are presented as both livestock and meat. Unquestionably the most compelling speaking subject the viewer is asked to identify with is a mother whose child died of contaminated meat.

Barbara Kowalcyk became a food safety advocate after her son, Kevin, died of *E. coli* poisoning from eating hamburger meat. In this episode in the documentary regulatory government agencies are held responsible for the reduction of slaughterhouses in the United States to a mere thirteen, resulting in a high number of cattle from different locations being consolidated into hamburger meat provided to the consumer. This increases the odds that animals that carry pathogens will contaminate a large volume of meat, compromising food safety. Despite the many images of animals and meat in the film, the moral (or emotive) center of *Food, Inc.* is constituted by Kowalcyk's face, voice, and perspective as she details the event of her son's death. Kevin died only days after being admitted to the hospital. The images cut between Kowalcyk's face and footage of a family holiday that, in subdued, almost black-and-white tones, shows Kevin playing on a lakeside. The sequence is framed by Kowalcyk's visit, with her own mother, to Washington to advocate on the issue. The risk that the production of poultry and meat pose to the consumer is personified and Kowalcyk's grief, apparent in her retelling of Kevin's death, is a potent site of identification. Moreover her advocacy work presents a participatory mode of citizenship, offering a surrogate for the viewer's potential self-recognition as a citizen. The rhetorical function of the human body here differs from that in *King Corn* or *Supersize Me*. Rather than the immediacy of the (contaminated) body of the filmmaker/narrator in the frame, this section of *Food, Inc.* offers the grieving face and historical footage that is seemingly mediated by a home movie camera, of a healthy boy. While Kevin is posed as a site of loss that the viewer perceives through his mother's perspective, this site is tied to the contaminating potential of dead animals. As with *King Corn*, the body of the animal is abstracted into arguments about human vulnerability.

In the scenes described, the problem of food is figured as an issue of contamination from meat as a bio-object, produced by unchecked commercial interests. The human face and body are visualized or referenced in the narrative, while the body of the animal is cast as a reference point beyond the frame, unfocused and abstracted in the human imagination. In this respect the documentaries situate the speaking subject and the body of the consumer as the core strategy for rendering an argument about food. Identification is with the likeness of the spectator, the place occupied by the consumer onscreen and thus the sequences reiterate the established codes for representing the political in documentaries. However, while *Food, Inc.* and *King Corn* elevate the thinking, speaking subject in these sequences, this subject becomes inseparable from embodied knowledge—the corporeal effects of consuming meat and, in the case of *Food, Inc.*, grief and loss. Significantly, intercorporeality is again central in this mode of identification, yet the contaminating potential of the animal is present only through a focus on the body of the consumer in the frame.

Documentary Realism and Nonhuman Charisma:
Living with Herds

Greater attention is given to animal life in the final mode of identification I discuss. This dimension of animal ontology is less frequently explored in food documentaries, which tend to forgo close attention to animals and focus more substantively on questionable farming or processing practices and the negative consequences of these. There are a handful of films, however, that concentrate on alternative agrarian practices while directly referencing food. These include *The Moo Man*, *American Meat*, and *Animals*. Andy Heathcote's *The Moo Man* lingers on the environment of livestock and the relationship between farmer and animal, throwing the objectifying impetus of the previous examples, with their focus on an industrial imaginary, into stark relief. It also comes closer to invoking a multispecies environment, in which animals exist as part of a web of relationships that includes humans, than the other films I have discussed in this chapter. While this documentary does reference the negative impact of corporate control over the food system, it does so by focusing on the alternative of traditional and small-scale farming. *The Moo Man* is highly populated throughout with bovine animals, including cows, heifers, calves, and steers and it invites the consumer to encounter the "creatureliness" of animals, existing in a cruelty-free environment, in ways that encourage affirmative responses to drinking the milk and eating the beef produced on the farm.

The Moo Man is a feature length documentary, largely shot on a small family dairy farm in East Sussex in England. Central to the film is the principle farmer, Steve Hook. The farm is run as a boutique business with Hook selling organic unpasteurized milk via farmers' markets, online orders, and doorstep deliveries instead of through supermarkets. As Hook notes in the film, the low retail price of milk in Britain means that farmers are only paid 27 pence per pint (a pint costs 34 pence to produce), pushing smaller farms out of business. Larger operations prosper through generous tax credits. This is noted briefly in the film and explains the scenes in which Hook is shown at markets speaking to customers and personally delivering milk. Hook's own family members feature only briefly and are not introduced to the viewer.

The style of the film is strongly observational and the camera follows Hook as he works on the farm, attending to cows in an enduring routine as they are herded through different paddocks, give birth, become sick, and must be nursed and fed by hand, and occasionally die. Images dwell on the paddocks at different times of the day and the year. In one scene the cows are let into a fresh pasture after the winter and play, jumping with vigor and animation in the misty light. The film is composed of long takes, reflecting the measured pace of life on the farm. The camera dwells on events, producing extended sequences, whether it is a cow experiencing a difficult birth with Hook leveraging the calf out with a rope or coaxing a sick cow to stand up or drink water. Hook's prize cow, or "queen of the herd," is twelve-year-old Ida. In one scene she is taken to the beach at Eastbourne to be photographed for promotional material. Ida is clearly Hook's favorite and this is demonstrated by the manner in which he relays her idiosyncratic behavior to the viewer. In this section I focus not on select scenes from different films, but on the broader address of *The Moo Man* and how it builds a picture of shared ecology based on Hook's many interactions with the herd and his descriptions. The film encourages an identification with animals through the focus on the human-animal relationship between cow and farmer.

While there is a strong observational dimension to the film, *The Moo Man* is structured by Hook's address to the camera and his voice in the sound track. It is a character-driven documentary, foregrounding Hook's compelling personality and his expressive relationship with his cows. The documentary exists in dialogue with traditions of ethnographic filmmaking, with Judith and David MacDougall's *To Live with Herds* (1972) offering a particularly resonant historical reference point. An accent on the every day and observation brings the film into line with the examples I discussed in the previous chapter. I draw again on Anna Grimshaw's reference to a lifeworld in which relationships are "made and remade through the ongoing, active

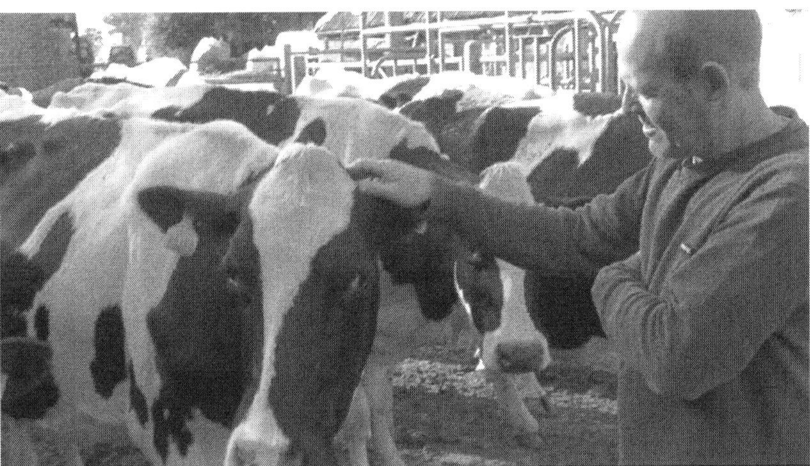

Figure 3.3. Farmer, Steve Hook, speaks in gentle tones to his prize cow, Ida, in *The Moo Man* (2012). This is just one instance of his close relationship with the animals on the farm.

engagement between diverse species and their environments" (256). Such an environment can be accounted for through employing, in Grimshaw's approach, a "sensuous, existential or phenomenological anthropology" (256). *The Moo Man* is integrally concerned with the relationship between cow and farmer, bringing a consideration of relations between species, and the tactile and material qualities of these relationships, to the problem of food and animals in the food production system.

As the camera captures Hook's movements around the farm the sound track is filled with overheard speech as the farmer talks to the cows, asking them questions and giving directions or encouragement. They are his wards and his tone suggests care and respect. This is married with the pragmatism of farm life in that the female cows, as milk producers, meet their full life expectancy while the male calves are killed after three years for beef. At a number of points Hook articulates the importance of the animals' quality of life during the time they are alive. For example, when one heifer is unable to walk due to a paralyzed leg and must be euthanized he laments that it is "not a nice way for a cow to finish its time on the farm." This is key to the ethical address of the film and structures the representation of the farm environment.

The cows in *The Moo Man* are afforded a certain elevated status as the viewer is asked to perceive them through the eyes of Hook, the farmer. They move beyond a simple objectification as meat or undifferentiated livestock. Jamie Lorimer's notion of nonhuman charisma provides an apt lens through which to read this characterization. His theory revolves around understanding the interaction and encounter between human and nonhuman. Lorimer is concerned with how the "ecological and affective dimensions to human—nonhuman interaction and environmental governance can help refine a 'more-than-human' understanding of agency" ("Nonhuman Charisma," 914). The nonhuman agency he refers to is one that recognizes the autonomy and singularity of animal species. Lorimer's approach privileges human sensitivity to and interpretation of nonhuman charisma, which can be "defined as the distinguishing properties of a nonhuman entity or process that determine its perception by humans and its subsequent evaluation" ("Nonhuman Charisma," 915). Charisma is subjectively perceived by humans in the encounter. This offers an understanding of animal qualities that is relational and contextual.

Adapting Lorimer's concept to the specificity of the documentary moving image, I propose that this encounter might be perceived as a "(non) human realism." In this case the viewer's desire for documentary verisimilitude is channeled through an engagement with the representation of nonhuman life. The viewer is asked to identify not simply with the animal, but with the encounter between animal and human. In the case of *The Moo Man*, Hook's descriptions of and onscreen interactions with the cows supply a lens through which to perceive the charismatic qualities of his animals. This charisma is constructed relationally, in the context of the environment of his farm, which is rendered as a social, stress-free and cruelty-free environment for the cows.

The fact that the relationship between the cows and human food is largely articulated in the film by way of milk production makes this an easier proposition and distinguishes *The Moo Man* from other films I have discussed, which are more concerned with animal meat. There are scenes, however, early in the film that visualize the animal as meat for consumption and despite their ironic framing, they sit awkwardly in the film. The viewer is informed that the Hook family eat beef from the farm as Steve Hook is seen in the farmhouse kitchen preparing and eating a plate of what seems to be spaghetti bolognaise. This is further reinforced when an animal that was sent off the farm for slaughter returns in the back of Hook's car as rolls of meat. The scene cuts to the farmer cutting up the rolls into portions in the kitchen. As he does so he relates his personal history with the animal, a foot infection as a calf and personality traits, stating "he was never 'friendly friendly' like some of the others, some of the others you'd go up to and pat, but he was always a bit wary, I don't know why. He was castrated so that normally quietens them down." While the viewer might perceive this as a departure from the respectful, nurturing ethos of the human/animal relation (and too explicit a visualization of the cow becoming food), the overarching trajectory of the observational address locates it as further affirming the ethical use of animals within human endeavor, suggesting self-aware consumption of beef. This is reinforced when Hook concludes he "had a pretty brilliant life for a dairy bull calf born on a farm."

The film assures the viewer that there is an ethical alternative to factory farming in which the consumer citizen's responsibilities and right to healthy food can be realized in ways that do not perpetuate animal suffering. This address is orchestrated through the prevalence of images of agrarian harmony and the slow rhythm of life on the farm, which is echoed in the long takes of the camera. This is an aesthetic that affirms viewers' choices to consume beef and dairy from sources similar to the Hook farm. In the two previous sections, animal meat is presented as a site of difficulty—it is either a threat to the body of the consumer (with the body as the locus of sensory meaning), or the process by which animals and animal meat becomes food is disturbed (either through abjection or abstraction) to the degree that meaning breaks down and confronts the viewer, vacating the link between animal and food. *The Moo Man*, however, encourages intimacy (partly through the duration of shots), presenting a (non)human realism in which animals trigger "emotions, affections and motivations," and perhaps even "a moment of awe-full or enchanting proximity to another animal" (Lorimer, "Nonhuman Charisma," 918). *The Moo Man* again entails identification with the human as the subject of knowledge and Hook is the central conduit for this identification. However, more than simply motivating a recognition of the human other, the film also engages the viewer, through Hook's point of view, in a realism that facilitates a sensuous and sensible proximity with animals. Cows dominate the frame throughout the film. Their bodies and their sounds multiply across the landscape of the farm. In this respect, the film seeks a somatic engagement with the viewer, foregrounding the sensible qualities of animal bodies and visually rendering the tactile experience of being in the presence of animals, and healthy animals in particular. In *The Moo Man* ways of knowing about the farming practices that are at the heart of the argument are conveyed through identifying with the *experience* of intimate proximity with the charismatic nonhuman other.

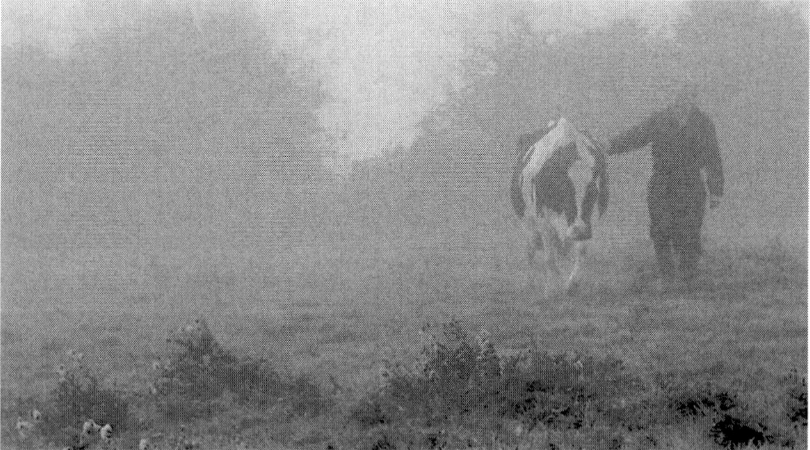

Figure 3.4. A misty morning with farmer and cows in the fields—*The Moo Man* (2012) conveys agrarian harmony and the tactile experience of being in the presence of animals.

Intercorporeality, Embodiment, and Consumer Moralities

All the documentaries I have discussed share an address to the citizen food consumer and invite identification with the possibility of coming to know about the facts or horrors behind the problem of food. There is a vital interaction between the social status of the consumer (as an avenue of self-identification), the address of the documentary and the shared experiential and embodied practice of eating (and eating meat specifically). At times these documentaries lead the viewer through a clear argumentative imperative and the release of some of the films I have discussed has been followed by public or governmental action.[12] Some films offer less explicit argumentation, such as *Leviathan* or *Our Daily Bread*, placing greater emphasis on what can be inferred from the film experience. Yet all play to what the sensory charge of cinema can achieve, especially the material and temporal functions that convey embodied life and its relation to matter.

To comprehend citizen consumers through intercorporeal or embodied modes of identification also suggests the social import of understanding spectatorial processes. The informing social narrative for contemporary food documentaries is, as noted earlier, a new morality, or remoralization, of consumption allied in recent years with notions of consumer activism or ethical consumption more broadly. The narratives and ideals that accompany this remoralization offer weight to the citizen food consumer as a legitimate subject for popular and political concern. As Barnett et al. describe, ethical consumption reconciles a privatized and individualistic form of action with public and collective modes of participation (84). Food is the first frontier and most quotidian dimension of individualized consumption. Many food documentaries address viewers in a manner that assumes they are already aware of the popular rhetoric and potential power of consumer activism.[13]

The relative popularization of ethical consumption offers further explanation for the rise of food documentaries in the context of the documentary renaissance. The widespread commercial success of a film such as *Food, Inc.* owes a debt to audiences' identification with the potential for consumer activism. The film encompasses an omnibus of narratives that circulate through ethical registers in the public sphere such as labor exploitation and alienation, the health of the consumer, the concentration of wealth and ownership, the disappearance of traditional economies and ecologies and, to a lesser extent, environmental concerns[14] and animal welfare. The range of narratives in *Food, Inc.* point to the proliferation of linked issues in the political imaginary that food documentaries seek to address. The alternative food politics of an older example, such as Jennifer Abbott's[15]

1998 documentary *A Cow at My Table*, which addresses animal rights and the meat industry, sits within a different paradigm of food activism. This is one indication that moral issues concerning eating meat and animal rights have been eclipsed by a more substantive and popular consumerist narrative around responsibility, citizenship, consumer agency, and market power.

As Cowie's work demonstrates, documentary studies has considered how the discourses of reality encourage identification, including through affective and desiring relations, in ways that center on human identity. Further, Nichols and Gaines point to the genre's capacity to evoke a mode of viewing that is affectively engaged with the events onscreen. Recent food documentaries, however, disturb the straightforward application of these theories and necessitate a new approach, one that accounts for the viewer as consumer and the embodied and social knowledge of food that this subjectivity is founded on. To use Csordas' words, food documentaries invite "somatic modes of attention" (151). The scenes and films I have described foreground materiality, inviting modes of identification that play to the equally material status of the viewer as "subjective matter" (Sobchack, *Carnal Thoughts*, 65). If documentary addresses us, and thus asks us to identify as "the one who knows," this knowledge is both embodied *and* localized to particular social arguments. I have explored a revised specificity for Sobchack's understanding of primary and secondary identification noted above by describing how the social and the somatic are mutually constituted in processes of identification.

Steven Shaviro, whose work informs Sobchack's analysis, usefully extends identification to foreground the body. He argues against the opposition of body and thought, preferring a theory, informed by a Deleuzian approach, that "posits a parallelism between them: it affirms the powers of the body, and it sees the very opacity and insubordination of the flesh as a stimulus to thought and as its necessary condition" (*The Cinematic*, 257). The examples I have explored demonstrate that it is not only embodied knowledge, but more crucially, the power of the body that is key to understanding identification here. The body is pivotal to the experience offered by the films, not only the human body, but also animal bodies. In this respect, the documentaries extend and speak to a feature of nonfiction that has, since early cinema, engaged the viewer's senses in animal life and death.

Food documentaries harness the power and meaning of animal bodies to institute an intercorporeal sensibility that is mediated through the film and the process of viewing. By this I am referring to the ways of being and knowing that emerge through particular documentary encounters with the corporeality of animals, their vitalism, their flesh as matter, or the unsettling intersection of both life force and materiality. Providing a way of understanding this intercorporeality in terms of cinematic reproduction, Shaviro theorizes how the cinematic apparatus itself is a form of embodiment. His approach is formulated in ways that enable a contemplation of nonhuman bodies, describing the experience of cinema as

> [. . .] a continuity between the physiological and affective responses of my own body and the appearances and disappearances, the mutations and perdurances, of the bodies and images onscreen. [. . .] Film theory should be less a theory of fantasy (psychoanalytic or otherwise) than a theory of the affects and transformations of bodies. (*The Cinematic*, 255–257)

The films pose the viewer's relation with animal others as bodily and tangible. This is the case whether they confront the boundaries of the (human) self with the inedible materiality of animal bodies, present the body of the consumer, the surrogate of the viewer, in ways that signify the contaminating potential of animal bodies or offer the sensual material experience of corporeal proximity of charismatic animals.

In all cases the formulation of the relationship of the body of the animal and the body of the human function on a continuum, reminding us, crucially, that human and animal are both flesh and blood. This shared state of being is highlighted in Shaviro's formulation by the continuity between the bodily transformations onscreen and the spectator's embodied ways of knowing and accessing the world. Such a proposition presents a much stronger challenge to anthropocentrism than the films of the "long take" discussed in the previous chapter—in that case the human lifeworld and identity were stable and encompassed animals in a visually fluid way. The continuity between animal and human in the food documentaries provide an avenue to momentarily contest cinema's anthropomorphic function encouraging identification not simply with human forms and knowledge, but with materiality itself. Moreover, the documentaries contribute a distinctive visual imaginary and documentary aesthetic to the new morality of ethical consumption, with animals featuring at the sensory and somatic centre of this contribution.

The new morality, as I have noted, addresses environmental questions in inconsistent ways. Moreover, the films addressed in the previous two chapters focused on agricultural food production gesture to environmental politics as a marginal concern. This is an observation also made by Helen Hughes in her study of environmental documentary and she remarks that this omission occurs despite the fact that current debates about food and agriculture "are closely linked to environmental debates about land management" (*Green Documentary*, 62). She goes on to note that there exists "an interesting parallel with nature documentaries that typically have excluded environmental issues, and those that have included them or focused on them have become re-categorised as environmental films" (*Green Documentary*, 62). The next two chapters take up this point, examining the complex legacy of wildlife filmmaking (its erasures and long-standing conventions) and its relationship to the contemporary terrain of nonfiction that represent animals in the polar regions.

Chapter 4

Arctic Futures and Extinction

Loss, the Archive, and (Wildlife) Film

The nonfiction film project has consistently been tied to the possibility of verifying life for the viewer. Documentary filmmakers are motivated by the possibility of bringing the historical world into view, giving weight to the substance of bodies and events in time. In the case of endangered or extinct species, the moving image, and especially the nonfiction moving image, is profoundly imbued with the potential for capturing and preserving life. Jan-Christopher Horak, the director of the UCLA Film & Television Archive, draws attention to the activity of recording nature in moving image form, outlining the powerful role such human activity might have in an age of accelerating extinction:

> Today, the impulse to document nature is augmented by the much higher stakes endeavor of "preserving" animal life in a virtual world. Looking over the precipice of an earth depopulated of its wildlife, the goal of nature filmmakers becomes the capture of animals, at least in images, so that society and science have a record of what was lost. Every moving image can potentially be the last "living" image of a species, in the truest sense of the word. (459)

For Horak, the rise in wildlife film and television can be seen as a proportional response to the demise of species in the wild. To record and classify animals in order to preserve them in the face of disappearance is to maintain at least the likeness, or index, of the animal, its movement and biotic traits. While the stakes of this preservation function might be high, I suggest there are further consequences, beyond those outlined by Horak. In this chapter I pursue what is at stake in perceiving the purpose of the moving image representation of wildlife in this way, examining how different filmic examples work toward different biopolitical ends—by this I mean how they feed into ways of imagining the future of endangered species by organizing and presenting life.

In an era that is marked by increasing awareness of the global magnitude of human induced species loss,[1] the Arctic ecosystem is known to be more precariously balanced than any other. Over recent decades the Arctic has become intensely associated with narratives of decline, whether in relation to the melting of Greenland's ice sheet, the acidification of the Arctic Ocean or mining and the exploitation of natural resources and attendant habitat destruction. The ecosystems in polar regions support much fewer species, often making single species more vital and sustainable ecosystems less resilient in the face of declining diversity. The life that is supported by the fragile ecosystem includes at least fourteen species that are threatened with extinction.[2] The previous two chapters mapped how clusters of films instantiated animals and humans (including the spectator) within the industrial institutions of food and agriculture and through the functions and expectations of the documentary real. This chapter and the next illuminate how animal life in (nonhuman) nature is brought into being by circuits of knowledge, including those relating to science, exploration, and species loss. Attending to the animal in the wild, these studies necessarily move away from human lifeworlds and investigate the narratives that construct the very notion of "the wild" against and in relation to the human. Thus, they also wrestle with an additional framing paradigm—the filmic language of the wildlife mode and the way an array of documentary storytelling conventions bring life into historical representation. The Arctic and Antarctic offer rich avenues for exploring how nature is perceived in relation to human history, including human and nonhuman futures.

Drawing on the work of Deborah Bird Rose, Matthew Chrulew writes that while extinction is part of evolutionary processes, "the rate and scale of contemporary 'man-made' extinction is the definitive double death: the irreparable loss not only of the living but of the multiplicity of forms of life" ("Managing Love").[3] Stories about extinction entail a particular capacity to draw attention to life in the face of definitive death. Such narratives are becoming a point of interest for documentary filmmakers, particularly those working within and adjacent to the highly popular natural history and wildlife subgenres.

In this chapter I focus on the documentary representation of the definitive death of extinction and its precursor, species endangerment, exploring what is at stake in the way the future of the nonhuman world is narrativized and thus imagined. There are (at least) two ways in which documentary might operate in this respect: representations of loss and decline have the potential to reduce the likelihood for imagining alternative futures, entrapping us, and our nonhuman others, in a narrow spiral of apparent decline that only anticipates loss. Alternatively, representation can tend toward advocacy or rendering species loss in ways that are allied with a more complex and open future.

With this in mind, I single out two contemporary examples, *Being Caribou* (2004) and *Arctic Tale* (2007). These two films provide two different alternatives or propensities for considering species endangerment and both draw on and adapt specific elements of the wildlife film genre. *Being Caribou* is a feature length documentary produced by Canada's National Film Board (NFB). It seeks to present the habitat and migration practices of the Porcupine caribou herd by following the five-month journey of the herd far into the frozen Arctic. The documentary explicitly references the threat posed by oil drilling in the Arctic, an activity that will devastate the migration and the existence of the herd. Director Leanne Allison and her husband, Karsten Heuer, are central to the onscreen events as they make the journey alongside the caribou. In contrast, *Arctic Tale* is a "Disneyfied" wildlife film that follows the life, from birth to adulthood, of a polar bear and a walrus. The animals feature as human-styled characters, who, as they progress through the narrative, become negatively impacted by the changing climate conditions in the Arctic. The Arctic provides a particularly important case study, not only because of the fragility of the ecosystem, but also because this geographical region has long held a particular fascination for documentary filmmakers. *Nanook of the North* (1922) is the most striking early precursor and I trace how this film poses Arctic life in the face of potential (human) species loss, binding animals and humans together in the historical imagination. However, I begin with the problem of the archive, questioning what is at stake in perceiving films about endangered species as a form of preservation, archived for the future. If the moving image submits to this role, what kinds of film worlds might it engender and how might it be seen to shape stories and sensual experiences for the viewer?

Life, Cinema, and the Problem of the Archive

It is the work of archives to preserve and order objects and events. When the moving image is perceived as a form of preservation, it takes on an instrumental status. For Jacques Derrida, the most well-known scholar of the archive, archiving does not guarantee memory or living knowledge, "on the contrary: the archive takes place at the place of originary and structural breakdown of the said memory" (11). Derrida writes that the archive does not conserve "content of the past" (16–17), it alters the status of the object or event, producing as much as it records the event. In the case of the recording of endangered life, an archive of wildlife imagery creates stasis, mummifying the animals it represents, even if the species is constantly re-created in new moving image forms. This is not the only way of perceiving and using archives—seed banks offer an interesting example of an archive that is founded on the potential for life, with seeds held in reserve partly due to their promise for generating new life. But this is not realized, at least in straightforward ways, in moving image archives.

Classifying and ordering potential loss can become a singular activity of preservation for a possible future in which life is extinct, rather than one focused on life and its maintenance.[4] It may be the case that responsibility for and emphasis on the more easily achievable activity of archiving eclipses or alleviates responsibility for maintaining life. Describing the visual dimension of this, or the public optic of preservation, Kathryn Yusoff writes, "ironically, in the aesthetic orders of species protection and extinction, an inverse relation exists between multiplication and subtraction: the more we see of a thing stabilised in the archive of protection, the less likely we are to see it in the play of the world, and vice versa" (81). Species that are well documented, especially those on the edge of extinction, can become popularized and recognizable, chronicled and embalmed into a predictable form.

In other words, endangered species can take on a status in the archive that resembles that of animals already extinct. Following this point, it is instructive to consider an example prominently represented in the archive of extinction. In an Australian context, perhaps the most well-known filmic image of an extinct animal is offered by the black-and-white footage of the thylacine, or Tasmanian tiger, in the Hobart Zoo in the early 1930s. In this sequence, which runs no more than two minutes, a female tiger paces and lies in its cage, at one point yawning with its huge jaws.[5] The "thing" captured on film, or the referent, is one of the last of the last. Ricardo De Vos discusses the thylacine in his account of "extinction stories," noting how the function of writing, another form of representation, effects a "spatial and temporal removal from its object" (190), an object that is absent. "Stories of existence which focus on the demise of the last remaining animal utilise evidence of an historical absence in realising the presence of an ideal form" (190) De Vos writes. In the case of cinema, the ideal form becomes that which is caught on camera, forever mythologized and distanced from the "reality" of an embodied animal that might produce multiple and divergent inscriptions. Photographic evidence, however, complicates De Vos' characterization, folding together the animated material presence and an ideal form. This play of absence and presence presents an uncanny animal revenant, animating life that is now gone—not only this single animal, but also its species obliterated. It evokes uncertainty for the viewer in the sense that it is animate but is without future, testifying only to the past.

Cinema's ontology has the capacity to intensify the viewer's relation to loss—this comes with the recognition that there is always a spatial and temporal distance from the filmed object. Access to the referent is always impossible—it is lost in the moment of registration. It might be said that cinema is consistently engaged in a process of extinction, or death, as it extinguishes potentiality, fixing the index and suggesting only the trace of what was there. The viewer is attuned to this and is asked to constantly grapple with the play of absence and presence that defines the process of photographic representation. In her book, *Death 24x a Second: Stillness and the Moving Image*, Laura Mulvey emphasises the stasis of the inanimate still image, twenty-four of which are featured every second in cinema projection, producing the moving image.[6] Further, Mulvey claims that cinema combines two human fascinations: "one with the boundary between life and death and the other with the mechanical animation of the inanimate, particularly the human figure" (110). Akira Mizuta Lippit brings this latter fascination back to a focus on the animal, and species loss in particular. He argues that early cinema developed "embodied animal traits as a gesture of mourning for the disappearing wildlife. The figure for nature in language, animal, was transformed in cinema to the name for movement in technology, animation" (196). Lippit's approach extends Horak's observations by perceiving not only the phenomenal rise in wildlife filmmaking, but also cinema's very epistemological origins, as a response to species loss.

To highlight cinema's place at the interstices of life and death is to understand it as continuously implicated in its own archiving function. To tie cinema to the negative function of the archive completely, however, is to reject its productive possibilities and the powerful role of the photographic image in the construction of an interventionist imaginary. For this reason I move away from the problem of the temporality of the film process (the stasis of the image and loss of the object) to seek out the generative capacity of the moving image, focusing on the imagery and storytelling conventions of the wildlife mode. How might wildlife film engage the phenomena of unfolding life, creating an "effect of material presence" (Stern 321) rather than emphasizing absence? I wish to confront the problem of the archive, exploring the prospect of a more open set of possibilities for the representation of species loss. Before focusing on moving image examples, I offer some background to the challenge of rethinking the anthropocentric motivations of the archive that privilege preservation in the interests of human knowledge. These motivations intersect with the equally humanist inclination to foreground human identity and aspiration in historical narratives of species loss.

Species Loss and History: Stories about Disappearing Animals

The staging of animal life for the purposes of rendering species loss within modern paradigms has a long history. The first species extinction to be documented as it occurred was that of the dodo in the seventeenth century, a flightless pigeon found on the island of Mauritius. According to reliable accounts, the dodo was first sighted in 1589 (Van Dooren 2) and it is estimated the bird was extinct by 1690.[7] The dodo has become emblematic of a human connection to a crisis in nature, emerging as a culturally significant species, burdened with the weight of signifying much more than simply is own biotic existence. Thom Van Dooren asserts "while this was by no means the first species in whose loss humans were centrally involved, the dodo inhabits a peculiar and iconic place in many contemporary accounts of extinction" (3). Ursula K. Heise further specifies the importance of the dodo, arguing that at the moment the dodo disappeared, human impact on flora and fauna first entered the modern imagination, instituting a new relationship with the nonhuman world. Since this time, the dodo has become "a recurrent symbol of the destruction of nature wrought by the imperialist expansion of European modernity—a destruction that, it should be added, also generated the first initiatives for conservation" (Heise 61). The dodo offers one of the earliest examples of animals becoming iconic due to their relationship to modernity and human induced extinction.

In recent times, singularly recognizable animals, such as the dodo, have come to metonymically stand for contemporary species loss in greater proportions. Such animals are endowed with cultural or iconic significance and are visible in a manner that is often proportionally at odds with their role in the ecosystem; these may not be the most important animals for sustaining the biodiversity necessary for ecological stability, but they excel when it comes to evoking human fascination and identification. These are often large mammals, sometimes referred to by geographers and conservationists as "megafauna." Some of these, as I will discuss in relation to the polar bear, are strategically utilized to rally support for conservation and, where possible, ensure continuity into the future.

Culturally significant animals that are deployed for the purposes of raising public awareness are also termed "flagship" species.[8] The giant panda, for example, is a flagship species *par excellence* due to the way it looms large in popular culture and serves to stimulate conservation awareness and support. The quintessential representation of animal life for political purposes, flagship species are an amalgamation of biopolitical discourse and mediatized dissemination. This amalgamation is disparaged by some conservationists and biologists and yet perceived as highly strategic by others. As a wealth of critique has made clear, flagship species claim precedence in the media sphere and eclipse more complex understandings of ecologies and biodiversity and how to sustain these. For Steve Hinchliffe, charismatic flagship species encourage the "Hollywoodisation of conservation" (89), marginalizing the importance of evolving ecosystems and the different roles that less visible organisms play in sustainable biodiversity.[9] Yet, these species offer a crucial example of the staging of animal species within discourses of extinction and conservation. This terrain of representation begins to indicate what is at stake in making life, and its potential for extinction, available to a popular audience in mediatized forms. Central to this is the problem of perceiving species loss in particular ways that are defined by human concerns, identities, and politics.

If species important to human narratives have more visual currency, they also play to a tendency to perceive narratives of extinction as a reflection of human identity and history. In this frame, changes in biodiversity become apprehended as human loss and animals are enlisted to perform human narratives of decline. This is, as Heise notes, a way of rehearsing histories of modernization, often in order to contest particular forms of progress and developmentalism. At historical moments of accelerating change, the loss of a particular species becomes a placeholder for "the vanishing of nature and the weakening of human bonds to the natural world" (68–69). Declining nature, its end or disappearance, is rhetorically tied to social decline caused by development in this formulation. The weakening Heise describes plays into more pervasive narratives of decline that have intensified in recent years and frequently fuel environmentalist movements. Moreover, declensionist narratives can be seen alongside the archiving impulse to preserve the likeness of endangered animals—they frequently frame decline as inevitable, offering a single story about biodiversity loss and deny the possibility of uncertainty, contingency and complexity in nature.

While in chapter 2 I discussed the notion of teleological decline as it underpins observational films focused on agriculture, here I am interested in how declensionist narratives structure the representation of biodiversity loss, tending toward singularity, denying the possibility of uncertainty, contingency, and complexity. Alternatives to the perceived movement toward the utter impoverishment of the natural world for Heise would acknowledge that while facts about species extinction and the causes are often irrefutable, "enough uncertainties and open questions surround these facts that the narrative of nature's decline turns out to be one possible, but not the only conceivable way of telling the story of biodiversity loss" (Heise 53). She goes on to note that "facts do not in and of themselves add up to the narrative of the decline of nature in the modern world such as it is often told in connection with biodiversity. The declensionist narrative is underdetermined by the facts—it is one possible but not the only way of translating them into story" (58). I am interested in the multiple ways in which this story might be told in popular (cinema) culture. If the dodo was the first figuration of crisis in the human interaction with nature, the Arctic brings this crisis to bear on a whole geographical zone in the contemporary epoch. While *Arctic Tale* and *Being Caribou* are, as I discuss later, examples of documentaries made in an era of increasing awareness of climate change and habitat destruction, they contribute to a pedigree of Arctic film history that has seen the staging of nature and loss since the earliest days of documentary.

Arctic Histories, Animals, and Disappearing People: *Nanook of the North*

Nanook of the North exists as the most enduring image of the Arctic in cinema's past across any genre. Flaherty's film offers a crucial reading of decline and modernity, but is underpinned by a human/animal relation that is unlike that described by Heise. By way of contextualizing the film in the history of polar representation, it should be noted that while *Nanook of the North* is the most famous, even paradigmatic, film to bring Arctic life to the screen in the silent period, a number of nonfiction films, including U.S., French, Italian, and German productions, preceded Flaherty's 1922 film.[10] Moreover, there were other significant long-form nonfiction films made over the 1920s and 1930s, including *The Romance of the Far Fur Country* (*Hudson's Bay Company*, 1920), the Norwegian film *Mot ukjent land* (1930), *From the Pole to the Equator* (1929),[11] and Friedrich Dalsheim's *The Wedding of*

Palo (1934). Representations of life in the Arctic continued on, in different permutations, throughout the twentieth century.[12]

Nanook is an early example of salvage ethnography. Focused on the daily life of a family of Itivimuit, a group of Quebec Inuit, the film was, in part, intended as a document of a culture believed to be dying out. Cinema's power to archive was to achieve what history could not—the abeyance of the death of a race of people. Rather than the change and progress of modernity being implicated in this extinction, the demise of the Inuit was seen to be located (and perhaps caused by) their location outside of history. It was believed that indigenous peoples were at risk because they were unable to adapt to the inevitable progress of the modern world.[13] *Nanook* offers a racialized depiction that was well suited to the imperial imagination of the time—the Inuit are depicted as insulated from modernity and aligned with the primitive and the animalistic. Thus, in this case animals are not the expression of human identity, as in Heise's formulation—instead humans are produced as primitive through their alignment with animals. This operation in *Nanook* provides a crucial role for Arctic animals.

With *Nanook*, Flaherty endeavored to show audiences of the time a culture outside the influence of progress and modernity. Much of the film is staged for the camera with Nanook played by Allalariallak. Nanook's Arctic is a multispecies environment, including dogs, fish, walruses, and seals. Rather than conveying animal ontology, the central function of these animals is to enhance the rendering of primitivism in the film. As Fatmah Tobing Rony indicates, in one scene this is achieved through the manner in which the Inuit are visually and narratively (through the use of intertitles) allied with dogs. This is primarily achieved through intercutting images of dogs and images of Nanook and his family. The family is described as on the "edge of starvation" and shots of them eating raw seal meat are juxtaposed with images of fighting dogs, aligning the two against the polar landscape. These scenes fed into the widespread assumption of the time that due to their diet of raw meat, the Inuit were closer to animals, savage and cannibalistic (Rony 105). In another sequence early in the film Nanook "displays" his young huskies, "the finest dog flesh in all the country round." Directly following this is a well-known shot of Nyla (Alice Nuvalinga), Nanook's wife, with her young baby nestled on a fur skin among husky puppies. The intertitle states, "Nyla, not to be outdone, displays her young husky too—one Rainbow, less than four months old." The image of puppies and baby are designed to charm audiences yet they also pose a zoomorphism, transposing canine identity and status onto the *Itivimuit* baby.

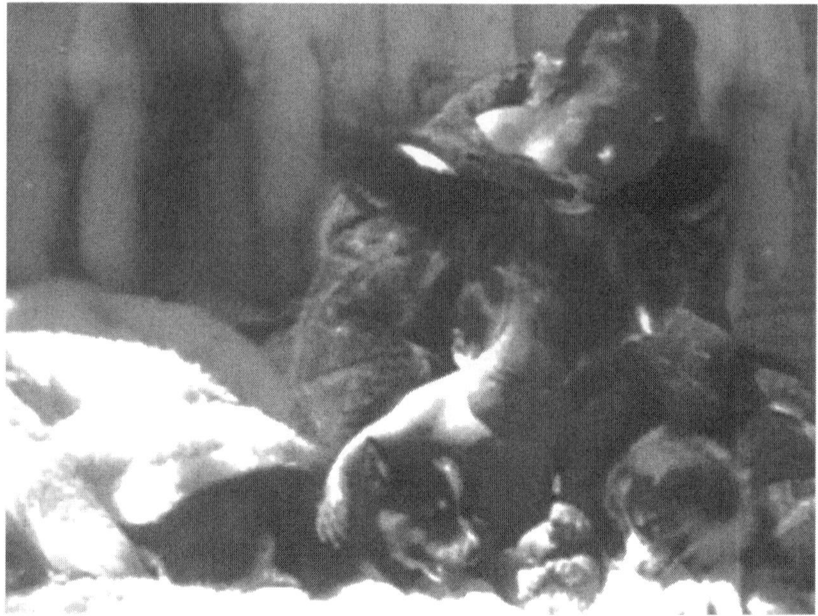

Figure 4.1. Nyla and her baby, Rainbow, are shown nestled among husky puppies. Aligning baby and puppies contributes to the primitivization of the Itivimuit in *Nanook of the North* (1922).

Further, polar bears and walruses serve, alongside the Inuit, to authenticate the representation of the Arctic—their exoticism highlights the isolation and strangeness of the Arctic vista. Moreover, the story of the film incorporates hunting and animals in a way that, for Rony, "abolishes" history—the death of the hunted animals, through repetition, becomes iconographic and supports the figuration of a time outside of (modern) history while presaging the supposed death of the Inuit people. In this critique, Arctic animals are companions to Inuit humans, both tied in a pre-historic frame. Alternatively, from a film historical perspective, animals function as referents that contribute to and help verify an imperialist ethnographic agenda. To the extent that *Nanook* is a preeminent film artifact, animals and humans are bound together in the archive through the parts they play in the rationalization of stasis and, thus, loss.

Keeping with this film historiographic perspective, it is instructive that Flaherty was an explorer and prospector before he was a filmmaker. His work, while far exceeding the simple format of the travelogue, is founded in this tradition of filmmaking. Such a tradition is, in turn, inspired by the imperial and romantic age of exploration of the nineteenth century, infused with sensibilities that celebrated nature, the mapping of new lands and the collection of evidence of foreign peoples, flora, and fauna.[14] The filmmaking influenced by the romantic age of exploration in the early twentieth century, as I discuss in more detail in the next chapter, perceived both "exotic" peoples *and* animals as valuable objects for the camera's gaze, both equally fascinating for Euro-American audiences at home. Due to their particular attention to animals in the wild, these travelogues represent unmistakable precursors to wildlife and natural history filmmaking, as it was to evolve in the century to follow. The following sections consider Arctic life in a contemporary frame, with examples that are part of a more recent paradigm, but one that responds to modes of wildlife filmmaking while also presenting animals within and against human history and knowledge.

Walking the Arctic: *Being Caribou*

Written and directed by Leanne Allison and Diana Wilson, *Being Caribou* is a film that chronicles the five-month journey of Allison and her husband, Karsten Heuer, as they follow the annual migration of the Porcupine caribou herd across 1,500 kilometers of Arctic tundra.[15] The two undertake the journey on foot, requiring them to walk from Canada to the caribou's calving grounds on Alaska's coastal plain. The migration of the 120,000 caribou and the journey is documented not only in the film but also in print—a nonfiction first-person account written by Heuer, *Being Caribou: Five Months on Foot with an Arctic Herd*. The book is informed by Heuer's expertise as a wildlife biologist. The documentary is motivated by Allison and Heuer's stated objective to learn more about the caribou and reveal to audiences the nature of their lifeworld while also publicizing immanent threats to the caribou habitat. *Being Caribou* does not fit the mold of traditional wildlife or natural history filmmaking. This is due to both the political motivations of the film and the strongly subjective affective commentary of the filmmakers. Historically wildlife film has been defined by a proposition that "authentic nature" (the defining object for wildlife narrative) is resilient and harmonious, insulated from human activities and impacts. While the onscreen figure of the human narrator as adventurer and biologist is not unusual, in *Being Caribou* the role of the narrators is distinct—they not only follow the caribou, their journey is structured around an intensifying affective relationship and this is channeled into heightening the advocacy role of the film.

The journeyers are Anglo-Canadians but indigenous people also play a role in *Being Caribou*. The township of Old Crow and its inhabitants, the Gwich'in people, feature as the pair set out and return from their journey. They meet Randall Tetlichi at the beginning of the film and he offers them advice for the journey. The couple spends a day with Tetlichi, following as he hunts and skins a caribou. This sits awkwardly with Allison and Heuer's careful, respectful proximity with the caribou that characterizes the rest of the film. It is offered context with Allison's statement in voiceover: "For thousands of years Gwich'in culture has revolved around caribou," which serves to align the Gwich'in and caribou in the long-standing ecosystem. Importantly, the timelessness, or primitivizing impetus, of *Nanook* is subverted and this is made especially apparent as Tetlichi rides off on his Ski-Doo snowmobile, leaving Allison and Heuer to begin their journey on foot. The two are left isolated in the snowy landscape while Tetlichi is accorded the trappings of modernity, consciously reversing the established typology of ethnographic film.

The journey is also framed by sequences that indicate the U.S. government's plans to enable oil exploration and drilling in the Arctic National Wildlife refuge. The planned development concerns an area that will affect the calving ground of the caribou. The opening images include archival footage of President Herbert Walker Bush and President George W. Bush advocating for drilling in the refuge in press conferences. Addressing a news camera at one point, George W. Bush encourages those present to travel to the area in order to "decide how beautiful it is" for themselves with the inference that there is only barren land to be found in the Arctic. Allison and Heuer take a plastic doll of George W. Bush on the journey under the pretense of showing him the migration. Allison articulates the motivation for the journey and its documentation early in the film when she states in voiceover that she hopes to bring the "story of the caribou alive so people will finally realize what's at stake and they'll care." In the final scenes the pair travel to Washington to lobby on behalf of the caribou and the documentary closes with Allison surmising that they may have seen and recorded the caribou before their numbers begin to decline: "Maybe we really did see one of the last times that they migrate." The possibility of species loss is not articulated until this final scene, which gestures to, in Bart Welling's words, the function of the film as a eulogy. Prior to this, *Being Caribou* is more fully focused on the lifeworld and experience of the caribou herd, despite the fact that the film begins with information about human incursions into caribou habitat. The film seeks, as Allison notes, to "bring the caribou to life." This is a very different gesture to that seen in *Nanook*, in which (human) life was purposefully embalmed in the stasis of history.

Being Caribou achieves this goal by appropriating the wildlife narrative trope of the journey and, within this, posing the animals as agentic, not fully appropriated to human knowledge or representation. The staging of human and nonhuman animal encounter over the course of the journey, moreover, draws awareness to what Kracauer describes as cinema's power to "register material phenomena in their otherness" (257). It presents a shared ontology or a "mode of attention," in the manner that Haraway describes, recognizing multiplicity and otherness and setting the film apart from those I described in chapter 2. For Welling, this institutes a critical anthropomorphism, produced through the engagement between human and nonhuman animal:

> Heuer and Allison's version of critical anthropomorphism is grounded in a healthy respect for the irreducible physiological, behavioural, and emotional differences as well as the continuities between human beings and caribou beings [. . .] Allison and Heuer resist touching caribou when the opportunity presents itself, but their attempts to make sense of "caribou being" are informed by corporeal feedback from the animals. (89)

This self-reflexive interaction is rendered, in the comments of Heuer and Allison, as an affective experience.

The narration and the point of view constructed by the camera highlight Heuer and Allison's ongoing attempt to comprehend the caribou in an affective manner and the magnitude of their trek while also being alert to the schism between their knowledge and their embodied encounters with the nonhuman. This is apparent in the opening sequence of the film, which is composed of different shots of the caribou against the vibrant colors of green mountains. In one shot they move out of view as they cross a ridge. Heuer states in voiceover:

> It's almost like a rhythm. You get up in the morning and the landscape that was just so alive last night is just vacant and empty. And then there is the mystery pulling you forward of where are they, where could they be? And it isn't just tracks we're following, trails on the map, it's something else and I truly believe there is something else keeping us on the general

> trail of these caribou—coming together, being pulled apart and
> then coming together. So I guess I have faith, a faith that we
> will happen upon them again.

The two narrators approximate the role of pilgrims as they follow the enigmatic caribou to their almost sacred calving ground, creating a mystical
portrait with romantic overtones of inspiring awe and discovery. Moreover,
this opening passage, introducing the viewer to the themes of the film,
highlights both the structuring importance of the *activity of following* that
is key to the narrative, a feature that allies the film with the wildlife genre.

Classical wildlife film is renowned for organizing the representation
of the nonhuman world through familiar storytelling conventions and there
are clear indications that *Being Caribou* follows this tradition. Derek Bousé
points to one narrative prevalent in wildlife film: "a variation on the ancient
theme of the quest, which had already given rise to a kind of standardised
narrative that could be traced from the *Odyssey* to *Don Quixote* to the nov-
els of Raymond Chandler" (*Wildlife*, 128). The quest or journey, however,
is most often presented in wildlife films through individuated characters
whose biography is developed in the course of a single film. *Being Caribou*
resists individuating or personifying the caribou by offering the structure of
a human biography. Instead it is the humans who maintain human qualities, articulating their quest as a human one rather than transposing it onto
the caribou herd.

To allow the caribou to lead, taking the human pair with them, produces a means of rendering animals which emphasizes their self-determina-
tion and undermines a fully realized anthropocentrism. The two narrators
are more followers than companions to the caribou. The quest takes the
filmmakers across vast areas of the Arctic region and the land, the seasons
and weather perform in the film as much as the animals. As the title suggests, Allison and Heuer's endeavor is to capture not only images of the
caribou but also the experience of being a caribou as it migrates through the
harsh conditions. Heuer concedes that they do not, in fact, become caribou:
"We're trying to be caribou. We're not being caribou. We're following caribou. We're being left behind by caribou." For Pamela Banting, this notion of
following, or more specifically walking, nevertheless institutes an alternative
experience: "a five-month walk places contemporary humans such as Heuer
and Allison in the position of being 'carried away,' carried out of themselves
and into another reality by the sights, sounds, smells, tastes, and contacts
they experience" (416). This reality is strongly conveyed through the words
and bodies of the pair as they move through different parts of the wilder-

ness. The viewer is asked to identify with their perspective as they observe and live in the same sphere as the caribou and other animals.[16]

The relationality between human and nonhuman produced by the documentary quest, one that is tied to the attempt at "being caribou," is certainly inspired by a romantic ethos. However, I am interested in reframing this encounter and understanding it not as a mystical pilgrimage, but as an encounter with nonhuman otherness. In chapter 3 I discussed Jamie Lorimer's notion of nonhuman charisma, which recognizes the appeal and distinctiveness of nonhuman species and how that might translate into a (non)human realism, facilitating an understanding of the documentary moving image. Here I wish to underline the potential for animal agency in this formulation. Lorimer is centrally concerned with embodied encounters between human and animal in the sphere of biodiversity conservation and in this context animals might be perceived in an anthropocentric manner (because the scientist is the source of knowledge and perception), yet this does not necessarily reduce animals to human and humanizing knowledge:

> Ontologically, nonhuman charisma blurs the modern subject object dualism to provide a new approach to understanding nonhuman agency. In particular, although the charisma outlined here is resolutely anthropocentric—it emanates from the human body—it does not elevate nonhuman organisms to the humanist status of subjects. Neither does it reduce them to the instrumental domain of the objects of natural science. Instead, an awareness of nonhuman charisma opens analysis to nonhuman difference and to the vast diversity of agency potentials performed by different organisms. (927)

In some respects Lorimer's account is compatible with Haraway's work on the complex asymmetrical encounters between animals and humans, however the notion of nonhuman charisma brings with it a form of human perception that is couched in the narratives of diversity preservation. Heuer and Allison encourage the audience to encounter the caribou as they do, by way of attention to lifeworlds, animal agency, and self-reflexive relationality. In other words, they seek a recognition of nonhuman difference.

In filmic terms, the encounter between the narrators and the caribou produces moments in which the materiality and vitalism of the caribou is heightened for the spectator. This is especially the case when death and dying is rendered in the documentary. In one scene Heuer describes having come across a cow standing in a shallow creek, noting that it takes him some time to realize the cow has its nose pressed into moss next to the creek because it has been infested with botfly and is in extreme distress. The camera cuts from Heuer's face, as he relates the story, to a close shot of a caribou, standing in the creek, swaying on its feet. He continues: "almost without question she's going to die there. The thing that struck me was that there wasn't a sound. It was just quiet. I guess what we're learning as we follow the caribou is that fate for a lot of them, is that they die." Heuer's words express the harsh conditions of the migration and the ecological factors that will necessitate the death of many caribou; however, this death is distinct from the stasis of the archive and *Being Caribou* draws attention to death as only one dimension of the life of the caribou herd. More than this, the footage of the dying caribou achieves what Miriam Hansen describes in her discussion of Kracauer's theory of film—it " 'addresses the viewer as a corporeal-material being'; seizes the 'human being with skin and hair' " ("With Skin," 548). In this case, the material phenomena Kracauer refers to is animal life—the skin and hair of the spectator's physiology are addressed by the equivalent materiality of living animal skin and hair, even or especially as it approaches death.

Significantly, in these instances the materiality of the image and signification, in the form of narrative, function together to produce an emphasis on life and its indeterminate qualities.[17] The quest narrative emphasizes movement and as each shot follows another, walking figures proliferate frame after frame. The film unfolds as a relationship between temporality and the movement of bodies in space (echoing the movement of the image) in a way that foregrounds the mutability of humans and animals. To return to Mulvey's point, this occurs in a way that harnesses the lost referent and the static image by acknowledging the impossibility of fixing the changeability of life when rendered in its material dimensions. The narrative quest and the narrator's spoken descriptions of the sensuous and tactile presence of the caribou highlight and bring the spectators' awareness to "the corporeal-material layers" ("With Skin," 462) of the film.[18]

By accentuating the caribou's agency *and* materiality, the documentary decenters the human, seeks a shared ontology, and allows the caribou to lead the narrative. In order to address species endangerment, the filmmakers draw attention to life and lifeworlds in the present, rather than foreclosing on the possible future of the herd by reducing the animals to a performance of decline, posed in predetermined ways. Moreover, the oscillation between presenting the caribou as objects of scientific knowledge and as enigmatic, beyond rational accounts, echoes this openness and suggests an animal charisma that appreciates the irreducible complexity of nonhuman organisms.

This is achieved through a documentary narrative that formulates the quest into a story of following and the caribou as a living material presence, rather than already archived into the catalog of extinction in a way that anticipates species loss. With a very different approach, *Arctic Tale* focuses on the highly recognizable image of the polar bear and incorporates this flagship animal into the commercial frame of Disney-oriented wildlife film.

Polar Bears in an *Arctic Tale*: Companions in Decline

The polar bear occupies an exceptional place in the popular imaginary. Yusoff captures this when she describes the white polar bear as "a mythic and biophysical storyteller, figuring the complexities of changing climates and habitat loss, and conjoining the biophysical and emotional worlds of humans and animals" (74). The capacity of this flagship species to encapsulate the richness of public feeling about climate change, animals, and the biosphere indicates why it has become a key figure in recent "blue chip" wildlife documentary. *Arctic Tale* places the polar bear at the forefront of its representation of Arctic ecosystems and underlying commentary on anthropogenic climate change. With Yusoff's observation in mind, I examine how *Arctic Tale* harnesses the storytelling potential of the polar bear and fuses it with the traditions and conventions of wildlife film to mythologize and thus co-opt the animal into the archive of extinction. This orientation toward myth, and Disney-esque humanization of animals, inflects the film's agenda to raise awareness about habitat destruction and species loss.

Examples that fall into the category of blue chip wildlife film are few in number and, as high cost and high return documentaries, are produced to circulate internationally to maximize audiences and profits.[19] As a joint production between Paramount Classics and National Geographic Films, *Arctic Tale* fits the blue chip mold. It was shot and directed over the course of ten years by Adam Ravetch and Sarah Robertson. The film is organized into two parallel story threads and follows "Nanu" the female polar bear and "Seela" the female walrus. The documentary offers close visual attention to polar bears and walruses in their habitat by compiling footage of different animals to represent the life, from infancy to adulthood, of a newborn polar bear cub and a newborn walrus. The story is unified through the voiceover, narrated by Queen Latifah, which organizes the images of various animals into a narrative. The voiceover furnishes the two lead animals with names and human-like qualities, contributing to the film's ambiguous location at the intersection of fiction and nonfiction. *Arctic Tale* was released soon after *March of the Penguins* (2005), one of the most commercially successful documentaries of all time with worldwide box office returns of $127 million.[20] *March of the Penguins* has a somewhat similar stylistic approach to *Arctic Tale*, yet does not reference the impact of climate change. Nevertheless, Gregg Mitman cites *March of the Penguins* as an important driver in mobilizing the rise of ecologically oriented film over the past decade, a phenomenon he terms the "green wave."

Arctic Tale exhibits textual qualities that align it with wildlife film traditions, particularly American traditions outlined by Bousé, in which artifice, story, and anthropomorphism are made explicit. This compares with the category "natural history film," which signifies a longer history of filmmaking now associated with British examples that, while focused on entertainment, draw more on references to established science. While these are identifiable categories, there is much overlap between the two, particularly in the contemporary, internationalized industry. *Arctic Tale* and *Earth* (2007),[21] a blue chip Disney production that also features polar bears, indicate a move, discernable in examples across both traditions, toward referring to the existence of climate change. Cynthia Chris maps how to some degree, in the postwar era, wildlife film and television acknowledged habitat destruction and encouraged conservation—albeit in ways that emphasized the resilience of the natural world. While since the 1970s this message has been more explicit, in most cases examples "evade discussion of specific causes and political solutions to environmental problems" (Chris 201). As I discuss in the next chapter, recognition of the definitive conclusions of climate science has been similarly protracted[22] and *Arctic Tale* offers a further example of Chris's point regarding the tendency for commercially distributed film to side step political controversy—*Arctic Tale* depicts how warmer, longer summers and deteriorating ice coverage affect the animals' ability to find food and refuge without stating the causes of the changing conditions.

Unlike *Earth*, *Arctic Tale* does not have a formal relationship with the Disney brand. Nevertheless, the film's formal and narrative concerns locate it squarely in the Disney tradition, particularly the True-Life Adventures series[23] and the 1958 film in this series, *White Wilderness*, is an important foundation. The adherence to Disney wildlife conventions, and the blurring of the line between fiction and nonfiction, places *Arctic Tale* at the forefront of the contested relationship between documentary and wildlife film.[24] While the focus on plot and artifice does not offer an easy fit with some definitions of documentary, I argue that wildlife film exists in a distinct category that draws on documentary techniques and, frequently marketed as documentary, makes use of viewers' desire for audiovisual evidence of the nonhuman world. These blue chip examples build on Disney's emphasis on storytelling and marry this with documentary realism in order to pose an inclusive address that appeals to younger viewers as well as adults. Moreover, with its environmental undertones, *Arctic Tale* makes this address explicit in ways that utilize the child demographic in the promotion of green consumerism: over the closing credits individual children relay choices they can make in their efforts to reduce environmental impact on the Arctic.

Mobilizing a green polemic in this way might be considered strategic, given the political climate of the time and controversy concerning the exploitation of natural resources in the sub Arctic. Mitman follows this view in his reference to the film: the "decision to use children and target individual consumption in addressing the politics of global warming was a safe one. It wouldn't draw heat from the Bush administration or alienate potential corporate sponsors" (216). Claire Molloy supports this assessment in her critique of Disney's corporate narrative of environmental concern, charting how the films under the Disneynature brand resist posing radical environmental messages while encouraging consumer activity and ensuring profitability ("Nature," 180–183). If *Arctic Tale* employs the adventure narrative in ways that offer a more veiled assertion of environmental politics than *Being Caribou*, this should be considered in light of industrial and narrative contrasts between the two. There are significant industrial differences between *Being Caribou*, a less commercial, publicly funded NFB production with a limited audience, and *Arctic Tale*, an intensely commercial exercise seeking broad international audience appeal.

Both examples reference standardized classical human narratives, a common practice in representing wildlife. However, in the case of *Arctic Tale* the animals are consistently humanized, manufactured to perform human storytelling conventions in a way that coheres through the disembodied voice of the narrator. In *Being Caribou* it is more predominantly human characters that perform the narrative, following the undifferentiated herd of caribou. The journey narrative is more conventionally depicted in *Arctic Tale* in the sense that it constructs individual (animal) characters through a biographical chronology. For Bousé, this mode of storytelling has been a long-standing feature of wildlife film that more widely includes "the focus on the life experiences of a single endearing character, the orphan theme, the journey motif, and the overall coming of age story with its drama of trial and initiation, separation and return, struggle and exaltation" (137). Both *Earth* and *Arctic Tale* begin with the moment at which two polar bear cubs emerge from their snow cave for the first time. Their mothers, who have been in hibernation for six months, accompany them. While *Earth* inserts the bears into a patriarchal nuclear family,[25] *Arctic Tale* personifies the animals by offering them human qualities and maintaining a coherent coming of age narrative throughout the film.

Nanu, as a cub, is protected and fed by her mother for the first half of *Arctic Tale*. During this period, particular reference is made to the warmer autumn, impacting on the bear's ability to hunt on solid sea ice. This is a problem perceived by the cubs' mother. As the bear walks over fragile ice the voiceover states: "Something is different this year. The ice isn't hard at all. This is not like any winter mother bear has seen before. They'll have to go back and wait for the ice to thicken. And until it does they'll remain hungry." During the winter, the male cub dies of hunger and fatigue in a storm; in a highly emotive sequence the mother and female cub huddle over him after death with the voiceover offering their grief in human dimensions. Soon, Nanu is shown at two years old and at this age her mother drives her away, separating from the cub a year earlier than usual, unable to provide for both of them in the changing climate. A shot reverse shot sequence is crafted to show the two bears looking at one another, as the voiceover interprets: "One look tells her that life with her mother is over. Mother bear can no longer provide for them both. In order for them both

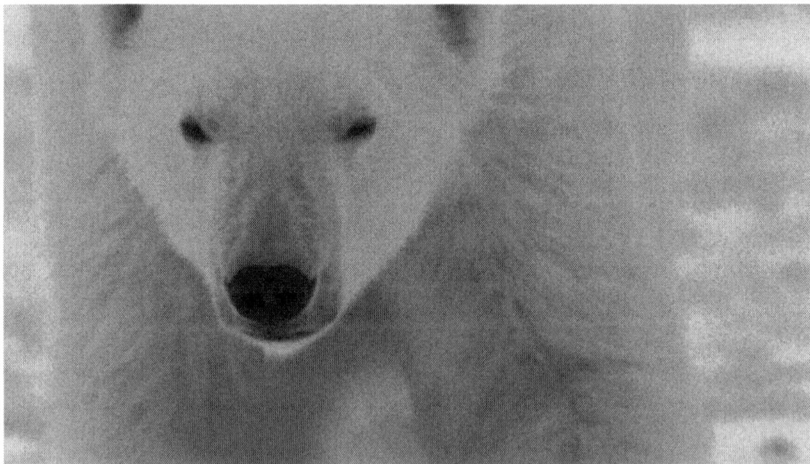

Figure 4.2. In *Arctic Tale* (2007) Nanu's mother, we are told, gives her cub a menacing look to drive her away as she cannot find enough food to support both of them in the warming climate.

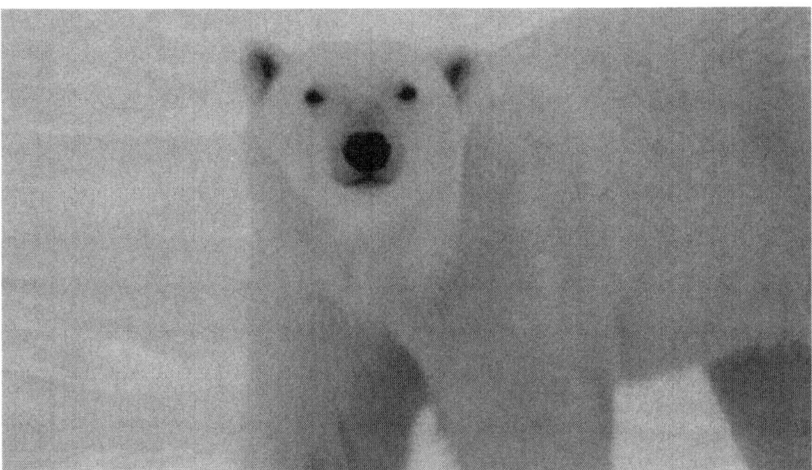

Figure 4.3. The next shot in *Arctic Tale* (2007) depicts Nanu responding to her mother, stationary for a moment before she bounds off into the snow.

to survive she must drive Nanu away. [. . .] Leaving is the hardest thing Nanu has ever done, but it's also hard for her mother. She can't protect her young one anymore." At this point the coming of age story is also realized as an orphan narrative.

The polar bear in *Arctic Tale* exemplifies Yusoff's concept of "companion species," a formulation that appropriates Haraway's well-known use of the term. In Yusoff's sense, however, animals can function as companion species in that they accompany humans in the journey towards environmental decline: "As companions in the experience of abrupt environmental change, polar bears have become a space in which to project, negotiate and comprehend a shared fate" (75–76). In this respect, flagship animals are "prosthetics" for human experience, standing in for our own somatic and epistemological access to the nonhuman environment. *Arctic Tale* takes not only the polar bear, but also the walrus and co-opts them to advance the journey through an Arctic affected by climate change. What it means to be an animal in the Arctic is rendered in striking visual detail, yet this visualization is deployed in understanding bears and walruses as cohabitants and companions to humans, rather than as causalities, victims of anthropogenic climate change and in need of protection. Symbolizing human social traits, the bears become characters in their own human story, eclipsing and displacing responsibility for the more crucial human story—the reasons for and actions to mitigate pending environmental catastrophe in the Arctic.

Loss is then projected onto polar bears but does not lead to recognition of the reality of species loss. They are made present through human markers of identity and sociality and are an index of the impact of habitat destruction, making it their own and eclipsing human causality and responsibility. The Arctic supports only a small number animals and no vegetation, resulting in an ecosystem perpetuated by violence: animals survive by eating each other. Only one such act of violence is shown in the film, and this is shown at a distance with the signifier of bloodied snow. Choosing not to show this violence maintains the film securely in the G-rating classification for its child audience and reinforces the sociability of the animals. It also feeds into the style of narrativization in the film, one that humanizes rather than drawing attention to the distinctive corporeality and material presence of the animals.

Molloy argues that, more broadly, Disneynature reworks earlier Disney wildlife films to accentuate the brand's relationship to nostalgia. The new emphasis on conservation that permeates many Disneynature films draws on this nostalgia to frame contemporary environmental destruction as a shared narrative, changing through time, with promotional material noting that "There was a time when most people viewed nature as something apart from themselves. In the 21st century, there is an increasing awareness that we are all part of nature" (cited in Molloy, "Nature," 182). For Molloy, Disneynature is "the communicator of an overarching, even universal story of nature and its films provide points of orientation from a "past nature" to the current fragile environment" ("Nature," 182). The Disney brand expressly constructs a relationship with the audience that allows them to perceive themselves to be sharing in a benign nature, across time, reinforcing the notion that animals are long-standing companions and dispersing responsibility.

In *Arctic Tale* Seela and Nanu are figured as human prosthetics for experiencing climate change, co-opted into a human rationale of decision making. They do not have the opportunity to be figured as animal agents. De Vos observes that in stories about the thylacine, the animals are not afforded "agency in adapting to a suddenly hostile environment. The thylacine, in its ideal form, is cast as unable to adapt to change, a victim of evolution and marsupial inferiority/innocence, helpless in the face of progress" (191). *Arctic Tale* does not explicitly depict animals as unable to adapt. However, nor does it recognize, in Lorimer's words, a kind of nonhuman charisma that infuses the public sphere of conservation with a nonhuman difference and "the vast diversity of agency potentials performed by different organisms." Instead, the possibility of observing and contemplating polar bear behavior and corporeality is thwarted by the imposition of humanizing qualities, minimizing the potential to understand these animals as agents or as outside the narrative trajectory of decline in which the story places them.

The coupling of the humanist biographical mode and the depiction of climate change is integral in this film. Nanu's character draws on the mythologizing impulse of classical (Disneyfied) wildlife film while also tapping into audience knowledge about potential species loss. Such a synthesis draws on and promotes the role articulated by Yusoff—the polar bear as a mythic and biophysical storyteller in climate change narratives. Posing the embodied animal as a mythological type again evokes De Vos' approach to the representation of extinct species in which he describes how the absent referent or inscribing subject is replaced with an idea: "The death and subsequent absence of the last specimen requires the absence of the inscribing subject. The reader is connected with the idea of the animal rather than its 'reality.' A first notion of the extinct animal is produced from a theory of last instances" (190). While the inscribing subject is always absent in film, often its living likeness may exist and be accessed in the world again. In the case of the definitive death of species loss, however, it is absent for all possible future inscriptions—it is frequently replaced with mythologies to which images become subservient. The polar bear is not yet the last of the last, but, significantly, it is brought into being in the film in ways that gesture to extinction narratives, presaging its death, anticipating last instances by minimizing its materiality and difference, co-opting it to a singular idea.[26] *Arctic Tale* attenuates the potential for film narrative to amplify viewer's awareness of the corporeal and material worlds that it can engender.

Documentary and the Future

More than simply an iconic film about Arctic life, *Nanook* crystallizes death, in the form of the dying Inuit race, in the documentary project from its beginnings. It does so in ways that gesture to imperialist prejudices of the time. Contemporary documentaries, such as *Being Caribou* and *Arctic Tale*, continue to frame the Arctic territory through the interplay between life and death but with reference to a different teleology—habitat destruction and ecological change. I have described the distinctive ways the two films express the problem of species endangerment, with *Arctic Tale* offering a more negative set of possibilities for the future. It is, in many respects, not controversial to indict the Disney-inspired format and elevate the product of a public institution such as the NFB. Yet, the specific mechanisms by which they produce images of animal life as a resource for conservation politics, and the way they resonate with the ubiquitous and constantly transforming genre of wildlife film, is less predictable.

Moving image recordings inevitably reproduce animals as archivable reproductions. However, the animal/human relations they encourage, the way the human is factored into this relation and the ease with which such images produce events that can be recruited into human narratives of decline are more open. It is possible to record endangered species without prematurely anticipating their extinction and elevating the stasis of representation over the dynamism of life. Recounting histories of extinction in ways that center the human produces narratives of nature in crisis that account only for the loss to human worlds and concerns. It also produces perceived situations of inevitable spiraling decline and while the scale and import of environmental crisis must be recognized, the possibility of imagining alternative futures will not be realized by mythologizing endangered species in familiar ways, even if it succeeds in raising revenue for conservation programs. If Nanook and his family were excised from modernity and history by Flaherty, and cast in a position outside Western progress, animals are similarly absent in anthropocentric conceptions of the history (and present) of extinction.

Nevertheless, the notion of significant, iconic, or flagship species (which are easily mythologized) is an important hinge that joins the conservation movement and the popular imaginary. They function as what Nichols refers to as a "dominant concept" or "strategy of containment" (143) around which it is possible to structure a delimited documentary narrative. I have elaborated on two films that, in some respects, present two such documentary narrative contingencies, encapsulated in approaches by Yusoff and Lorimer respectively. For Yusoff, while flagship species might raise funds and awareness in a way that fuels protection for less popular animals, she questions the kinds of practices and epistemologies that might be engendered by this approach to the politics of (species) loss, claiming that animals that have "sociable aspects, traits, characteristics, quirks" ("Aesthetics," 586) become the object of social power and care in ways that other animals do not. This critique focuses on how flagship species exist as a technology of representation that aestheticizes environmental issues, making them easily consumable and facilitating negatively selective conservation practices. In contrast, for Lorimer the charisma of particular animals, including flagship species, presents more open-ended possibilities for relating that also might operate as dominant concepts in textual representation. These possibilities are based in the appreciation of nonhuman difference and agency.[27] This formulation points to the way the science of ethology, of animal behavior, might feature in the shaping of flagship representations, drawing out the more than human attributes of different species, and thus, recognition that animals are not compatriots, equally contracted into the campaign of preservation as humans.

In chapter 2 I discussed the avant-garde agricultural films of the "long take," concluding that they assert human worlds and the values of humanism. Yet they do so in ways that ask the viewer to stay with animals, their distinctiveness and mutability. The nonhuman difference I have described in this chapter functions in a similar way, yet in the case of the representation of wildlife I have described in *Being Caribou*, human stories are subordinated to the movement and life cycles of wild animals, challenging an absolute anthropocentrism of the documentary narrative and image. In the case of *Arctic Tale*, the weight of the narration imposes anthropomorphism on the figure of the animal in the frame, discouraging or even eclipsing viewer curiosity about the distinctiveness of animal embodiment.

The problem can be understood as one that references layers of time: cinematic time and the chronological progression from life to extinction. In cinematic time the filmed object is lost following the moment of registration, the image becomes only an index, with time and space separating the two. The loss or death that is at the heart of documentary apparatus' inability to fully capture the referent accentuates the loss that constitutes extinction. Documentary representation, however, need not be caught in the loop of repeating death, at the expense of life, affirming loss in the past and foreshadowing it in the future. It is possible for documentary film to render significant species in ways that advance a biopolitical situation in which death is not certain, decline could be otherwise, and the referent offers animation and an emphasis on life rather than the multiplication of death. I have outlined how this might occur in the case of images (and their relation to physical presence) and conventions that draw the viewer's attention to nonhuman agency, materiality, and difference.

Chapter 5

Antarctica, Science, and Exploration

Encounters at the End of the World

Antarctica has produced some of the most marketable images of wildlife in the contemporary era. *March of the Penguins* (*La Marche de l'Empereur*, 2005) and the animated *Happy Feet* (2006) have secured a place for the topology of the continent in the cinematic imagination in a manner that is unprecedented. Yet, there is a clear disparity between these constructions that utilize Antarctica as a backdrop for popular storytelling and the experience of Antarctica as a continent unlike any other: it is the most isolated landmass in the world, the most sparsely populated with wildlife, and, along with the Arctic, the most vulnerable to global warming. It was also the last continent to be discovered and mapped, a fact that affords it a special place in human history.

In his discussion of Captain James Cook's unsuccessful attempts to infiltrate Antarctica and conquer the South Pole on his 1772–1775 expedition, Mariano Siskind proposes that the territory persists, symbolically, as a site of difficulty for globalizing modernity. Its very existence is a critique of the colonial process of globalization:

> Antarctica becomes, since Captain Cook's symbolic failure, the ultimate exception to the universal premises on the basis of which globalisation is imagined, discursively formulated, and carried on. Witness of a dozen colonising waves, Antarctica remains an irreducible particularity, or, in more extreme terms: read, historically, as the ultimate exception of the universal premises of a globalising modernity. (Siskind 9)

Crucially, the exceptional status attributed by Siskind constitutes a barrier that leaves Antarctica "outside modernity" (19). The natural characteristics of the territory, its temperature and geography, were central to Cook's decision not to attempt further incursions into Antarctica. For Siskind, this natural world overwhelmed the explorer, eliciting fear and horror and thus annulling the possibility of discovery. He frames Cook's experience, with Edmund Burke's notion of the sublime in mind, as an encounter with nature that is horrifying and fundamentally destabilizing as it eclipses reason and the ability to comprehend the perceived object. Thus, it "destroys the boundary between subject and object" (Siskind 18). The examples I discuss in this chapter transform Antarctica from a barren inhospitable landmass into a biopolitical stage that filmically organizes human and non-human life. They do so with reference to the motivations and discourse of science, replacing sublime experience with a representational frame that reinstates reason.

This chapter perceives the language and gaze of science as it is filtered through the aesthetic concerns of three different documentary outliers—the adventure/exploration film of early cinema, contemporary blue chip natural history film, and the essay film. While all nonfiction, these modes sit outside the realist norms of observational and expository documentary cinema. I am interested in what kinds of relationships between and across humans and animals these documentary appropriations of science produce given the unique historical and geographical stage provided by Antarctica. The "science" these examples pursue is most often ethology, the study of animal behavior, which is the prime driver of the wildlife mode, visualized and narrativized across the idea and embodiment of animals. Nevertheless, climate science, evolutionary biology, and zoology more broadly also feed into these narratives.

I begin with the films of the early era of heroic exploration, especially those that draw on Herbert G. Ponting's cinematographic record of Captain Scott's expedition to the South Pole. These works are fundamental constituents of the historical (visual) archive of Antarctica. They contribute an explicit cultural reference point, a thread that is woven through two later examples made nearly a century later. David Attenborough's *Frozen Planet* (2011) series about the Arctic and Antarctic and Werner Herzog's *Encounters at the End of the World* (2007) both refer back to the expeditions of Scott and Shackleton, binding them not only through a shared preoccupation with Antarctica, but through an interest in an earlier age of exploration and its visual expression. All three films are intensely concerned with the nonhuman world, animal life in particular, and how it might be rendered in relation to different phases of human endeavor in the continent. In this respect, this chapter is crucially concerned with the time of exploration, its failure and success, and how moments linked to the spectacle and ideology of the age of exploration echo through history.

Life is framed not only through the discourses of science, but also the profoundly important narrative of rationalism and modernity articulated by Siskind: exploration and the expansion of reason. Animals become integral to the process of assimilating overwhelming nature and recuperating Antarctica back into the frame of modernity and reason, posed through the aesthetic and narrative properties of documentary. I investigate how differing (documentary) conceptions of science might produce revised understandings of animals and animal/human relationships. In particular, Charles Darwin's work on the genealogy of the species not only inspires the scientism of wildlife film and television, but also provides a platform for evaluating how these films pose animal life and its relation to the human. While they have much in common, the examples discussed differ greatly in their approach to science. Ponting's films offer early amateur naturalism. *Frozen Planet* presents well-established film and television conventions that synthesize zoology and ethology into narrative forms while pushing into the new terrain of climate science. In *Encounters at the End of the World* Herzog challenges established orthodoxies with an essayist critique of the relation between nature, conquest, and reason with Antarctic scientists and animals as the vehicle for this critique. All films, significantly, share one further important quality—the embodied and subjective presence of a narrator who lends authority and authorial identity to the interpretation of events onscreen. This offers a particular documentary response to the challenge to the boundary between subject, or the self, and the object of the sublime Antarctic environment.

90° South and the Era of Heroic Exploration

The "heroic era" of Antarctic exploration began in the final years of the nineteenth century and spanned two decades. During this time of intense exploration, ten countries initiated seventeen different expeditions. The "heroism" of this era is characterized by not only the achievements in scientific and geographical exploration, but this nomenclature also alludes to the notoriety of the poets, artists, and photographers involved in the expeditions who conveyed to a distant audience the romanticism of the polar landscape. History has elevated three of these expeditions in the popular imagination. While Roald Amundsen's Norwegian contingent was the first to reach the pole, Ernest Shackleton and Captain Robert Falcon Scott's missions have secured a firmer place in the history books. Both of the British expeditions were captured on film. Frank Hurley, a member of Shackleton's 1914–1917 expedition and Herbert Ponting, who accompanied Captain Scott on his 1910–1913 journey, are the earliest cinematographers to shoot footage in Antarctica. Hurley's film, *South*, was released in 1919. I focus on the silent feature composed of Ponting's footage, *The Great White Silence* (1924) and the sound version of the same film released in 1933, *90° South*, which features Ponting's narration.

Ponting began his career as a cinematographer on the Antarctic mission and consequently became a key figure of travel filmmaking. His most renowned work, shot on Scott's expedition, had multiple filmic incarnations and included not only the two versions of the feature, but also newsreels and an illustrated lecture undertaken by Ponting. Footage also appeared in Gaumont's *The Undying Story of Captain Scott* (1914) a film released a year after news of Scott's death reached England. Given his historical achievements, Ponting might be understood as what Eric Barnouw terms the "documentarist-as-explorer" (30). He was a figure who, despite the growing popularity of the newsreel format by 1910, continued to work in a manner that laid the groundwork for the emergence of documentary proper in the 1920s, making way for Flaherty's success with *Nanook of the North* in 1922. Moreover, the persona of the filmmaker as explorer and as an identifiable authorial presence is accentuated in the sound version of the film with Ponting appearing onscreen, with Vice Admiral Edward Evans who was also part of the expedition, to introduce the film and offer opening comments. This marks the voiceover to follow as the voice of the filmmaker.

In this introduction Ponting evokes the power of the geography the explorers faced. These same words appear in intertitles in the silent version:

> The Antarctic Continent is an ice-clad wilderness of dazzling whiteness and appalling silence. It is the home of nature in her most savage and merciless moods, and it is there that the hurricane and blizzard are born . . . at the heart of that dread and sterile desolation only ten human beings have trodden since God made the World.

The BFI's rerelease of *The Great White Silence* with the original tints to the black-and-white footage is eerie in its depiction of looming icebergs, standing straight against the sea. The images do more to evoke the sublime than Ponting's hyperbolic rhetoric, yet both soon give way to the documentation of the everyday life of the men at the camp and the observations of wildlife that take up a significant portion of the first part of the film. *90° South* and *The Great White Silence* work to bring the drama of Scott's expedition to audiences by framing it as both an unfolding adventure/exploration narrative and, to a lesser extent, an educational natural history film. For Derek Bousé, Ponting produced an unusual separation of historical events and animal behavior, composing an awkward fit between the two. I suggest that the two sit side by side as twin manifestations of narratives of modernity—together imperial exploration and popular science offer form and drama to the Antarctic expanse. They do so by foregrounding and framing life, human and nonhuman, in ways that historicize Antarctica through complementary motivations.

Ponting faced a number of difficulties in realizing his agenda to both promote the expedition in the minds of the public and entertain, whether through the lecture or film format. Not only did he face the challenge of making the everyday lives of the men in the ice compelling, the heroism of Scott's achievement and the tragedy of his death were not captured in moving images. Ponting only stayed with the expedition while they were camped near the coast and did not embark on the trek inland with Scott's party of five men. The quest to the pole had to be re-created and dramatized from still images and reenactments. The resulting film seeks to appeal to audiences by offering narrative detail about exceptional subject matter, both in regard to wildlife and the unique situation of the men in the camp.[1]

The scenes of wildlife in *90° South* are conveyed as compact and eventful moments. In one shot a Waddell seal clambers over a rock and then moves back again in the other direction. The action is narrated by Ponting: "strolling across the shore, this one met with a little obstruction . . . when he had got over it he had changed his mind, didn't want to go that way at all, so he back paddled." The narration draws attention to the body in motion, doubly inscribing the tactile animal gesture in the shot. The scenes of *Adélie* penguins are the most extended in the film, visualizing the detail of animal behavior while assimilating this to the gendered codes of the time:

> One often sees a gentleman picking up stones and laying them at a lady's feet. Penguins make their nest with stones and the offering of them is a proposal of marriage. This lady seems disdainful of her admirer's attentions, then she hesitates. After all she thinks, perhaps she may not get a better offer. So, exercising the privilege of her sex, she changes her mind and accepts him. Then the newlyweds immediately settle down to rear the family.

This depiction not only documents penguin behavior not previously captured on film, it also humanizes the activities, presenting them as parallel to the narrative moments that create drama in the representations of the men at the camp, such as a football match or a special meal. The purpose of the scenes with seals, penguins, and killer whales also has a stated ethological motivation, educating the audience in the "hitherto unknown habits" of these animals in the wild, as is noted in Ponting's voiceover.

The scenes of wildlife address an audience already accustomed to safari and adventure films of the time, some of which I referred to in chapter 2. As Bousé notes, safari films, such as *Native Lion Hunt* (1909) and *African Animals* (1909) were popular as expeditional films, combining adventure and animal imagery, often with a focus on hunting and killing. For Elizabeth Leane and Stephen Nicol, Antarctic species, such as Waddell seals, Adélie penguins, killer whales and skua gulls, presented a further challenge for Ponting—they posed too little threat to humans and could not be easily incorporated into a human adventure narrative (132).

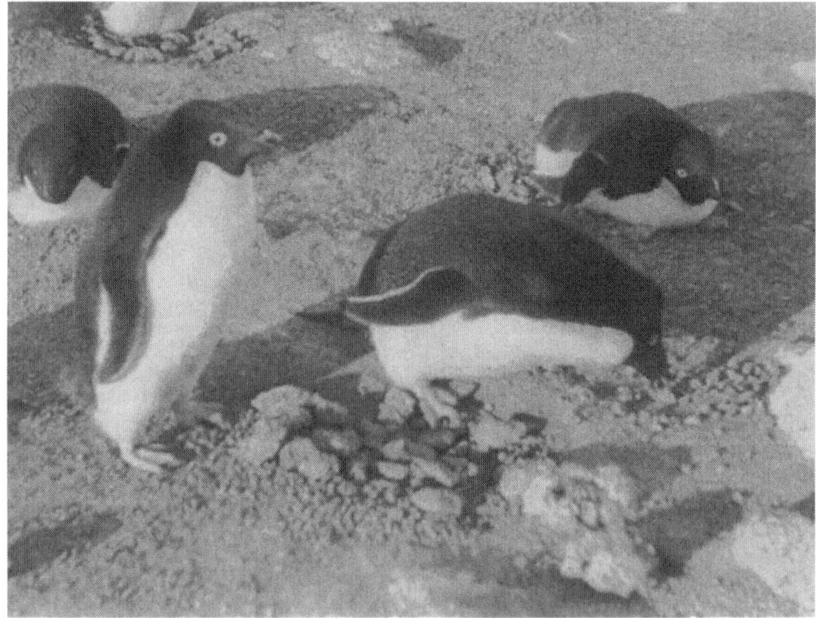

Figure 5.1. A male *Adélie pengiun* lays stones at the female's feet, preparing a nest in *The Great White Silence* (1924).

90° South does not attempt to follow the generic lead of the safari film and the dramatic substance of the film is not anchored in dangerous encounters between humans and animals. While Leane and Nicol argue that Ponting nevertheless manages to create a dynamic of human/animal encounter, I suggest that the narrative action is most striking when it occurs between animals, reinforcing the film's emphasis on wildlife and the spectacle of animal behavior, bringing it into line with contemporary natural history film. The most dramatic scene captured on film in *90° South* (given that Ponting's camera did not capture the journey inland to the Pole), is shot from the view provided from the deck of the *Terra Nova*, Scott's ship. This single wide shot follows killer whales as they hunt a baby seal. The seal cannot leverage itself out of the water and onto an ice ridge. Its mother dives into the water a number of times to distract the whales and push the baby seal out. Ponting narrates: "frenzied with fear she leaps onto the ice, and the little cub tries to struggle out too." Without editing, the thrilling scene relies on the relation between, and possible collision of, bodies in the expanse of sea and ice. The drama and movement comes to an end with human intervention—a harpoon is fired into the whales from the ship and they disperse.

The film's turn to animal observation in preference to the adventure narrative of the safari film was surely influenced by Ponting's interest in ethology, which can be traced back to his earlier work photographing wildlife. The structure of these animal sequences, moreover, offers a realism that is shaped by dominant modes of natural-historical "ways of knowing" in the sciences. With this I refer to an approach to nature that is observational and descriptive, locating the object in a world that science has the tools to investigate and explain.[2]

Science has been intimately tied to nonfiction film since its earliest manifestations and this relationship has continued with science one of the "discourses of sobriety" (Nichols 3–4) underpinning audience expectation of documentary's alignment with the real. The work of Eadweard Muybridge is well known but there were also lesser known figures working only slightly later, in the early twentieth century, such as Charles Urban and Francis Martin Duncan, both of whom specialized in microcinematographic studies.[3] Another important figure in this British movement was Frank Percy Smith. Drawn to the scientific expression of nonhuman life (including mites and insects), Timothy Boon refers to these figures as "amateur naturalists" who contributed to the activity making science available to a lay audience.[4] Such filmmakers can be considered together with Thomas Edison who, as noted in the first chapter, produced actualities in the same period, many of which focused on animals. They enabled a public culture of science that was both visual and participatory, emphasizing display in a way that only the early medium of cinema could achieve. Ponting's work, especially the films produced in the 1920s and 1930s, offers a fuller emphasis on narrative than the early examples and this turns to narrative gestures to an emerging tradition of narrativized wildlife film.

The comedy and the suspense Ponting sought to infuse these scenes with is supported by both the strangeness of these animal gestures and bodies and the threat symbolized by wild animals. It is also founded in the drama of animals in contestation with one another, struggling to survive. In the case of the penguins, this is realized through the pressure to build nests, mate, protect themselves and their eggs from predators such as gulls. The encounter between seal and killer whale again concerns the capacity to triumph in a life or death situation. Charles Darwin's *On the Origin of the Species*, published in 1859 and fifty years prior to Scott's expedition, provides a lens through which to read Ponting's animals. While the film does not directly reference his work, it is supported by the proposition made popular by Darwin that life is the result of natural selection and the struggle for existence. Yet, this proposition is seen through the prism of an anthropomorphizing lens. *90° South* and *The Great White Silence* present an early example of what has become a staple of wildlife film: the characterisation of individual animal personalities in the struggle to survive in adverse circumstances.

The scenes in question demonstrate how Darwinian principles can be adapted with some rhetorical ease to serve dramaturgical purposes. Derek Bousé describes this as a "symbolic Darwinism." Animals are "personified" and existence is structured by events occurring between or concerning individual animals. In this mode species' evolutionary "fitness" to survive is replaced by single incidences of momentary struggle that attest more to luck than the genetic environmental aptitude of species in the face of changing conditions. In this respect, these early vignettes share much with the central tenets of the wildlife genre through the twentieth century, especially the lineage of film and television aligned with Disney.

Ponting sought to gain a wide audience for his films and was concerned as much with the way science was fostered in public culture as bringing Scott's achievements to the screen. These unusual embodied creatures from a distant and inhospitable place were novel species when Ponting first began his lecture circuit soon after the expedition, if not in the ensuing decade. Leane and Nichol link the emphasis on animals specifically to Ponting's desire to entertain *and* educate: "Ponting believed that 'the masses' needed to be entertained if they were to be educated, and that key to this was the introduction of 'numerous animal scenes, without which the "show" would be a total failure'" (131). By 1920, the popular appeal of penguins had escalated and they were dubbed "Charlie Chaplains," (Leane and Nichol 137) caricaturing their physical attributes in ways aligned with popular culture.[5] The films framed animal life by promoting pleasure in the aesthetics of ethology and evolutionary biology and assimilating these to familiar and anthropomorphizing codes. What cannot be underestimated here is the indexicality of the image and its capacity to testify to the grainy black and white embodied presence of seemingly remarkable animals in the landscape. If Ponting was the "documentarist-as-explorer" he must also be considered what Boon refers to as the "amateur naturalist as an adventurer" (14). This persona is important as it offers a subjective compass, guiding the viewer through animal and human stories in ways that are attuned to the discourses of science and those of exploration.

Significantly, the films of the expedition feature not only wildlife but also service animals, with Siberian horses, huskies, and a cat ("Nigger," trained to catch mice on the ship) occupying a prominent place in the depiction of the sea journey and life on the ice for Scott's men. While *The Great White Silence* and *90° South* seek to tell a human story, it is the visualization of animals, not humans that is the most appealing spectacle in this drama. The film places animals at the center of the drama while also humanizing them in the popular imagination, serving to both displace and restage anthropocentrism respectively. Rather than an awkward fit between human history and storytelling about nature, I suggest the film achieves the task of bringing animals into history, visually and narratively, in ways that more expansively acknowledge the core role of nonhuman species in the popular history of geographical exploration. The twin narratives of animal science and heroic adventure compose Scott's expedition as a story about encountering the nonhuman environment, not just the conquering, and mapping, of the continent.

Frozen Planet and the Greening of the Blue Chip Format

If Herbert Ponting exemplified the notion of the documentarist-as-explorer, in *Frozen Planet* this figure is replaced by the subjectivity of the natural history celebrity. David Attenborough[6] has become an archetypal presence in natural history television, not only in the United Kingdom but also in the international media sphere. Featuring Attenborough's distinctive narration,

Frozen Planet was produced in 2011 and focuses on both the Arctic and Antarctic in each episode. It brings the polar regions to the screen through the transnational vehicle of blue chip production and through the tradition of British natural history programming. I focus in particular on the representation of Antarctica in the series. In the previous chapter, I outlined the distinction between the American wildlife tradition and the tradition of the BBC, which demonstrates closer associations with popular science. I am interested in how this series frames Antarctica and its animals for a contemporary popular audience through both the scientific orthodoxies of natural history and wildlife film and the emerging credibility of climate science.

Frozen Planet was produced by the BBC's natural history unit, with significant financing provided by the Discovery Channel. The executive producer, Alastair Fothergill and series producer, Vanessa Berlowitz were also responsible for *The Blue Planet* (2001) and *Planet Earth* (2006). The series achieved considerable audience reach, with 48 percent of the British population watching at least fifteen minutes of the broadcast (Richards, "Greening Wildlife," 174). As a high-cost product that seeks to maximize audience interest,[7] the wildlife blue chip mode of documentary is formally conservative, marrying technological innovations with many long-standing aesthetic conventions. The expectation that the scientific knowledge explicated in blue chip examples will be undisputable by a lay audience further echoes the orthodoxy of the form.[8] However, Morgan Richards understands the *Frozen Planet* series as part of the "greening" of the form. As an example of what she refers to as "green chip" programming, *Frozen Planet* was released on the heels of a string of high-budget examples that revised the conventions of natural history programming to include attention to environmental issues. Richards' discussion focuses on the question of how the interrelation of industry and audience expectation enabled this shift. As "the science behind anthropogenic global warming became more solid, allowing BBC producers to present this information more unequivocally, it was accompanied by a subtle shift in how environmental issues were framed" ("Greening Wildlife," 182). This indicates that audiences were ready to accept climate science as credible and "uncontroversial," to use Richards' term, enabling global distribution.

This emphasis on the acceptance of climate science should be tempered by an acknowledgment that the first five episodes of the series are little concerned with anthropogenic questions—they are largely conventional, blue chip wildlife productions, with one introductory episode and four subsequent episodes that focus on the four different seasons. The sixth episode, titled *The Last Frontier*, examines human life in these inhospitable conditions, including scientists working in Antarctica.[9] Only the seventh episode, *On Thin Ice*, discusses the impact of climate change. Despite greater audience acceptance of climate science, this structure allowed the BBC to offer the final, most controversial, episode of *Frozen Planet* as an optional broadcast extra internationally. The Discovery Channel had initially proposed to broadcast only the first six episodes but eventually reversed this decision. This was complicated by the onscreen presence of the narrator—the first six episodes for the British market featured Attenborough's voice in the soundtrack but he did not appear in shot, enabling the Discovery Channel to replace it with the voice of Alec Baldwin for U.S. audiences. The final episode could only be broadcast with Attenborough's voice and image maintained because he appears onscreen and his experience working and filming in the Antarctic is discussed in ways that are integral to the episode.

I focus here on the British version of the series. In this example, different episodes offer different manifestations of science, and authorized scientific investigation, casting life in Antarctica through different frames of knowledge, albeit all facilitated by the persona of Attenborough and, thus, the scientific credibility of the BBC.

Attenborough's particular brand of science (and the programs he lends his name to) extends amateur naturalism into the highly codified paradigm of zoology or natural history.[10] This paradigm provides an accent on plants, animals, and other organisms, attending to their biotic characteristics and evolution. For Michael Jeffries "BBC wildlife programmes have increasingly come to depend on the presence of Sir David Attenborough as the embodiment of scientific authority" (543). Helen Wheatley refers to the distinctive "whispery reverent timbre" (329) of Attenborough's voice. This voice and his occasional onscreen appearances are central to how this embodiment has become familiar to viewers. They perpetuate his authorial signature and its alignment with trusted analytical knowledge and the consistent access he has offered to the spectacularization of nonhuman life over the decades. Further, documentary knowledge is facilitated for the audience by a rhetorical function through which Attenborough is identified with particular markers of social subjectivity.

Observing the imperial and classed dimensions of his persona, Jeffries refers to Attenborough's "patrician manner" that, however subtly, echoes "the traveller from the days of empire, well connected with the government and national institutions, travelling the earth to bring back objects of interest to those at home in Britain" (534). Attenborough is easily cast in the mold of "the heroic naturalist" (Jeffries 534) and this imperial, colonial sensibility resonates with the amateur naturalists of early scientific public cinema that

I described earlier. These naturalists, while distinguished as artisans, also often included wealthy gentlemen specialists who were not only consuming, but also "doing" natural history (Boon 15). Like *90° South*, much of *Frozen Planet*, especially the first five episodes, brings Antarctica into the popular imaginary (but to a significantly larger popular community) by assuaging the awe of experiencing the continent with not only the rationality of zoology, but also the masculine sensibility of mastery, exploration, and empire. The familiar outline of Attenborough's "old world" establishment persona offers a point of view that is a stable ground for perceiving the alien location of Antarctica and its animals.

In the blue chip representation of Antarctica, hypercolored and detailed images of animals, other life forms and geography offer viewing pleasure and stand in for the firsthand experience of the sublime. In particular, it accentuates sensory engagement, by way of the camera, with the movement, sounds and sensuality of animal bodies. Contemporary wildlife photography excels in offering spectacles that slow the movement of animal

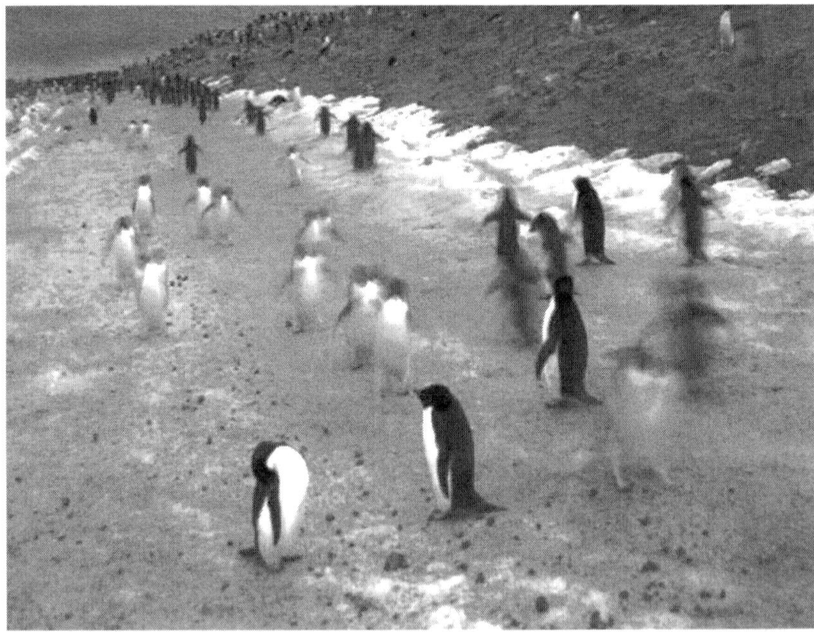

Figure 5.2. Stop motion techniques appear to speed up the penguins' progression to the sea in *Frozen Planet* (2011).

bodies or speed up scenes to present animal populations and their environments in order to provoke fascination about not only nature but also the means by which it is captured and visualized. Mastery over animals is manifest in filmic terms as virtuosity in manipulating the technology of the spectacular, and the capacity for mastery over the temporality of the image in particular. Speeding up and slowing down life offers the illusion that it is possible to manipulate material phenomena in order to grasp its meaning more fully. The voiceover adds to this function: the first six episodes of *Frozen Planet* feature the archetypal "voice of god," with an omniscient narrator, albeit inferring Attenborough's embodied presence outside the frame, explicating the world onscreen through the rationality of science.[11]

In the traditional mode, natural history programs offer a world in which these visual and analytical components are deployed to express an environment beyond human history and activity. Indeed, the first five episodes of *Frozen Planet* largely adhere to the expectation that wildlife and natural history programming will provide drama, spectacle, and education in a way that is isolated from the unpredictability of the social world. In this isolation the ecology of animal life is in harmonious balance, com posed of a natural order of birth, death, mating, and migration. Jeffries categorizes this as "Old Ecology," aligning it with a mid-twentieth-century conception of biological science that emphasized balance, equilibrium, and renewal (528). Cynthia Chris identifies this rhetoric of harmonious balance as a more pervasive feature of the subgenre, one that plays to an ideological image of nature that is reassuring and predictable:

> By masking its political stakes, by diluting its environmental messages, the wildlife genre provides an illusory picture of the pleasurably ordered, harmonious, resilient natural world; that is the comforting image of an eternal "natural," depoliticised and heterotopically whole world. (202)

The focus of *Frozen Planet* in the early episodes is on the succession of the seasons and how each brings challenge, cyclical change, and vibrant display where nonhuman life is concerned. These cycles are implicitly ageless and unchangeable.

Many scenes reprise Ponting's preoccupation with seals, penguins, and killer whales. One vignette in the first episode captures a seal on a small ice floe as a pod of killer whales work in unison to destabilize the ice until the seal falls prey to the sea and the predators. In another episode, *Frozen Planet* depicts the exact same activity that Ponting observed and described:

while building their nests Adélie penguins take coveted stones from neighboring nests while the owners attention is directed elsewhere. In both cases this is anthropomorphized, becoming an activity of theft and criminality. While many scenes in *Frozen Planet* stage episodes of drama between individual animals, the narration couches this synecdochally, with a firm relation between the example and the behavior of the species. In one narrative thread that extends across winter and spring episodes, Emperor penguins are shown marching into the Antarctic interior, in advance of the coldest part of the year. The female lays a single egg and the male incubates it as the female returns to the ocean to feed for the winter, only returning in the spring to the near starving population of males and chicks. While the editing and imagery lead the viewer to believe they are observing one couple across seasons, the narration makes clear reference to the species as a whole and constructs the small family as exemplifying the species' struggle for survival. In this respect, the series points to the ways in which contemporary blue chip natural history programming is more moderate in its production of a symbolic Darwinism of the kind Bousé describes, while still exploiting the power of the focus on interactions between individualized animals.

Popularized Darwinism haunts the series to the degree that questions of survival are foremost in many sequences and their narration. The central premise of Darwin's work, however, is necessarily rejected in a construction of the natural world that is insulated from the human. Crucial to Darwin's genealogy of species is the fundamental continuity between humans and all other living species. Wildlife modes function contra to this premise by disaggregating human and inhuman worlds, thus implicitly privileging the human paradigm above all others. In his own time, Darwin observed the convention in work by naturalists to place humans in a different order: "If man had not been his own classifier, he would never have thought of founding a separate order for his own reception" (*The Descent*, 170). In Darwin's words, this becomes a question of authorial power and self-perception. Similarly, in wildlife film human activity is only present via authorial sovereignty, which is manifest as the license to name, categorize, and thus master all other forms of life (and to revise the temporality of life through audiovisual virtuosity). Indeed, Attenborough, as the conduit of such knowledge, marks this separation through his distinctive persona, infusing the series with the further hierarchicization of imperial and masculine subjectivity.

Given this, it is significant that the sixth episode of *Frozen Planet* focuses on the human presence at the polar regions. However, because it is a separate episode, the possibility of incorporating humans as one of many forms of life, separated only by degrees of difference is not realized and civilization is ultimately set apart from and above nature. It is notable, however, that the *first* episode is not solely focused on animal life—it emphasizes the harshness of the conditions by recalling Scott and Amundsen's trek into the interior. The vista shot from a helicopter fills the frame and landscapes of glaciers and mountains unfold in front of the camera as Attenborough narrates:

> We are following the route of Scott and Amundsen as they struggled to become the first humans to reach the South Pole. They were travelling on foot and the first sight of these mountains must have been daunting indeed. In front of them stretched one of the world's longest ranges, spanning 2000 miles from one side of the continent to the other. The winds up here are the fastest on earth. They reach speeds of 200 miles an hour [. . .] This is the Beardmore Glacier, which Scott and his men somehow traversed on foot. It is over 100 miles long and one of the largest glaciers on earth. But this is nothing compared to what lies beyond the mountains [. . .] From here to the South Pole there is noting but ice for 700 miles.

The mountains referred to are part of the Transantarctic Mountain Range. The images render these, the glacier and the 700-mile ice cap in stunning visual detail. If Ponting's films expressed a movement between the events of the heroic age of exploration and (anthropomorphized) animal behavior, this episode binds these same events, as history, to threatening geography and the geological sciences. Indeed, the last two episodes not only reference human endeavor in the form of explorers, they also include present-day scientists, thus explicitly posing Antarctica as an ongoing site for human mastery, discovery, and knowledge.

If Cook's confidence in the advancement of reason to every corner of the globe was thwarted by his failure to infiltrate the continent, natural history series' about Antarctica, such as *Frozen Planet*, are successful in this mission, bringing the spectacle of landscape and life to a global audience in high quality cinematography. *Frozen Planet* not only achieves this through the long-established codes and conventions of BBC natural history television, in the last episode of the seven part series it also accords with a new paradigm in Attenborough's establishment approach to science and television. This new paradigm accounts for the ecological entanglements between human and nonhuman worlds by acknowledging environmental politics and, implicitly, the capacity of the viewer to participate in this political agenda.

I now focus on aspects of this episode, *On Thin Ice*, which might question the position of humans as outside the ecologies of nature. It significantly departs from the convention of rendering an unchanging and reassuringly harmonious natural world, acknowledging the conclusions of climate science alongside the work of ethology and zoology. This episode alone brings the series into line with the "green chip" programming described by Richards. It does so in ways that offer moderate assessments of the impact of climate change, and in this respect, proclamations take a cautious approach to the audience and its notionally conservative expectations.

Only the final third of this episode is dedicated to the Antarctic. The foremost animal examples discussed in this segment are penguins. Noting the way that the earth's warming is occurring more rapidly in Antarctica, ten times the average rate of anywhere else on the planet, Attenborough's narration describes the decline of Adélie penguin populations. The decrease in numbers has occurred with the reduction of sea ice: "Many colonies have been emptying fast. It may be that penguins are starving or it may be that many are heading south to colder climes where there is still plenty of ice on the sea. But as in the Arctic, while ice loving animals are feeling the heat, animals that like it a bit more cozy are moving in." Rather than following the drop in the numbers of the Adélie with a conclusive discussion (for example, one that might consider the potential for extinction due to habitat destruction), the episode moves on to discuss the way another species, the Gentoo penguin, has begun nesting farther south, with ten times more Gentoo on the Antarctic peninsula than thirty years ago. In this characterization, while the balance of migration has changed there are no explicitly negative ramifications of this change.

The clearest negative evaluation offered in this segment of the episode devoted to Antarctica is afforded by new and unprecedented footage of the disintegration of the massive Wilkins ice shelf. The producers managed to obtain this footage via helicopter and it shows the massive 200-meter-thick ice sheet, broken into chunks as an awestruck scientist speaks of the implications of this from his seat in the helicopter.[12] Thus, the focus is on the occurrence of change rather than emphasizing the notion of decline. This is in keeping with the moderate approach to and conservative interpretation of climate science that might be well suited to expectations of the genre. It also, however, can be viewed as a refusal of narrowly rendered declensionist narratives that view decline as inevitable, discussed in the previous chapter, narratives that have been shaped by environmentalist movements over decades.

The last scene offers the culmination of the episode, and perhaps the series. It features Attenborough in direct address to the camera with the rocky Antarctic geography behind him:

> We've only started to see changes in the Arctic and Antarctic, so it's hard to predict exactly what impact these changes will have, but we can see for ourselves that these places are changing and on a scale that is hard to ignore. The poles, north and south, may seem very remote, but what is happening here is likely to have a greater effect on us than any other aspect of global warming.

He proceeds to emphasize the negative impact on humans, privileging them above other life, by referring to the destruction caused with the melting of the ice shelves and rising sea levels on low-lying coasts. If the goal of this statement is to encourage action against climate change, the rationale appears to be that viewers are motivated most powerfully by self-interest and effects that damage human existence. Yet, within this frame, animals become a model for evolutionary adaptation rather than the casualties of anthropogenic climate change: "We've seen the animals already adapting to these changes. But can *we* respond to what is happening now to the frozen planet?" Reference to the changes to the penguin colonies reprises the focus on adaptation rather than animal extinction, replacing an awareness of the impact of changes to the natural world with a reference to the singularity of human suffering. Moreover, it aligns with the notion discussed in the previous chapter that animals can be considered partners or companions in climate change, rather than its victims. But interestingly, Darwinism haunts this characterization, with humans and nonhumans rendered in relation to a single cohering paradigm, both evolving in relation to changing conditions, albeit evaluated in relation to different ends.

Another notable aspect of this episode is the use of not only science, but other technologies of modernity to offer evidence about, and to locate Antarctica in, human history. This brings changes to the natural environment (if not animals) into alignment with human history. After his ship, the *Endurance*, was crushed by ice, Shackleton and five of his crew went to the island of South Georgia to find help. Attenborough describes this, noting that exploration of this area only began one hundred years ago, and the images show the *Endurance* in the ice, footage surely shot by Frank Hurley for *South*. The photographs taken during Shackleton's 1916 journey across the island provide an index for measuring changes to the geography over time and echo the reference to Scott and Amundsen in the first episode. A team of Royal marines is shown retracing Shackleton's journey in a tribute to the explorers. However, the ice has changed to such a degree they cannot take the same path and must alter their course. Hurley's photographs, spectral black-and-white plates, offer visual verification of the typography in 1916. These are juxtaposed with contemporary images of South Georgia, with its glaciers significantly receded. Attenborough's own personal history is set alongside this as he also refers to his visits to the island over thirty years. Most of the changes have occurred, he notes, over this short time. More recent photographs illustrate this point.

This episode not only presents, and thus validates, climate changes, it also situates changes to the nonhuman world in human history. It does so through reference to both heroic exploration and the historical veracity offered by the photographic image. The representation of climate science and the ongoing data being collected in the polar region does not include any reference to the anthropogenic causes of rising temperatures or make claims about the potential for animal extinction. The episode does, however, pose the rapidly changing conditions as impacting on both humans and animals, thus implicitly posing both as part of a mutual ecology. In this respect, *On Thin Ice* is part of a broader body of natural history and wildlife media that departs from a reassuring representation of nature that insulates the struggle for individual survival from the connections between all living forms (and the material universe) and the potential for irreparable biotic and geographical change. From the perspective of the lineage of Antarctic representation, *On Thin Ice* also echoes the function of *90° South* in the way it locates animals in history, albeit in this case it is the contemporary history of climate change. Rather than the representability of the age of exploration relying on animals for drama and the expression of the landscape, the potential for human catastrophe is figured through the adaptations (or decimations) of penguin species that are already underway. Moreover, in some respects it achieves the reverse of Ponting's two films—instead of bringing animals into the humanism of the heroic age of exploration, it brings human activity into the wildlife mode and ties animals (however briefly) into the disintegration of Antarctica and the ramifications of this for human life on the planet.

Encounters at the End of the World:
The Essay Film and the Auteur

Werner Herzog is arguably the most discussed documentarian in contemporary film studies. His work frequently features individuals who grapple with their relationship with nature, including animals, in ways that offer meditations on the human condition more broadly. *Grizzly Man* offers the most well-known example of this. Here, however, I focus on *Encounters at the End of the World*, Herzog's film about, ostensibly, his excursion to Antarctica's McMurdo Station, a U.S. research center on the southern tip of Ross Island. *Encounters at the End of the World* constitutes a very different approach to how animals might be viewed through the lens of science and documentary representation. If Ponting facilitated a view of Antarctic animals through the eyes of the amateur naturalist, and Attenborough from the perspective of the environmental celebrity (albeit in the mould of an "old world" establishment persona), Herzog frames the same animals through the lens of the artist and the essayist auteur more specifically. Rather than the verification of zoology and ethology, or even climate science, *Encounters at the End of the World* frames the continent by taking up existing narratives about science, humans, and animals and destabilizing their authority, gesturing to alternative (albeit at times obscure) meanings through recourse to poetic truth rather than rationalism.

Herzog himself rejects the label of documentarian (Praeger 8) but it is instructive that *Encounters at the End of the World* was nominated for an Oscar under the category of best documentary feature.[13] I follow Timothy Corrigan's lead and read the film within an essayist tradition, one that, in particular "renegotiates assumptions about documentary objectivity, narrative epistemology, and authorial expressivity" (Corrigan, *The Essay*, 6). Herzog's films depart from offering any rewards to the epsitemophilic viewer who desires a clear path to documentary knowledge. Instead, as Corrigan notes, drawing on a well-known phrase from Theodor Adorno, Herzog's films engage the viewer with the provocation that "the thinker does not actually think but rather makes himself into an arena for intellectual experience, without unraveling it" ("The Pedestrian Ecstasies," 82). I suggest that *Encounters at the End of the World* stages the "encounters" of the title in ways that critique the values and practices of modernity. This critique is made available to the viewer as vignettes of Herzog's own subjectively rendered interactions with people, animals, and numerous narratives in popular culture and occurrences in history. An example of this critique, and one that is key to the concerns of this chapter, is provided by Herzog's commentary on the expeditions of Shackleton, Scott, and Amundsen.

Like *Frozen Planet*, *Encounters at the End of the World* returns to Hurley's footage of the *Endurance* trapped by ice. The similarities end there as Herzog's film follows with shots of the preserved interior of Scott's hut and his voice referring to the era when the "scientific exploration of Antarctica began":

But one thing about the early explorers does not feel right. The obsession to be the first one to set his foot on the South Pole. It was for personal fame and the glory of the British Empire. [. . .] But, in a way, from the South Pole onwards there was no further expansion possible, and the Empire started to fade into the abyss of history. [. . .] On a cultural level, it meant the end of adventure. Exposing the last unknown spots of this Earth was irreversible, but it feels sad that the South Pole or Mount Everest were not left in peace in their dignity. It may be a futile wish to keep a few white spots on our maps, but human adventure, in its original sense, lost its meaning, became an issue for the Guinness Book of World Records.

The images explore the material culture of the every day and the hut as an archive. The camera lingers on the tinned food that remains, with "minced scallops" clearly visible on one label. Herzog imagines the Heroic Age of Polar Exploration in a way that is very different to Ponting or even Attenborough. Rather than marveling in the ability of the men involved and what they were able to accomplish given the geography and climate, the achievements and even the aspirations are deemed futile and couched in relation to the banal everyday detritus left behind by the explorers. The very act of "conquering" the pole is posed less as a triumph in the global expansion of reason, and more through the way it reveals the limits of such a preoccupation.

Corrigan eloquently describes the sentiment expressed in this sequence in his description of the film more broadly: "Exploring these worlds becomes exploring the limits of experience as the experience of limits, which invariably leads to a kind of failure or collapse: the bombastic extremity of human efforts and gestures before the massive indifference of the world able only to call attention to the intense longing for significance" ("The Pedestrian Ecstasies," 13). I want to draw attention to his phrase "human efforts" and Herzog's own reference to "human adventure," which indicates what is at stake—an allusion to the aspiration to master the human *and* inhuman world, thus revealing it as an intensely anthropocentric endeavor.

Herzog's interest in nature throughout his career has been well documented. Scholars have consistently drawn a relationship between this interest and German romanticism. Herzog himself, however, explicitly rejects the influence of romantic thinkers (Cronin 135–136). Yet, he maintains that his approach to landscape begins with what might be considered a romantic impulse—that the natural world can be rendered in ways that express the complexities of human psychology and sociality: "For me a landscape is not just a representation of a desert or a forest. It shows an inner state of mind, literally inner landscapes, and it is the human soul that is visible through the landscapes presented in my films [. . .]" (Cronin 136).[14] Rather than edifying, for Reinhild Steingröver Herzog's landscapes are indifferent to the many humans who are drawn to nature as a way to "pursue their passions, express their idiosyncratic ambitions, and invariably encounter great tragedy and loss along the way" (468). I do not dispute this reading of the function of nature in Herzog's *oeuvre*, but I ask a different question of the poetic approach to nature in *Encounters at the End of the World*—rather than illuminating the human condition, what does the representation of nature convey about nature, and the relation between animal and human life in particular?

In the first instance, the expression of nature can be understood through the ways in which sound and image respond to established modes, such as the wildlife film or the environmental polemic of, for example, *An Inconvenient Truth* (2006) (released one year prior to *Encounters at the End of the World*), in their presentation of the natural world. Herzog's work consistently seeks to create a new visual archive of the landscape. His images of Antarctica avoid the extreme wide shots of icebergs and penguin colonies or vistas that can be seen from helicopters. He also eschews the manipulation of time-motion that both highlights the artistry of wildlife filmmaking and renders life as extraordinary visuality. Much of his framing is relatively tight with mid-shots focusing on humans, animals, and the interior of McMurdo station or its exterior—a jumble of buildings and vehicles set against the snow. This converts the virtuosity of spectacle to the time of the everyday and the quotidian events of men and women. Rather than isolating nature from human sociality, the two are inseparable throughout the film. In addition to the imagery of the every day, Herzog reimagines Antarctica by making it strange. The first image is not a wide-establishing view of ice and snow. It is, instead, an underwater shot, taken from beneath the ice of the Ross Sea. The eerie, dream-like images are accompanied by choral music and together they present the viewer with an almost mystical vision. From the outset *Encounters at the End of the World* suggests that our ways of envisaging Antarctica will be turned upside down and made strange through the use of sound and image.

Supplementing this aesthetic, Herzog's voiceover adds a poetic and questioning, rather than explanatory, dimension to the film. Following the underwater shots, Herzog arrives at McMurdo on a military plane. He describes how the National Science Foundation had invited him to come to

Antarctica even though he had informed them that he "would not come up with another film about penguins." This comment makes reference to the phenomenal commercial success of *March of the Penguins* and the animated *Happy Feet*, and perhaps wildlife films more broadly.[15] Elaborating on his own questions about nature, Herzog notes:

> I told them I kept wondering why is it that human beings put on masks or feathers to conceal their identity? And why do they saddle horses and feel the urge to chase the bad guy? Hi-yo, Silver! And why is it that certain species of ants keep flocks of plant lice as slaves to milk them for droplets of sugar? I asked them why is it that a sophisticated animal like a chimp does not utilise inferior creatures? He could straddle a goat and ride off into the sunset.

Accompanying this commentary are archival images of the lone ranger galloping on horseback, natural history footage of ants in extreme close up and a highly colored caricature of a chimpanzee on a goat. This sequence refrains from any information about embodied humans or animals, or Herzog's motivations for coming to Antarctica per se. Instead it evokes a set of metaphysical questions that serve to render humans and animals on the same plane, with anthropomorphism and zoomorphism equally present. These opening questions alert the viewer to the film's orientation away from science and visual evidence, and toward abstraction, enigma and farce.

If *Encounters at the End of the World* expounds the futility of the age of exploration, it offers an even more sustained commentary on the institutions and discourses of science. Herzog, however, does not seek to deem science futile. Instead, the film draws out different dimensions of the geographical and biological sciences in ways that view them through the lens of the poetic, strange, and subjective. Rather than a narration imposing zoological knowledge on filmed events as in wildlife film, Herzog's voiceover and his onscreen interactions are aimed at revealing as much about the subject of science, the scientist, as its objects. One volcanologist, Dr. Clive Oppenheimer, is interviewed on the rim of a volcano. He is shown in a vintage tweed outfit, a significant contrast to the brightly colored cold-weather attire of others in the film. He wears it as "a tribute to the explorers of old" and is described as a "true Englishman from Cambridge University."[16] This draws attention to the idiosyncrasies of the scientist as an individual—he is no longer simply a depersonalized purveyor of verifiable geological knowledge.

It also ties his particular subjectivity to the histories of Scott and Shackleton mentioned earlier in the film.

Another interview encouraging the persona of the "quirky" scientist features a Dr. Ainley speaking about the penguin colony in Cape Royds. He sits in shot with the penguins behind him, slightly down a slope, and describes how the male penguins are sitting on eggs, waiting for the return of the female of the species. This is the same activity described in *Frozen Planet*, albeit by way of Attenborough's disembodied voice. In this shot the eye of the viewer is drawn from the face of Ainley, to the penguins in the distance and back to the scientist. Herzog is less interested in the standard ethological detail that Ainley has to offer and more intent on framing the personality of the scientist, who he describes as "taciturn" and notes his goal is to keep the man talking despite his clipped answers. This results in awkward pauses. It soon becomes apparent that Herzog is seeking to draw out irregular and inexplicable penguin characteristics, asking about "strange sexual behavior" and whether penguins go insane: "I don't mean that a penguin might believe he or she is Lenin or Napoleon Bonaparte, but could they just go crazy because they've had enough of their colony?" It is unnecessary for Herzog to explain what he means by insanity but by referencing what might be described as peculiar behavior in humans, he draws the penguins and the idiosyncrasies of the scientists together in to an unspoken web of human/nonhuman eccentricity.

The next scenes, perhaps the most discussed in the film, describe penguins that become disoriented and determinedly set out in the opposite direction to their colony: "one of these disoriented, or deranged, penguins showed up at the New Harbor diving camp, already some 80 kilometers away from where it should be. . . . And here, he's heading off into the interior of the vast continent. With 5,000 kilometres ahead of him, he's heading towards certain death." The camera lingers on the lone penguin, making its way out across the snow and ice as its tiny form recedes and shrinks in the white expanse of the frame.[17] This sequence differs from the previous scene, and many other scenes in the film, in that the penguin is not simply the quirky object of science—it is framed in ways that anthropomorphize and provoke empathy with the solitude and hopelessness of the penguin's undertaking. The animal behavior is cast as simultaneously inexplicable and poignant.

Encounters at the End of the World frames the scientist as the bearer of knowledge while also personalizing them with eccentric traits. In some moments, science becomes otherworldly, with evolution compared

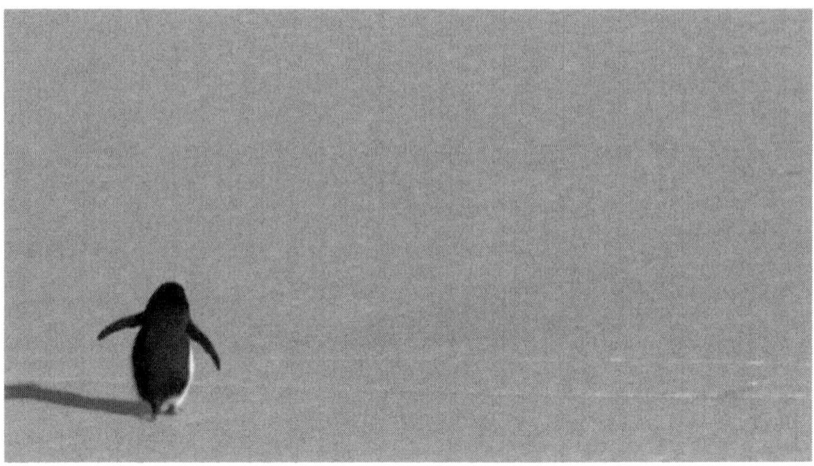

Figure 5.3. The much discussed apparently "disoriented" penguin in *Encounters at the End of the World* (2007).

to cosmology. The subjective and aesthetic nature of the scientific process comes into view and, to some degree, the rationalism of this endeavor is decentered. The disoriented penguin offers a symbol, in Herzog's hands, that speaks to the limits of ethology, indicating that full knowledge of the natural world has not been achieved by science. This presents the undoing of absolute human mastery over nature in a manner that is opposed to the traditions of natural history and wildlife film. In this respect, the film opens a space for perceiving an ethology that includes humans and animals, suggesting a more expansive appreciation of Darwinism.

Darwin developed a series of principles that apply equally to humans and other species. Pinpointing the profound implications of Darwin's thought, Elizabeth Grosz writes:

> The human, when situated as one among many, is no longer in the position of speaking for and authorising the analysis of the animal as other, and no longer takes the right to name, to categorise, the rest of the world but is now forced, or at least enticed, to listen, to respond, to observe, to become attuned to a nature it was always part of but had only aimed to master and control—not nature as a unified whole, but nature as ever-striving, as natural selection, as violence and conflict. (24)

As Grosz notes, Darwin's principles allow for "differences of degree, not differences of kind" (16) across species, thus allowing for variations and gradation within species. This notion of difference links species, rather than separating them into mutually exclusive paradigms.

The most striking example to illustrate this in the film is a short sequence that examines a single-celled sea organism through a microscope as it structures itself into a tree-like form. Another scientist tells Herzog that a century ago one debate advocated that at the time "every definition of intelligence that was being formulated could be fulfilled by these single-celled creatures [. . .] it is a manifestation of the best of our abilities, really, the way that they build their shells. It's almost art."[18] The reference to "our" is crucial—it frames intelligence as a feature across the human/nonhuman continuum. The microscopic images add another element to the alternative visual archive of Antarctica catalogued in by film. Pointedly, Herzog does not explore the conclusion of that debate, thus deeming the suggestions of the history of scientific thought more compelling than definitive and authorized knowledge.

Antarctica is the home of scientists *and* animals and Herzog "encounters" both, albeit with a greater attention to human interaction. While the microscope might be seen as a trope of vision and mastery, in Herzog's hands the motivations of science and those who undertake its work are equally put under the microscope and filtered through the director's version of sense-making. In a different way, the penguins, seals, and single-celled sea organisms are also reframed. Both science and animal life are cast as expressive and eccentric and similarly available to in the film's poetic brand of ethology. *Encounters at the End of the World* may be more concerned with constructing and stylizing nature through the aesthetics of the essay film than being attuned to and observing nature as Grosz articulates. Nevertheless, there is a case to be made that animals are rendered in a way that places them alongside and equally exposed to the indifference of the universe as humans: "man is not the centre of animal life, just as the earth is not the centre of the universe" (Grosz 24). Like Darwin, Herzog acknowledges a natural world (and a world that encompasses human and nonhuman) that is not harmonious, but characterized by tragedy, unpredictability, and the inexplicable.

Brad Praeger cites Herzog's stated interest in elevating aesthetics and the "truth-content of art over any form of overt political engagement" (*Cinema*, 3). *Encounters at the End of the World* does not advocate for or recognize environmental politics in an obvious way. It does not seek even a moderate acknowledgment of climate change and its effects as can be seen in *On*

Thin Ice. Herzog, indeed, abstains from explicit political positions, and the rationalized truth claims required for these, in favor of his version of poetic truth in which meaning emerges from the play of language and the conjunction of ideas and images. This is not to say that his films are apolitical. In *Encounters at the End of the World*, I argue, this aesthetic expresses, among other things, a profoundly radical perspective on the human/nonhuman relation. Eschewing rationality, it departs greatly from the popular scientific taxonomies of wildlife film, which cast the human paradigm as above and isolated from the nonhuman environment. In offering an alternative to both the imperative for global exploration and the mastery of the natural world through science, the film models rather than describes the relation between human and animal. It does so by way of Herzog's guiding voice, which is as distinctive as Attenborough's, effectively marking the film as the product of one of the most recognizable auteurs in European cinema.

If the previous examples reincorporated Antarctica into the auspices of modernity by appropriating its geography and animal life to the catalogs of science, thus ordering and mastering it, *Encounters at the End of the World* stands out as the film to most fully populate the continent with people (scientists) and nonhuman life as it is seen through the lens of scientific knowledge. As in the other examples, the boundary between the subject and object is reaffirmed as the presenter/narrator provides a point of subjective identification for the viewer to consume the impossible and sublime object that is Antarctica. However, in the case of Herzog's film, his accented voice does not guide the viewer through a clear and reassuring ethological or geological account. If, as Brigitte Peucker writes, Herzog's subjective expression and theatrical styling points to "the fragile boundary between subject and object, one that his films deliberately blur" (52), the problem of grasping the object is always in play. The Antarctic he chooses to present is amorphous and metaphysical, offering questions and critiques about human and animal life rather than scientific certainty.

Out of Nothingness and into History

Stephen J. Pyne describes the nineteenth century as the era of the romantic explorer, thus referencing a figure engaged in the fascination for natural history. This mode of exploration involved not only surveying landforms and cataloging the abundance of material objects and specimens, it also "celebrated that very profusion" (84). Antarctica, however, was an anomaly for early explorers. Echoing Siskind's description, Pyne writes that the ice,

> Challenged the philosophical precepts, artistic genres and scientific
> systems by which the era had understood the metaphysics (and
> metahistory) of nature. [. . .] The Promethean desire to embrace
> everything lost its meaning in a landscape of nothingness. [. . .]
> In place of abundant objects, there was only ice; and in place
> of tangible landmarks, such as mountains and lakes, there were
> only abstract concepts, such as the poles of rotation, magnetism,
> or inaccessibility, all invisible to the senses. (84)

I have established how animals might be made to confront this problem
of nothingness—in tandem with human life, they offer Antarctica a
representable form. If the sublime overwhelms the senses, the examples
I have discussed emphasize a film experience more focused on the more
wieldy sensuousness of human and animal bodies. Moreover, as the objects
of science they provide an avenue for exploring reason, and thus bring
humanism to the "empty" landscape. In addition, the material presence
of animals focus narrative and spectacle and, in the case of *Encounters
at the End of the World*, their bodies imbue the poetic reframing of the
continent. Crucial in the three examples discussed is the role of the persona
of the narrator in modeling the subject/object relation, whether it is the
documentarist as explorer and natural historian, the environmental celebrity
and naturalist, or the auteur.

Ponting, the first cinematographer to record moving images in Antarctica, was inspired by the preceding age of exploration described by Pyne,
one that emphasized the project of surveying and cataloging different natural worlds. This project was intimately tied to his quest to bring the heroic
sensibility of the time into representation. Like those to follow, he focused
on the fringe of Antarctica rather than the interior, showing it to be populated with humans and animals, contesting the notion that there is nothing
to be experienced in this place but abstraction. The two recent documentaries reserve a special place for the history Ponting was a participant in,
one peopled by the illustrious figures of Scott, Shackleton, and Amundsen,
offering it as a site of either homage or critique. In both cases they bring
history to fore as another way to recuperate the continent into the auspices
of reason. The films are indebted to the age of exploration, framing the
continent not only through the universalizing potential of science, but also
through particular historical narratives that are punctuated by individual
achievements and tragedy.

In a broader view, *Frozen Planet* and *Encounters at the End of the
World* contribute to a history of filmmaking in Antarctica that began with

Ponting but, in the postwar era, also includes the wildlife genre with its deep investment in the authority of the male adventurer. I have elaborated on this authority in relation to Attenborough, principally through the manner in which he evokes the British age of empire. This persona is one that is cemented in the postwar era. The 1950s and 1960s, as Cynthia Chris notes, saw a refashioning of the wildlife genre as filmmakers once again sought out animals beyond the studio and the zoo, thus revisiting the "masculine adventure saga reminiscent of expedition films of the 1910s and 20s in its predilection for action and the exotic" (46). Attenborough was one of the figures in this movement, alongside Jacques-Yves Costeau. These adventurer-documentarists were invariably white, male, and European or American, presenting "an authoritatively masculine rule that depended on feats of increasingly spectacular mastery of visual technologies" (46). Herzog revises this history, rejecting the very notion of adventure, conventional spectacle and indeed, the possibility of mastering nature. Despite this, he nevertheless shares with these men the status of the European masculine subject and his films reflect the surety with which he executes his own auteurist vision, posing it as a superior rendering, if not an authoritative expression, of the world.

While entrenched in this documentary history, Attenborough and Herzog bring a new understanding of animals to the history of the representation of Antarctica. Animals take on a position within a human/non-human ecology. This occurs through the new and recent (conditional and modest) acknowledgment of climate science in the blue chip format and through the metaphysical disruptions of Herzog's poetic, essayist aesthetics. The import of this departure should be considered alongside the fact that these two examples represent the most high-profile representations of Antarctic life since *March of the Penguins*. The theories of Charles Darwin offer the most incisive avenue to read the formulation of the relation between species, including human species, not only because the principles of this approach to evolutionary science are a key feature of wildlife aesthetics, but also because his work entails the possibility of moving away from anthropocentric, and toward biocentric conceptualizations of life that do not pose humans above and isolated from the natural world. In chapter 3 I argued that food documentaries can radically displace the anthropomorphism of the documentary camera by visually encouraging recognition that the body of the animal and the body of the human function on a continuum. Darwin's genealogy of the species decenters the human paradigmatically rather than visually, by posing nature as a unified whole. This mirrors the potential to decenter the human in understandings of history.

Erica Fudge extends a challenge to "the ways 'human' always relies upon 'animal' for its meaning. By refusing humanism, and, implicitly, anthropocentrism, we place ourselves next to animals, rather than the users of animals, and this offers a new way of understanding the past" (15). This gestures to an approach to history that is not simply concerned with attitudes to animals in the writing of history, but how a history, such as the filmic history of Antarctica, renders anew the very status of humans and animals. The three examples discussed achieve this in differing ways, each crucially revising the orthodoxy of wildlife film that poses nature as outside human history. My reading casts light on how this occurs, either through exploring the importance of animals in early polar expedition films, attending to the inclusion of human effects and activity in the wildlife mode or highlighting Herzog's critique of the humanist separation from and mastery over the natural world.

Chapter 6

The Nonfiction of YouTube
and "Naturecams"

Posthumanism and Reflections on Agency

The preceding chapters have outlined histories of representation and cycles of filmmaking that inform our understanding of the animal in the documentary moving image. This chapter departs from this frame in a number of ways. While I maintain the focus on wildlife established in the previous two chapters, I move away from the codified terrain of professional filmmaking in the interests of seeking out the more quotidian interactions with nonhuman life that might be represented in nonfiction form. This exploration of the quotidian is couched in a desire to examine the role of widely accessible audiovisual digital technologies in the circulation and rendering of animal life. These interrelated interests encompass a wealth of moving image examples, as I will explore, from Timothy Treadwell's documentation of bears in *Grizzly Man* (2005) to user-generated content on YouTube and sites specifically dedicated to "naturecams." In this investigation the informing paradigm is a more recent historical cinematic epoch to those in previous chapters, which I establish with reference to shifting assumptions about the digital film image and also a changing worldview concerning human/nonhuman agency.

Locating different media examples within this recent history, I ask what they might tell us about the changing role of the cinematic image in encounters with nature. How are perceptions of animals, particularly conceptions of animal agency, being reformulated? What are the consequences for human-centered forms of knowledge, perception, and embodiment? This last question, perhaps the most complex of the three, is inspired by an attempt to respond to Cary Wolfe's proposition, developed in the interests of locating animal studies in relation to the humanities, or the "posthumanities." For Wolfe, the task is not to break with the legacy of humanism, but "to attend to that thing called the 'human' with *greater* specificity, *greater* attention to its embodiment, embeddedness, and materiality, and how these in turn shape and are shaped by consciousness, mind and so on" (120). To the extent that this signals the possibility of perceiving the human in ways that move beyond (human) subject-centered paradigms, it also gestures to the value of attending more closely to the material world. Such attention requires an acknowledgment of the entangled, complex relations that constitute that world, encompassing humans, animals, the environment, and technology. I pose questions of nonfiction digital media through a film theoretical lens in ways that are guided by the capacity of the camera to function on biopolitical terms, not simply recording but also organizing life for the viewer.

The Videographic and Agency in a
Time of Ecological Existentialism

The move to theorize the digital era in film studies has focused on the shift to electronic projection, to videographic rather than photographic ontologies, and the "decentring of the theatrical film experience" (Rodowick 27) in film distribution. This belies the fact that the documentary has, for decades, been as much tied to the videographic as the cinematic. Documentarians were early proponents of video production while broadcast television has been the preeminent financing and distribution avenue for different incarnations of the documentary form since the 1960s. Further, the rise of nonfiction lifestyle and reality formats over the past two decades offers an example of the importance of the constantly transforming relationship between documentary and television. Nevertheless, the sensibilities and capacities encouraged by digital media and the web have enabled new nonfiction forms that present expanded cultures of documentary. I maintain that "documentary" remains a useful term to describe the examples I discuss in this chapter. As Adrian Ivakhiv writes, "much of what is digital remains oriented toward fulfilling viewers' apparent desire for photographic or perceptual realism and 'depictive credibility'" (330). If developments in digital technology can be considered part of a "postindexical" moment, it is a protracted moment that extends back to the early cinema experiments in illusion of Georges Méliès more than a century ago. I am interested in a parallel history, one in which, as Ivakhiv articulates, viewers' desire for the real, for verisimilitude and perceptual realism persist. I align this desire with Cowie's description of the appeal of documentary specifically and "the fascinating pleasure of recorded reality as both spectacle and knowledge" (3).

However, my interest in exploring the question of digital culture in relation to documentary does not revolve around "digital documentary" per se. This term is, at times, used to reference the influence of digital technology on conventional documentary films that circulate through well-established distribution channels, such as television, theatrical release, DVD, or the Internet (including downloaded or streamed). It is also, perhaps more commonly, used to refer to media artifacts that are purpose-built to take advantage of the online and interactive capacities of the web, producing new forms of largely auteurist documentary.[1] I am concerned with contextualizing yet another manifestation of the relationship between the digital and documentary—the more ubiquitous appropriation of the documentary image, its realist codes and indexicality, in web specific media, specifically user generated content and webcams. Alongside this circulation of the documentary image sits the now well-established accessibility and mobility of the means of recording high-quality video images. Cameras such as the GoPro are specifically designed and marketed for nonprofessional use and recording in outdoor action/adventure oriented contexts.

Central to my interest in this nexus of technology, documentary indexicality, and nature is the question of agency. To expand on what I mean by this, I hypothesize two interrelated cultural formations. The first relates to how, in the words of Thomas Elsaesser and Malte Hagener, "cinema has become a meta-reflection on agency" (185). As a meta-reflection, the examples Elsaesser and Hagener describe are as much concerned with enacting agency as its illusion or denial. They refer to not only cinema but also digital media. In the case of "doing" activities with a computer, the question of agency revolves around the action of doing. As Elsaesser and Hagener note, the digital "both stresses and represses the knowledge that 'we' are not doing the 'doing'" (185). The activity on the screen is not directly caused by a movement of the hand, biomechanics, and the senses, but is rather produced by electronic code. This pseudo-awareness of agency inflects contemporary cinema, especially that which uses new imaging techniques,[2] to question our "being in the world" (185) through the construction of different imaginary spaces for characters. Their further, related, example addressing the question of agency explores how animation, such as *Toy Story* (1995), offers new strategies of point of view, gesturing to nonhuman agency. This follows the proposition that the illusion of agency in cinema is facilitated by identification with our surrogates onscreen and their point of view. While classical cinema has consistently produced point of view for spectators in ways that are constructions, rather than reflections of human perception, Elsaesser and Hagener describe how digital cinema's "re-embodied manifestations of everything visible, tactile and sensory allow the digital to become much more closely aligned and attuned to the body and the senses" (174). This role for the digital, and its harmonization with the embodied spectator, can be deployed to rethink point of view, unhinging it from the realist human surrogate and creating more malleable identities and perspectives. Given this, their approach opens an avenue to consider posthumanism in cinema, offering specificity to Wolfe's call to think through not only nonhuman (animal) point of view, but also an interrogation of human, subject-centered point of view.

The second cultural formation I wish to consider is more explicitly tied to the position of the self in relation to the nonhuman world and how this connectivity finds parallels in media and representation. Deborah Bird Rose's notion of ecological existentialism offers a rethinking of, in particular, human agency in and over nature. Rose questions who we are as a species and how we fit into the Earth system in an age of accelerating extinction. She poses ecological existentialism in contrast to her reading of humanist existentialism—the latter arises with the absence or death of God and a struggle with human dread in the "face of cosmic isolation" (*Wild Dog Dreaming*, 43). Humanist existentialism separates the human from "all else on Earth" (*Wild Dog Dreaming*, 43) and is amplified by a loss of certainty and destiny that comes with the absence of God. Crucially, for Rose, while ecological existentialism also recognizes an absence of destiny or certainty for humanity, it works against isolation and fosters a posthumanist form of connectivity (by decentering the human)[3]:

> I propose that our condition as a co-evolving species of life on Earth, our kinship in the great family of life on Earth, situates us in time and place. We are still creatures for whom there is no predetermined essence or destiny; we are a work in progress. At the same time, as creatures enmeshed within the connectivities of Earth life, there is no ultimate isolation; we are thoroughly entangled. (*Wild Dog Dreaming*, 44)

While she does not describe it in these terms, this might be seen as a reflection on agency writ large, one that underpins and questions the very meaning of the human. This worldview subjugates human agency to the infinite processes of ecosystems: "our power exceeds our capacity to contain its effects, and thus we are constantly confronted with our own powerlessness" (*Wild Dog Dreaming*, 48). It directs us to interrogate historical knowledge paradigms that locate the human in isolation from nature. Humans are embedded in the planet's present and past. They are also entwined in the possible futures of the nonhuman world.

Leaving aside the issue of agency for a moment, the conjoining of ecological awareness and connectivity also offers an informing narrative for the increasing popularization of wildlife imagery, or Gregg Mitman's contemporary "green wave." As I described in the first chapter, Mitman elaborates on a significant expansion, in the twenty-first century, of wildlife media, with much of this film and television falling into the category of documentary. The rise of not only documentaries about wildlife, but also the concentration of representations of nature and wildlife on the web and in the subscription television market, demonstrates the considerable currency of such themes and imagery. This speaks to the interconnection across the world of human modernity, encouraged by the transnational media apparatus *and* an increasing attentiveness to the natural world. This avalanche of media and the way viewers experience it, however, may deliver multiple and divergent biopolitical possibilities, especially on the terms described by Rose. In the following section I explore a handful of these, considering how they might respond to Rose's question: "how to engage in world making across species" (*Wild Dog Dreaming*, 51) in filmic terms?

Grizzly Man as Epochal Text

If previous chapters have addressed the epistemological underpinnings of the genre in the twentieth century, this chapter is concerned with the twenty-first century and marking out a more recent frame of historical reference for documentary. In determining the sensibilities intrinsic to this epoch, there are a number of important films that stand out and might be perceived as exemplifying the intersection between documentary popularity, the green wave, and the use of digital spectacle. Chief among these are *An Inconvenient Truth* (2006) and *March of the Penguins* (2005). Both achieved great success commercially upon release and have been consumed by a high volume of viewers. Both, albeit in very different ways, are breakthrough films. One confirmed a new awareness of the impact of global warming in the popular imaginary and the other confirmed the commercial appeal of narrativized wildlife imagery. Both cemented this moment as one in which nonfiction cinema could compete with fiction feature film for audiences. Despite the success and visibility of both of these films, I turn to a less commercially accomplished example to expand on the specificity of an epochal moment for documentary film. Indeed, *Grizzly Man* is Werner

Herzog's most well-known and most discussed film and, in turn, Herzog has become one of the most prominent documentary auteurs of our time. *Grizzly Man* was released within a year of *An Inconvenient Truth* and *March of the Penguins*. It contributed to and benefited from the renewed popularity of documentary and an intensified, multivalent interest in the nonhuman world. It did so, however, on the terms of an auteur cinema aesthetic and via the formal play of the essay film, producing the most notorious example of the form in a decade.

Grizzly Man revolves around the events leading up to the moment when Timothy Treadwell, the leading human character in the film, is killed and eaten by a bear. This incident occurs after Treadwell had spent thirteen summers living in close proximity with bears in Alaska's Katmai National Park and Reserve. While Treadwell had given names to a number of bears, it is an unfamiliar animal that takes his life. His girlfriend, Amie Huguenard, who was camping with him, was also killed. The documentary was made possible by the fact that Herzog was able to gain rights to the footage shot by Treadwell with two camcorders during his time in the park and in the moment of his death. The film is crafted around this footage and the documentary's notoriety owes much to the fascination evoked by the autobiographical depiction of the late Treadwell.

In understanding *Grizzly Man* as an epochal example, I am as much concerned with the reception of the film, or the assertions and stated sensibilities that circulate alongside the text (including those that pertain to Herzog as the director), as with the detail of narrative and form. One viewer comment on the *Internet Movie Database* states, "Initially I thought that the story was a cross between *Jackass* and the Discovery Channel," offering a canny indication of how the film orients viewers in relation to its principle concerns: the natural environment and human folly. Roger Ebert's favorable account of the film states, "*Grizzly Man* is unlike any nature documentary I've seen." This statement co-opts the documentary into the category of wildlife film while simultaneously gesturing to the way it turns the subgenre on its head. It refers to the film's focus, which, rather than examining animal life, as per wildlife film, is concerned with how "human nature" might be manifest at the scene of an encounter with the natural world. In its preoccupation with human endeavor and selfhood, it exemplifies the concerns of Herzog's *oeuvre*. Subjects in Herzog's films, including Treadwell, personify the limits, and at times farcical disposition, of human sociality and aspirations.

There are further reasons, a number that are crucially connected to the points outlined above, for perceiving *Grizzly Man* as a film that sits at the cusp of a moment in the development of documentary cinema. The film encapsulates the focus on agency that emerges at the intersection of the acceleration of digital media and a growing consciousness that Rose refers to with the term *ecological existentialism*. Given that Herzog's approach, described in the previous chapter in terms of "poetic truth," offers a very different documentary experience to *March of the Penguins*, it performs this focus in ways that appeal to an openness to a more complex (or even perplexing) meditation on truth, agency, and the human among audiences.

Significantly, Herzog's film demands a renewed attention to agency in documentary across a number of different registers. At one level this concerns the agency of the filmmaker. With both Treadwell and Herzog contributing to the layers of crafting and the authorial voice of the film, this might be considered, as Undine Sellbach explains, as a "discordant collaboration" (42). Agency is shared, albeit with Herzog remaining the most powerful filmmaker-subject. At a more interesting level, for my purposes, the film contemplates the relation between the human and the nonhuman, the materiality of humans and animals. The ubiquity of the consumer-grade video technology used by Treadwell enables this contemplation, and notably the widespread take up of this technology only became the norm in the decade preceding the release of the film.[4]

In one respect, it is through the use of this technology that Treadwell relinquishes agency. Sueng-Hoon Jeong and Dudley Andrew note the way Treadwell, in his take up of the electronic camera, necessarily assumes an imagined audience: "he cannot be present to the audience instantly; he knows that whoever watches him belongs to a future in which he, Treadwell, will be excluded" (10). For Jeong and Andrew this is a ghostly encounter with spectators, a form of becoming-ghost that supplements Treadwell's other transformation, that of becoming-animal. In this "becoming animal," they describe how Treadwell's life, and death, with the bears might be seen to destabilize the boundary between human and animal. I believe *Grizzly Man* points more persuasively to a situation in which humans face an indifferent and enigmatic nature and, thus, it provides a scene for staging human agency as an illusion. Both human and nonhuman nature are mutually embedded in a drama that defies certainty, recalling Rose's ecological existentialism.

Moreover, *Grizzly Man*, as a film about a man being eaten by a bear (an event that viewers are usually aware of before they watch the film), exudes corporeality, offering a further dimension to the interrogation of human subjectivity. Glimpses of bears in the park, shot by Treadwell's camera and his own blonde-haired figure and accented voice (his American accent is cast in distinction to Herzog's familiar German accent) both equally stir the senses of the viewer in ways that are laden with the knowledge of the primal scene in which the materiality of man and animal meet in violent encounter. Indeed, the film circulates in ways that foreground the vitalism and threat of the bears. I couch the film in relation to a closer consideration to the human that, in Wolfe's terms, offers greater attention to embodiment and human materiality. This attention shifts a human-centric position by obliterating the subject/object relation and collapsing the relation between human and animal into a material dimension, one that places matter before subjectivity.

The moment of preeminent importance for the film, however, is the moment in which Treadwell loses control of the camera after he is attacked by the bear. The camera continues to record sound and image. It may be the most meaningful moment *for* the film, but it does not appear *in* the film—Herzog refuses to let the audience hear the audio of the bear attack. At this moment Treadwell does become spectral, and becomes part of the bear in an intercorporeal sense (perhaps a reversal of the intercorporeality evoked by food documentaries I describe in chapter 3). Both the death of the cameraman and Herzog's production of the film emerge from this moment. It also offers a different slant to the notion that in the case of digital manipulation, the use of technology "both stresses and represses the knowledge that 'we' are not doing the 'doing.'" In this instant the human cedes the agency of point of view, giving it not to the bear, but to an absent author as the camera alone is charged with producing perspective. In this pivotal moment, point of view moves beyond the human, allying the film with what has become a more prevalent possibility in the digital age, the displacement of a subject-centered point of view in ways that reassess the human.

The corporeal wrench that this moment evokes, perhaps a feeling that saturates the experience of viewing the whole film, is one that, in Sobchacks' words, questions the "dominant philosophies and fantasies that fix our embodied human being and constitute our identities as discrete and thus reminds us of our true instability: our physical flux, our lack of self-coincidence, our subatomic as well as subcutaneous existence that is always in motion and ever changing" ("Introduction," xii). Although Sobchack's reference point is a different relation between human embodiment and digital representation—computergraphic "morphing"—she aptly describes the malleability of human identity and agency evoked by *Grizzly Man*. It is a film that relies on digital video to highlight how moving images might draw attention to the taken-for-granted centrality of human knowledge and embodiment, refiguring it within and against the unpredictable natural world.

Infolding and Encounters with Cameras:
"Marmot Licks GoPro"

Moving from *Grizzly Man* to the markedly different sphere of the Internet presents a study in contrasts, highlighting the difference between the singular profile of Herzog's feature length film and the high volume of short nonfiction examples that populate YouTube and other sites supporting user-generated content. I seek to bring the two into a common orbit, exploring how particular examples from the web offer another way to consider how an admixture of the worldview articulated by Rose and the shifting point of view offered by digital media resonates in popular culture. The Internet and low-cost cameras allow individuals of relatively modest means to become filmmakers by producing and distributing their own work. For my purposes, it is also critical that most of these filmmakers decide to become documentarians. I am interested in how examples within this culture might further our understanding of the nexus between the documentary moving image, the constitution of animal agency in relation to humanism, and the function of moving image digital media as a world-making form.

It should be clear to even the most casual observer that in recent years moving image animals have proliferated across the web, transforming it into a digital menagerie comprised of farm animals, domestic pets, and wild animals. Given that my focus is on wildlife and its history of representation (rather than domestic animals), one striking development in this lineage can be found on YouTube and is constituted by clips that not only employ the digital as a medium for recoding and distributing images, but also include the matter of the apparatus, the camera, in the frame. This imagery often depicts encounters between wildlife and humans in which animals are "doing" things with technology. In this respect, the encounter is not simply between animal life and human life, but with the technological apparatus that extends or stands in for human perception. These depictions often have diverse effects in terms of the rendering of animal agency. In this exploration of agency I am less interested in actual manifestations of animal agency and how it might be observed in an ethological sense, and more concerned with how a space might be opened to mediate such agency and how it troubles human-centered assumptions and aesthetics.

Recordings of birds attacking "drones," or more accurately "quadcopters" with mounted cameras, provide a specific subset of examples of animal interaction with technology. In these clips, flying remote control devices with fitted cameras that are either engaged in the activity of observing birds or their nests, or unexpectedly encounter birds, are attacked and forced to the ground by large, predatory birds. In the daily web magazine, *Slate*, Ariel Bogle identifies this trend:

> The growing amateur use of drones, combined with increasingly cheap, lightweight cameras such as *GoPros* and their clones, has allowed humans to blunder into airborne territory that had been more or less restricted to professional wildlife photographers. Every man with a drone is an accidental David Attenborough—with discomforting results. Of the many, often beautiful videos of animals shot by drones on YouTube, there's an intriguing new sub-set. Call it "bird vs. drone."

Bogle observes that the comments sections that accompany these clips convey strong support for the birds, "cheering" them on in their battle with the drones. She notes, however, that "this doesn't seem to prove any comprehensive pro-environment sentiment as much as anti-drone rhetoric." However, rather than understanding the bird and the drone in opposition to one another, and thus opposing technological modernity to nature, there

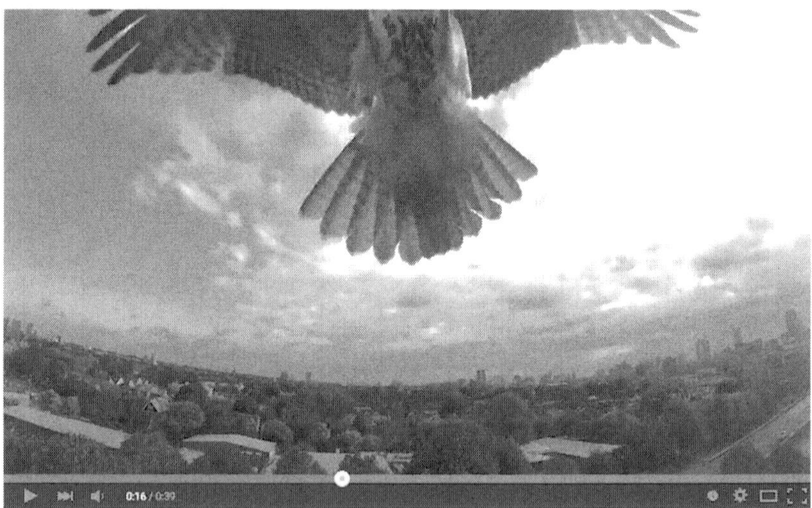

Figure 6.1. A hawk swoops down to unsettle a drone that has flown nearby and in the process reorients the horizon line of the camera in YouTube clip "Hawk vs. Drone! (Hawk Attacks Quadcopter)" (2014).

is much to be gained by looking more closely at what the encounter produces in aesthetic terms.

In an example such as "Hawk vs. Drone! (Hawk Attacks Quadcopter)," recorded at Magazine Beach in Cambridge, Massachusetts and posted by Christopher Schmidt, the opening perspective of the shot looks straight on to the curved horizon line as the camera hovers many meters above the ground. A hawk flies past the camera, returns, and, with only its tail and claws in view, swoops down to unsettle the drone and it falls to the ground. The final image depicts another horizon line, albeit this time inverted with the camera upside down. In this one-shot sequence, human vision and perspective is replicated by the camera (even if with a God-like vista in the sky), but is then disturbed by the encounter with the bird, resulting in a point of view that, because it is upside down, contests the camera's efficacy as a prosthetic for human sight. Within the six months after it was posted in 2014, this forty-second clip attracted four-and-a-half million views.

Encounters with rams offer another, albeit less prevalent, set of examples. In "Angry ram takes down a drone . . . and its owner" a drone confronts a ram on a hillside. The ram attacks the device and when its owner comes to retrieve it he chases the man, who records the ram attacking as he retreats with the drone. In another example, "Ramcam behind the scenes, how we got the angry ram to wear a *GoPro*" a more interventionist drama unfolds. A man is shown attaching a camera to a makeshift harness on a ram's back. The sequence then takes on the ram's perspective as he chases and butts the car of the man as it drives away. In this latter example, the animal does not simply reorient human perspective; it becomes the subject of point of view, albeit achieved through a questionable intervention into the ram's lifeworld.

All of these examples can be considered in relation to Haraway's approach to technology and embodiment in which

> technologies are not mediations, something in between us and another bit of the world. Rather technologies are organs, full partners, in what Merleau-Ponty called "infoldings of the flesh." I like the word *infolding* better than *interface* to suggest the dance of world-making encounters. (Italics in original, 249)

Haraway introduces the term infolding to preface her discussion of *Crittercam*, a 2004 television series on the National Geographic Channel that was promoted around the activity of scientists who attached camcorders to marine animals as part of their research.

Crittercam is a further example that highlights the potential for recognizing animal agency by inhabiting their point of view and infolding human and nonhuman worlds through the extensions offered by electronic cameras. Yet, the television episodes Haraway describes are more concerned with the interaction between bodies (human and human, nonhuman and human) and the materiality of technology (cameras, boats, light aircraft, and diving equipment) than with the footage generated by Crittercams and its uses:

> [. . .] perhaps most striking of all is the small amount of actual Crittercam footage amid all the other underwater photography of the animals and their environments that fills the episodes. Actual Crittercam footage is, in fact, usually pretty boring and hard to interpret, somewhat like an ultrasound recording of a fetus. Footage without narration is more like an acid trip than a peephole to reality. Cameras might be askew on the head of the critter or pointed down, so that we see lots of muck and lots of water, along with bits of other organisms that make precious little sense without a lot of other visual and narrative work. (258)

As a whole, the Crittercam footage does not provide the clear narrative structure that the short YouTube clips, crafted to accentuate their intelligibility, are able to achieve. Notably, in explaining the embodied pleasures of watching this "acid-trip" footage, Haraway couches it in a film historical frame, likening it to Jean Painlevé's surreal underwater films of sea creatures, in particular *The Love Life of an Octopus* (1965). While the raw underwater footage may be uninteresting for a television audience, its resistance to interpretation extends it more fully into the arena of a reflection on and contestation of the sensible perspectives of human-centered vision.

Further tapping into the relationship between film avant-gardes and animals doing things with cameras, Florian Leitner builds a compelling discussion around two moving image examples. The first is footage found on a digital camera that had been lost at sea for six months and posted on YouTube. It shows a sea turtle intercepting the camera, playing with it and apparently trying to eat it—the images were recorded after the turtle had triggered the video release button. The second is Michael Snow's film, *La Région Centrale* (1971), a renowned experimental film produced with a camera attached to a robotic arm that records a mountain landscape at different and constantly rotating angles. The similarities between the two are striking and for Leitner they suggest "a nonanthropomorphic way of looking—in which looking and moving become inseparable" (265). Like

Haraway, he argues the sea turtle footage is testament to a site of relations, but he refers to this not as a dance of encounters, but a "renunciation of monocausality" (270), an accidental outcome of human and animal actions that complicates subjectivity and agency.

A further example that extends the infolding promoted by Haraway into another realm of intimate encounters, "Marmot Licks GoPro" presents a more sophisticated aesthetic than the clips I have already discussed. While also hosted on YouTube, this example was posted by Greenpeace USA and has clearly been crafted by the organization for distribution. As described in the comments section, the footage was shot in the Glacier National Park in the state of Montana during production for a documentary. A camera set up on a tripod is positioned to provide a view from a mountain, looking down into a valley with more mountains on either side, leading the eye to a point in the distance and thus echoing Cartesian perspective with a clear vanishing point. The caption below the frame leads us to believe the camera is "unmanned" and recording the scene in order to create a time-lapse sequence for the documentary. The forty-eight second clip begins in time lapse, with clouds rushing through the sky and shadows moving quickly on the ground. After five seconds it reverts to real time and a marmot (a species of large squirrel) can be seen moving up the hill, approximately ten feet

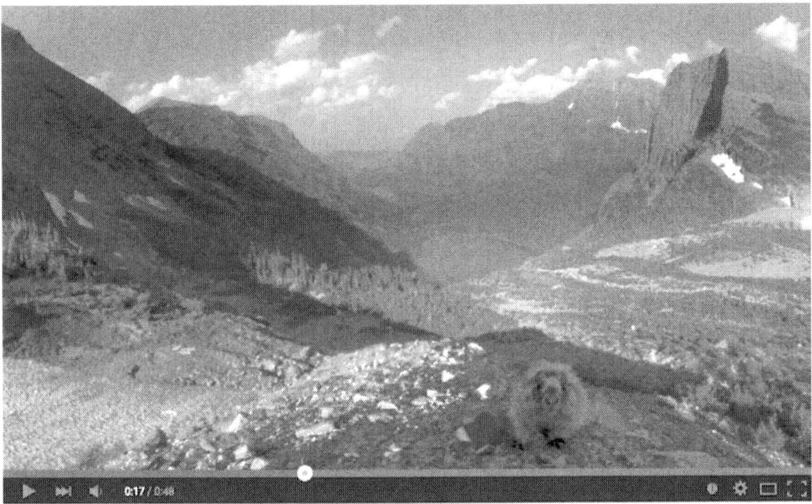

Figure 6.2. In a YouTube clip titled "Marmot Licks GoPro" (2014) a marmot approaches the tripod, hesitating for a moment before licking the camera.

from the camera. It stops, sniffs the air and progresses toward the camera and goes almost out of shot at the foot of the unseen tripod. The animal then appears with its face directly in front of the camera and the recording captures the marmot licking the lens and the lens housing, with its nose, tongue, or fur in shot. Both audio and image overwhelm the viewer with the materiality of the animal as it investigates the technology. The camera lurches to one side as the marmot retreats, the vanishing point is cast awry and the shot ends with the camera facing a rock.

Ostensibly, the marmot's inspection was unplanned but there is no way to verify this. A link appears onscreen during the clip with the notation: "click here to protect this little guy's home from climate change." The advocacy function of the marmot again features in the comments with a link to a petition: "This Marmot would like to give you a kiss for helping to save its home! [. . .] SIGN & SHARE if you think the U.S. Department of the Interior needs to keep coal in the ground so that marmots in Glacier can stay cool!" These indicate a context that contrasts with the "bird vs. drone" grouping in as much as there is both a strategic institutional agenda and recourse to environmental politics in play. Rather than the question of verisimilitude and whether this scene was staged or not, I am interested in how the animal is depicted as an agent, and posed in relation to human vision and embodiment, by Greenpeace.

As is the case with all of the clips I've mentioned, "Marmot Licks *GoPro*" lends itself to repeated viewing, and this is perhaps a reason for the high number of views (this clip had two million views over a three-month period in 2014). When watching, the eye is drawn to the gradual approach of the animal to the camera in the otherwise static scene. The animal is lent a seemingly contemplative agency as it ponders its response to the camera. The physical interaction with the camera is unexpected and once the short clip is over, a repeat viewing offers the potential to reexperience the proximity with this captivating animal materiality. The scene is organized in ways that seek to enhance the status of the marmot, maximizing the affective response from the viewer, for the purpose of revenue raising. This is effective because the marmot easily exudes "nonhuman charisma," a quality borne from human interaction that I have elaborated on in previous chapters via the work of Jamie Lorimer. This charisma is shaped by both human perception of animals that deems some species as affectively appealing *and* animal-centered qualities that allow for nonhuman difference and agency.

Again, the agency enacted by the animal when face-to-face with the camera produces a moving image artifact in which single point perspective is established and then obliterated. Contesting the conventions of perspective in this way also presents a challenge to familiar means of textually orienting vision, and centering the (human) viewer in relation to the scene presented, as I discuss later. For Leitner, the sea turtle footage asks us to consider a network in which what we encounter, beyond the human (gaze), is not the nonhuman (gaze) but a hybrid configuration of human and animal, technical, and natural "actors" (272). Yet I wish to take this beyond simply recognizing a site of relations to speculate how it might produce a revised conception of the nonhuman. These segments present a documentation of life, or encounter with life in the process of documentation, that revolves around a nonfiction narrative turn (present in all examples except the Crittercam), that offers a new way of seeing nature. This way of seeing emphasizes the unexpected and the agentic in the nonhuman world.

Further troubling established modes of vision, it is also notable that the time-lapse function in the Greenpeace example is halted part way through the sequence. Time-lapse, like slow motion, is a feature of blue chip natural history filmmaking, especially the spectacular television mode. These temporal manipulations are devices that amplify the sense of human mastery that this subgenre relies on. This mastery is underpinned by a separation from nature and is supported by a clear capacity to describe (through science) and produce or revision (through audio/visual and thus aesthetic means). With the single act of licking, this mastery gives way to mutual "world-making" to return to the phrase used by both Rose and Haraway. A world of meaning and action is produced in which the intimate proximity of animal embodiment interrupts and participates in the electronic fabrication of point of view and, thus, agency.

Knowingly or not, "Marmot Licks GoPro" reprises a number of other clips on YouTube that add to the phenomena of animal encounter with GoPro technology, such as "Cheetah Licks My GoPro," "Gopher Licks GoPro," "Komodo Dragon Licks GoPro," and "Fox Kills and Eats my GoPro." In these titles the sensible experience offered by the act of licking, and eating, becomes entangled with the industrial brand and the object that is the popular camera. The GoPro name and knowledge of the durability, mobility, and distinctive image produced by the camera, locate it squarely within narratives about the capacity of contemporary consumer-grade technology. As indicated by Bogle, "GoPro" signifies the phenomenal rise in the nonprofessional recording of the natural environment.

Yet, only the Greenpeace clip, with its activist undertaking, makes explicit reference to habitat destruction and, thus, the potential for extinction. It can be even further distinguished from the drone footage because it is easy to perceive the drones and their users as negatively interfering with the natural word and its inhabitants. There is value, nevertheless, in thinking about what these interferences might achieve as *media practices*. They are everyday encounters, often occurring in unplanned ways and beyond the certainty and ordered formula of most wildlife film and television. They privilege messy and entangled relations over the mastery and separation fostered by blue chip film. Documentary's appeal as both spectacle and knowledge in these cases is achieved through a closer alignment with disturbing our expectations of recorded reality. In this they might contribute to an ecological existentialism in which the boundaries between nature and culture are less fixed and more entangled. All of the examples remind the viewer that the doing of agency is not simply the preserve of culture, but also extends to nature. The examples I've described offer the viewer an embodied experience of the nonfiction moving image and a phenomenology of the nonhuman world that troubles, in some small way, the humanist familiarity of visual culture and its aesthetic paradigms. The currency and popularity of this online material gestures to a fascination with the nonhuman that is centered on the moments in which animals "surprise" us with their unscripted, agentic behavior and their materiality onscreen, with the "us" constituted by both the human on-site and the viewer. This fascination is assisted by the capacity of remote control devices and mobile digital cameras to function as prosthetics for human vision.

Africam, Alberti's Window and Speculative Realism

Webcams focused on scenes of nature and wildlife, also known as "naturecams," present a different example of the interaction between technology, agency and human/nonhuman encounter. This is, in part, because unlike the drones and Treadwell's camera, encounters between human and animal are configured through an emphasis on distance rather than proximity, serving to complicate the question of connectivity as I have posed it. Just as there are innumerable kinds of webcams, deployed for different purposes, so, too, are there many variations on naturecams. The greatest majority, however, are focused on recording life in zoos, museums, or wildlife reserves. Some offer close-up images of animals in enclosures or confined spaces for the purposes of relaying the process of rearing young or recovering from illness. Others present wide shots, offering a broader vista that frames a real-time landscape of activity. All provide a moving image representation on the web of events occurring simultaneous to the world of the viewer. The possibility or promise of the naturecam is the experience of viewing a scene of nature that is actually occurring and is geographically distant or remote. *Africam* is a site that offers six different cameras capturing scenes from around southern Africa. I focus in particular on a camera located at Tembe Elephant Park, a game reserve in Maputaland, KwaZulu-Natal, South Africa. The *Tembe Live Wildlife Channel* is focused on a watering hole.

Describing the world enabled by this naturecam requires an acknowledgment of the unique relation between the spatio-temporal location of the observer and the scene observed. Playing the moving image window on the site at 2 PM in my location, Melbourne, Australia, I see a darkened image and the scene of the waterhole at 5 AM, the local time in South Africa. While there is little movement in the image, the sounds of early morning can be distinctly heard, with birds, crickets and, atmospheric noise accompanying the scene. At 5:31 AM the sun has risen and a single giraffe moves into shot, stands motionless and then drinks at the waterhole. As it walks to the left of the frame the camera moves to follow and pans across the plane, zooming in for a closer image of the animal. The resolution is grainy, resulting in a blur as the giraffe moves away. Even with the blur it is possible to perceive the tilt of the giraffe's long body as it walks.

The most directly apparent formulation of agency in this instance concerns the positioning of the viewer—naturecams emphasize spectatorial mastery and pleasure. They promise the possibility of "dropping" in to distant and exotic or hidden and intimate locations. The mode of participation on offer encourages a sense of omniscience, a God-like accessibility that places human activity and sight at the centre. The *Africam* site states "get your nature fix," referencing the pleasure of spectatorship when the desired ethological scene is always unfolding, always available for consumption.

The format and function of the naturecam can easily be allied with the window metaphor that has structured Western modes of viewing since Leon Battista Alberti advocated an approach to renaissance painting that perceived the canvas as an open window. In her book, *The Virtual Window: From Alberti to Microsoft* (2006), Ann Friedberg observes how the window metaphor has persisted ever since in theories of painting, architecture, and moving image media. Crucially, for my purposes, this metaphor also remains a means of affirming the humanist subject of perspective, constructing space on a flat surface by assuming the viewer is positioned centrally in front of the single frame. As Friedberg notes, there have been many disruptions to single point perspective, particularly in twentieth-century modernism. However, "through most of the cinematic century, the dominant form of the moving image was, with striking consistency, a single image in a single frame"" (Friedberg 2). For Friedberg, the computer screen presents the greatest challenge in this history of perspective because it "has more in common with the surfaces of cubism—frontality, suppression of depth, overlapping layers—than with the extended depth of renaissance perspective" (3). I argue, nonetheless, that the naturecam retains a strong reference to cinematic visuality—the frame extrudes from the screen, enclosing a view onto an exterior world. By framing nature, moreover, the naturecam window fulfills expectations concerning the function of an actual window, merging the window as metaphor and practical device. Perhaps most importantly, the window metaphor *highlights the epistemological separation between observer and observed*. The function of the screen, as a substitute for the window, is to bring the distant, and temporally co-present, into view. Nature, as the object of this vision, is to be mastered and seen at a distance, working in contradistinction to Rose's notion of "a deep and abiding mutuality" (50) that characterizes the entanglement of life on Earth.

Yet, I suggest there is an alternate possibility, one that might emerge if emphasis is placed on the *temporality* and embodied life that constitutes the scene, and the different modes of viewing this requires, rather than emphasizing the *spatial* location of the viewer/viewed. This is also an insistence on technology as an enabling "infolding of the flesh," to borrow Haraway's term (in turn borrowed from Merleau Ponty), that does not mediate encounters but is part of the materiality of the encounter.

One way of viewing the *Tembe Live Wildlife Channel* is to "drop in" momentarily to get a "nature fix" observing the activity at a given moment. It is possible to register for "animal alerts," which send a message to subscribers, letting them know when an animal, a giraffe, elephant, or water buffalo, is present onscreen. These alerts accentuate naturecam spectatorship as momentary and event-oriented. Another mode of viewing makes room for the contemplative, the gestural, and the incremental. This requires watching for a sustained length of time. Such a conception of the moving image brings naturecam spectatorship into line with the recent art cinema aesthetic of "slow" cinema or a "cinema of sensation." "This slow, materialist cinema," as Elena Gorfinkel describes, "prizes the everyday rhythms of the phenomenal world and an immersion in dilated duration—through the use of long takes, camera movements, and static framings—over and above exposition, fast-paced editing, or narrative hydraulics" (313). But rather than the human bodies, postures, and gestures that Gorfinkel describes, the naturecam "intensifies the spectator's gaze, awareness and response" (Flanagan) in relation to nonhuman animals.

If, as discussed in previous chapters, wildlife film and television offers artificially "event-filled" versions of the rhythm and processes of nature, the naturecam extends to a new alternative, one in which seemingly nothing happens for long durations of time. It encourages two spectatorial possibilities—either viewing only long enough to ascertain that nothing is happening (a minute or two) or extended viewing for the purpose of engaging in the pleasure of waiting and the appreciation of minor and unplanned occurrences or sounds. It is in the notion of the unplanned and the uncrafted that the medium differs from both wildlife film and slow cinema. Only this latter mode of viewing presents the potential for a less human-centric reading of the naturecam. Bringing to the window metaphor a mode of contemplative realism locates the technology of the screen not in the possibility of momentary virtual travel, but in relation to an infolding, tying the time of the image to matter and attentiveness.

To return to my chronicle of events at the Tembe Elephant Park, at 4:21 PM Melbourne time and 7:21 AM South African time the camera focused on the waterhole shows a group of three impala standing near the bank that dips into the water. Despite the resolution of the image it is possible to make out the distinctive curve of their antlers and their muscled haunches. They graze on the grass and slowly walk in and out of frame. By 7:27 AM they have moved on and the waterhole is still. There is no wind and nothing moves for another two hours, including the leaves on the shrubs in the foreground, as the heat of the day takes hold.

I wish to consider agency in relation to the phenomenology of slowness and how it might encourage not simply an emphasis on the power of the viewer to perceive, but also the viewer's involvement in an experiential and sensory response to the tactile and corporeal phenomena beyond the frame. This infers an encounter that relies both on the specificity of the viewer and the object viewed. This can be furthered, however, by considering how nature might be more fully apprehended as in process and determining interpretation. In this I draw not on phenomenology, but on understandings of "speculative realism," and more specifically, Steven Shaviro's interpretation of Alfred Whitehead. Shaviro's reading rests on the manner in which Whitehead

[. . .] insists that "things experienced are to be distinguished from our knowledge of them. So far as there is dependence, the *things* pave the way for the cognition, rather than *vice versa* . . . the actual things experienced enter into a common world which transcends knowledge, though it includes knowledge." That is

> to say, the question of *how we know* cannot come first, for our
> way of knowing is itself a consequence, or a product, of how
> things are and what they actually do. (*The Universe of Things*, 3)

Following this, the impala drinking at the waterhole must be perceived (and thus, to a degree, known) as a consequence of the qualities of specific animal life and embodiment that it presents, with the way in which the viewing subject experiences this, as phenomenological knowledge, emerging from the impala's autonomous existence.

Shaviro goes on to note "Epistemology must be deprivileged, because we cannot subordinate things themselves to our experiences of them" (*The Universe of Things*, 3). This approach to speculative realism accentuates the real in a way that is strongly nonanthropocentric, emphasizing possible encounters with life in which we "do actually encounter things other than ourselves" (*The Universe of Things*, 8). The impala is not a projection of subjective knowledge, structured by humanist traditions of perspective and romanticism, but rather "things move or force us to feel them" (*The Universe of Things*, 8). Acknowledging the autonomy of things, in this case animal life, works to not simply distribute agency equally across the observer and the observed, it reformulates agency by insisting power is a property of all things. Indeed, in this mode of realism all entities share a common world in which they are deeply interrelated and in a constant state of transformation.

The contemplation encouraged by gazing, rather than glancing at the Tembe naturecam, echoes the principles of speculative realism in that one must be open to the unplanned and constantly altering scene of the wildlife park. Transformation and uncertainty come hand in hand. There are commonalities between Shaviro's discussion and ecological existentialism with Rose's assertion that all species are entangled and humans have as little predetermined essence or destiny as any other species. However, Shaviro's work brings a pivotal emphasis on the issue of encounter, a consideration that is useful for examining how the naturecam might move beyond the human-centric and advance a mode of viewing that reevaluates the relation between the human and the slow aesthetic of nature presented by this media.

Referring to James Benning's use of the long-take in his experimental documentary work, Malin Wahlberg observes,

> The effect of real time approximations is less bound to narrative
> and symbolic functions than to a mode of critical contemplation,

where the viewer is invited to reflect upon the different meanings and associations that the filmed motif may invoke, and to
engage in this perceptual play with camera optics and the time
based quality of the film image. (95)

Through the use of streaming technology the naturecam takes the "realtime approximations" and their address to the viewer so aptly described by
Wahlberg and pushes them into another register of temporal documentary
verisimilitude. Moreover, the perceptual play is quite specific in this case,
bringing to the fore an encounter with the mutability of nonhuman otherness. If glancing at the naturecam positions the animals in the park through
perceived separation, as the projection of human desires and humanist identity, I argue that the autonomy of the world through the window might
come into view with a closer gaze, of a longer duration, the grainy images
bringing recognition of the material phenomenon of animal life. This is a
question of embracing the potential of time, and extended duration, rather
than the web's ability to foreground the spatial paradigm of the window.

The Thrill of the Real: Embodied Vision

The examples I have discussed in this chapter not only realize the documentary project to invite the viewer to embrace a desire for the real, they
exemplify this project by proposing (ostensibly) unplanned (and unplanable) encounters with the natural world. The properties of videographic
technology are vital to the specific achievements of this media. This should
not be interpreted as a claim for a determining role for digital technology
(one that suggests technology singularly enabled the YouTube and naturecam examples), rather video technology has contributed to an increasingly concentrated interest in recording wildlife in sound and image. For
Wahlberg, in her discussion of the long take and isochronal representation
in experimental documentary, "the problem of time measurement becomes
more radically linked to a metacinematography of filmic representation
and voyeurism, of the thrill of the real and the pleasure of photographic
abstraction" (94). The single-shot sequences of animals interacting with the
camera invite repetition, constituting them as isochronal in the sense that
they occur in recurring or equal time. The naturecams are also singular in
their ongoing duration. Each is constituted by a degree of abstraction when
compared with the crafted product of feature length or television documentary. Yet it is an abstraction that fits easily with the popular culture platform

provided by the Internet—the examples I have described in this chapter are embedded in the way viewers (and producers) use digital technology at the level of the every day. Their appeal, thus, can be appropriately described, in Wahlberg's terms, via intensified links to "the thrill of the real and the pleasure of photographic abstraction." This pleasure finds a focus not simply in any staging of the real, but one that compels the viewer to participate in the sensory experience of the nonhuman natural world.

However, further consideration of this point should attend to the rise of spectaularizing technologies that mediate our experience of nature, which I discussed in chapter 4 in relation to blue chip wildlife film. Do the quotidian prosthetics for human vision I discuss in this chapter maintain distance rather than connectivity, allowing humans to claim proximity while, in actuality, mitigating our emotional distance from the problem of environmental change? In other words, do mobile cameras and access to nonhuman worlds on the web extend our sensory capacity, and thus our responsiveness, or replace it? To follow Haraway's formulation, the answer would be no, such technologies not only extend our embodied experience, they are a form of embodiment or infolding. Shaviro might respond to this issue by asking whether such technology allows us to encounter the autonomy of things. I have demonstrated how the naturecam and YouTube sequences of animal/technology might, on the terms these scholars suggest, gesture to "worldmaking" across species.

This media heightens the possibility for embodied perception or recognition of animal difference by emphasizing life as the product of movement (movement that obtains in agency) and materiality. For the last word I draw on Lesley Stern's proposition "that while the indexicality of the cinematic image creates an effect of material presence, the movement of the image simultaneously renders that presence potentially unstable and ephemeral" (321). Extending Stern's formulation of the moving image's potential to create affect through movement and temporality, I argue that in the examples discussed here such movement also institutes a new contingency, one that both generates the destabilization of familiar codes of humanist vision and underlines the corporeality of animal life.

Chapter 7

In Conclusion

Documentary, Science, and the Umwelt

When mosquitoes dance in the sunset, they do not see our big human sun, setting six kilometers away, but small mosquito suns that set about half a meter away. The moon and stars are absent from the sky of the mosquito.

—Jakob Von Uexküll, An Introduction to Umwelt

The first decade of the twenty-first century has seen the proliferation of film and media forms that draw attention to the interface between the nonhuman environment and the institutions of human endeavor. This increase across cinema, television, and the Internet has occurred alongside growing awareness of unprecedented anthropogenic changes to the environment and the precariousness of the world ecosystem. Chapters have detailed evidence and conclusions that specify how this documentary culture speaks to a multifaceted ecological imaginary, one that does not cohere within a single ideological agenda. I have elaborated on how a range of filmic examples, focused on modernity's biopolitical practices, systems and narratives, operate to provide multiple ways of reimagining animal/human relations and the work of documentary. We cannot understand the archive of documentary films that make use of the figure of the animal, past and present, without the contextualizing forces of the Anthropocene, such as habitat destruction, anthropogenic changes to the environment, and the use of animals as a resource for humans. Chapters have been informed by these forces and have attempted to unravel how the circuit of relations across the human and nonhuman are made and remade by the project of cinema, its ontology and aesthetic specificities. These include the long take, the encounters facilitated by digital technology, documentary identification and, more broadly, the structuring of wildlife spectacle. In this respect, it has tied the capacity of cinema to stage encounters with the sensuous materiality of life to the biopolitical, the human knowledge systems to which animals are subjected.

Describing Siegfried Kracauer's theory of film, Miriam Hansen proposes "If cinema has the power to stage encounters with the other, it can also, like no other medium, register material phenomena in their otherness, in their opaque singularity" ("Introduction," xxx). These words claim a visionary role for cinema in manifesting otherness. The reference is not simply describing material objects, but, more specifically, the "flow of life," its vibrancy, temporality, and indeterminacy. I have followed the contours of this claim, exploring what such a potential to register otherness offers the animal in cinema. In the first chapter I posed a challenge for film and media studies—to consider anew how the properties and economies of cinema center the human and human life. I have pursued this challenge, attending to what films and filmic moments might yield in the way of decentering the human and grasping the infinite entanglements between human and nonhuman worlds.

Conclusions have indicated that there is a delicate balance in play— rather than working outside dominant paradigms, many of the examples discussed work with the precepts of, for example, the industrial food system, the history of heroic exploration, and the capacity of new audiovisual technology, in ways that contest the settled status of the human. They do so by offering alternative (audiovisual) approaches to animal materiality and to the existential relation between human and nonhuman. Other examples, such as the unique, precarious lifeworld of people living and working with animals in films such as *Raw Herring* and *Los Hereredos* or the companions in environmental decline offered by *Arctic Tale*, offer a reaffirmation of human perspectives and worlds, albeit in very different ways. Complicating this, we can see how *Frozen Planet*, as a series, achieves both a verification of the natural history mode's mastery over nature *and* recognition of the anthropogenic effects on the planet. This translates into both a centering of the human, separating it from the natural world, *and* the identification of the connectivity that organizes all life in the planet, apparent and competing across different episodes in the series.

I have also posed the problem of cinema's anthropocentrism as a historical one, bound to how histories in/of cinema are rendered in humanist terms or might be rethought in ways that question the centrality of the human. Both of these lines of inquiry have been crucially informed by a critique of cinema's default anthropomorphic function, questioning the way it operates to perpetuate subject-centered worlds, which offer human perspectives and human singularity for spectatorial engagement. Furthermore, close attention to the animal in the documentary frame leads to a rethinking of principles of documentary theory, requiring them to become more malleable in order to account for the problem of nonfiction's archiving function, identification with nonhuman materiality (especially in the case of the food documentary), and the explication of nonhuman agency.

The notion of nonhuman charisma has been a recurring interest across a number of chapters. In chapter 3 I extended Jamie Lorimer's formulation of the term into a film studies frame to begin thinking anew about how animals are encountered in the process of spectatorship, proposing a "(non) human realism." This is a verisimilitude that places emphasis not only on the nonhuman animal, but the body of the perceiving human (the viewer and the human in the world of the film) as a way of encountering the real of nonhuman materiality. It is relational and thus brings the methods of scientific inquiry to the question of locating subjective perception, a core consideration in documentary studies and a point I explore later in this chapter. This encounter with nonhuman charisma, moreover, appropriates anthropocentrism, maintaining that human embodiment can be the source of a human recognition of nonhuman difference.

I have charted how core examples of the nonfiction tradition, antecedents to the new wave of documentary such as *Nanook of the North* and *The Great White Silence* establish animals as central to the representation of particular historical human worlds, troubling the humanism of documentary's past. Conversely, attention to histories of extinction shows how these are rendered as markers of human crisis, rather than a crisis that far exceeds the human. Documentary that attends to the materiality of life in the face of extinction works to bring this focus back to the nonhuman.

The question of history, both film history and the past and present of human and nonhuman interactions on the planet dovetails with a recurrent theme in this book—the numerous ways in which the temporal inflects the rendering and ontology of animals. This includes the time of exploration and the time of habitat destruction as images and narratives confront the progression of changes to the planet. The question of futurity underpins every chapter because each is structured by attention to humans and animals as co-evolving species, bound up in various kinds of mutual ecologies that have a relationship with the future. Also, perhaps more pertinently, the duration and motion produced by the length of shots and the rhythm of editing contribute to the filmic understanding of animal being in crucial ways. The long duration of the shot emphasizes the materiality and charisma of animals as they unfold in time. There are also moments when life or corporeality surprises the viewer, whether it is the unexpected agency of animals interacting with cameras in an instant or the momentary identification with the materiality of flesh as food. The filmic relation to extinction, in some senses, manifests as the nontime of loss as the camera registers an index of life that may soon be gone, its likeness and species obliterated. Time is allied with our sensory response to the cinematic image and it plays a special role in structuring our understanding of animals.

More to this, many of the films discussed provide important cues for questioning the status of the human as defined earlier and against other (nonhuman) animals. They trouble humanist histories and show that there is a fissure in the anthropomorphic totality of cinema. They do not, however, recalibrate representation to the fullest degree. In this final chapter, I take the opportunity to further the discussion of new documentary ontologies began in the previous chapter to ask: What would it mean to fully revise the gaze of the camera, and more significantly, the film world, in a way that was structured by nonhuman agency and perceptual perspective?

In posing this question I am inspired by Janet Walker's notion of "eavesdropping." Walker develops this term in her analysis of *The Cove* (2009), the Oscar-winning documentary that explores, and advocates against, the annual commercial killing of large numbers of dolphins in a cove in Taiji, a Japanese fishing village. Walker's approach to the documentary invents an interdisciplinary film studies method that draws on geography and animal science. She takes the underwater observation of dolphins by scientists as a starting point, a practice of data gathering they refer to as "eavesdropping." Walker synthesizes this eavesdropping with "observation" as "a documentary function or mode" (211) to understand how the filmmaker's process of collecting footage in the cove (a process documented in the film) "makes visible the capacity of documentary film not only to sense and to represent but actually to remap and remake the natural environment" (211). In part, this analysis is one that recognizes a space for viewers to "think across species" (211) in an empathetic manner that is scientifically informed.

Importantly, Walker makes a case for anthropocentrism in a scientific frame. She draws on the work of Sandra Mitchell to suggest that fields such as cognitive ethology have found productive ways of considering animal physiology in relation to human physiology: "Mitchell explores claims of human-to-non-human causal isomorphism—that is, similarities in 'neurophysiological structure, sensory apparatus, and so on'—and finds them valid in certain cases" (213). Taking this one step further, I am interested in thinking not simply about physiological commonalties, but the less anthropocentric possibility of, in the words of Buchanan, Bussolini, and Chrulew, "ways of knowing—empirical, phenomenological, ethnographic, otherwise—that prove insightful regarding other forms of life, and indeed transformative of our own" (2). In chapter 2 I posed the notion of lifeworld, drawing from Husserl's *lebenswelt*, a concept that poses an experiential world that is both objective and mutually perceived but understood through the senses. While it does not discount the possibility of the nonhuman lifeworld, I argue it does not allow for the perceptual differences between species. For this reason I turn to the work of Estonian biologist Jacob von Uexküll[1] to build on Walker's synthesis of film studies and science and explore the possibility of a nonhuman filmic world.

With the term *Umwelt*, Uexküll makes the case that each species has its own perceptual world, its own "island of the senses" ("An Introduction," 107). Yet more than simply a way of perceiving, the Umwelt recognizes the way each different animal constructs its own environment, as Brett Buchanan describes, "out of the midst of its perceptions, actions, and relationships" (2). Indeed, for Buchanan, Uexküll "introduces us to a new way of thinking about reality as such," (2) not only moving beyond the notion of one physical world, but making a case for the distinct subjective reality of the animal. *Umwelten* are akin to soap bubbles—vessels that house single forms of life. Describing a scene in which one strolls through a meadow, Uexküll writes that each animal might be encased in a bubble, which is:

> filled with the perceptions accessible to that subject alone. As soon as we ourselves step into one of these bubbles, the surrounding meadow is completely transformed. Many of its colourful features disappear, others no longer belong together, new relations are created. A new world emerges in each bubble. (*A Stroll Through*, 5)

Given this, Umwelt translates into "environment," but in a manner that is attentive to the disposition, functionality, and activity of the organism that is embedded in that environment. Not all features in the surroundings are included in the Umwelt—it is partial and actively selective, constituted by only those features that are relevant to the subject, producing a multiplicity of physical worlds and realities.

For Uexküll, then, reality is subjective—organisms construct an environment that is meaningful to them. This contrasts to the speculative realism discussed in the previous chapter, one that recognizes the physical autonomy of perceived objects. Elizabeth Grosz understands Umwelten to constitute the organism's agency: "The Umwelt is the sensory world of space, time, objects and qualities that form perceptual worlds for living creatures, the

world that enables them to effect actions, to exercise their organs, to act"
(175). Considering how the concept of the Umwelt might be transposed
onto cinematic representation and spectatorship presents a revolutionary
proposition. Because Umwelten differ essentially in their make-up, they are
not limited to any spatial, auditory, or temporal (or tactile and olfactory)
frame. The ontology of cinema might be entirely rethought in replicat-
ing nonhuman Umwelten. Objects placed in different Umwelt, moreover,
are intrinsically transformed, resulting in a changed reality for the viewer.
Further, Umwelten produce nonhuman subjects (they are a form of subjectification), and if film worlds were able to account for this, they would
function as the source of profoundly intersubjective encounters.

Following this thread, one might imagine what it would be to produce
the Umwelt of the honeybee in cinematic terms. This would entail a shallow
depth of field, given the limited spatial plane of the bee. They are among
animals that have "smaller Umwelt horizons" (Uexküll, "The New Concept," 108) than humans. Flowers would loom large, taking on particular
significance. More than this, the form of flowers dictates the morphology of
all objects in the honeybee Umwelt: "[. . .] honey gathering bees can only
distinguish two shapes: open and closed. Ray shapes and many sided shapes
of all kinds attract the bees, while circles and rectangles repel it" (Uexküll,
A Foray, 180). Dividing objects into open and closed forms, buds are rejected by the honeybee as it privileges the spatiality of blooms. According to
Uexküll's determinations about color, bees transform the visual palette and
fill it with only ultraviolet, blue, green, and yellow ("The New Concept,"
120). Bees have limited hearing, sensing sounds as vibrations but only if
they are very close by (Grosz 181). The film world of the honeybee would
be much simpler, with fewer embellishments.

It is notable that in his descriptions of different Umwelten, Uexküll
emphasizes not the inferiority of such spheres, but rather the melodic tones
of life. The adaption between life form and surroundings is discussed by
way of the "harmony" of life[2]:

> The theme of the music for the honeybee is the collection of
> nectar and pollen. To find them the path that leads to them has
> to be marked with perceptual cues. This explains the choice of
> properties of flowers that become form, colour, smell and taste
> perceptions to the bees. A honeybee meadow is something very
> different from a human meadow. It is a honeybee composition
> made up of bee notes and is much easier to comprehend than
> our human Umwelt compositions. ("The New Concept," 120)

The musical metaphor employed here may not necessarily offer a soundtrack to Umwelten, but it does suggest a sense of rhythm and temporality that enhances the ethological detail of honeybee subjectivity. To extend this, one might imagine the visual and auditory experience of the hive, including the complexity of honeycomb.

Speculation about a nonhuman documentary cinema Umwelt provokes questions about examples I have discussed in previous chapters. How would a film such as *Sweetgrass* be posed—the ranch, the mountains and other animals—in a sheep Umwelt? How might changes to the Arctic habitat be perceived given the polar bear Umwelt? The hawks' encounter with drones as they knock them out of the sky? In the previous chapter I discussed Haraway's description of the Crittercam (a camera attached to marine animals), which she notes is "usually pretty boring and hard to interpret, somewhat like an ultrasound recording of a fetus. Footage without narration is more like an acid trip than a peephole to reality" (258). How intelligible would texts designed with Umwelt in mind be, filtered as they are through the mechanics of human production? They would certainly privilege rhythm, sharing something with naturecam footage. Yet the reference Haraway makes to the "peephole into reality" is central to documentary concerns. With no objects that are stable or consistent across different Umwelten and no shared physical field, the discourse of the real that structures the expectations and institutions of documentary must be rethought. The photographic image, the basis for cinema's relation to the real, is no longer a reliable indicator of the reality in the case of nonhuman Umwelt.

Assuming this presents an experimental rather than a popular cinema, intelligibility is less important than how such a cinema might throw into relief human ways of knowing and perceiving, triggering a fuller understanding of the specificity of human perception (rather than perceiving it as universal). Beyond this, there is scope to add to scientific endeavor, further extending the interdisciplinarity outlined by Walker (and others) and bringing a new efficacy to documentary as an apparatus of human endeavor. Most importantly, while this cinema is subject-centered, it is not human-centric. Indeed, it reveals the human to be one subject among many with the recognition that nonhuman perception is entirely distinct. In comparison with previous chapters, a documentary Umwelt asks the viewer to not only to engage with otherness (recognizing the animal difference in a shared world), but to become other through the transformation of perception.

Notes

Chapter 1. Introduction

1. The preeminent documentary in this respect is *An Inconvenient Truth* (2006), the first film to generate widespread interest in and establish documentary as a formidable tool for raising awareness about environmental crisis. See Lage (2014) and Shoard (2009) for further discussion of this category in the popular press.

2. See B. Ruby Rich (108–109) for a discussion of the renaissance in 2006, and the new culture of production and criticism, particularly in a North American context.

3. French examples include not only *March of the Penguins* but also a precursor to the boom (and another wildlife-oriented documentary), *Le Peuple Migrateur* (*Winged Migration*) (2001) and *Etre et avoir* (2002). *Touching the Void* (2004) was a British film to achieve success internationally while *Bowling for Columbine* (2002), *Inconvenient Truth* (2006), *Fahrenheit 9/11*, *Supersize Me* (2004), and *Spellbound* (2003) all dominate in this period.

4. *Chimpanzee* (2012), *Oceans* (2010), *Bears* (2014), *African Cats* (2011), *Monkey Kingdom* (2015), and *Earth* (2009) all feature in the top fifteen films in terms of U.S. theatrical release success. See www.boxofficemojo.com/genres/chart/?id=documentary.htm

5. In this book my reference to nonhuman life is largely concerned with animal life. I employ the term "nonhuman" with an awareness that a number of other terms also exist in the conceptual taxonomy that accounts for life or "living-ness" that is beyond the human, such as inhuman, infra-human, more than human or ahuman. I employ "nonhuman animal" to gesture to the indecisive boundary between human and animal, recognizing the animality of humans and the way humans are situated as simply one species among many.

6. While Cubitt's work has achieved the most impact methodologically, two further important studies of popular, primarily Hollywood, cinema-influenced scholarship about ecological issues in the first years of the twentieth century—David Ingram's *Green Screen: Environmentalism and Hollywood Cinema* (2000) and Pat Brereton's *Hollywood Utopia: Ecology in American Cinema* (2005).

7. Beyond the titles I discuss in the next paragraphs, this body includes work by Catherine Russell (1999), Morgan Richards (2013a, 2013b), Palle B. Petterson (2011), and Claire Molloy (2013).

8. For a detailed review of the field of critical animal studies see Kari Weil (2010), Matthew Calarco (2008), or Cary Wolfe (2010).

9. *Creaturely Poetics* was followed by an equally groundbreaking collection edited by Anat Pick and Guinevere Narraway, *Screening Nature: Cinema Beyond the Human* (2013). Moreover, Pick's focus on cinema is preceded by work by Jonathan Burt, most notably his book, *Animals in Film* (2002), and Akira Mizuta Lippit's *Electric Animal: Toward a Rhetoric of Wildlife* (2000). The field of work addressing film and animals beyond wildlife film now includes work by Janet Walker (2013), Robin L. Murray, and Joseph K. Heumann (2009), Claire Molloy (2011), and Jennifer Ladino (2009, 2012) and the edited collections, *Framing the World: Explorations in Ecocriticism and Film* (2010), edited by Paula Willoquet-Maricondi, and *Ecocinema Theory and Practice* (2012), edited by Cubitt, Mohani, and Rust.

10. Barry Keith Grant explores the controversy that erupted around the film and notes that Wiseman did not feel compelled to defend the film and did not have strong opinions about animal research (111–112).

11. Thomas W. Benson insightfully describes Wiseman's endeavor: his "rhetorical talent is to help his audiences identify with oppressors and oppressed: we feel pity, fear, and rage on behalf of the victims, with whom we identify; and we feel the shock of horrified recognition in realising that the oppressors are acting in our name, as members of this society [. . .]" (195).

12. See Cottle (94–97) or Blewitt (100) for more elaboration and evidence of this point. In chapter 5 I discuss some of the ways blue chip wildlife film is now giving more weight to climate science and environmental change.

13. Offering a different perspective on the limitations of television, Thomas Austin notes how with the "ongoing segmentation of audiences and markets, commissioners and schedules have the option to place some documentary programming on smaller, specialist channels" (22), effectively allowing more challenging material to be ghettoized on minor channels. He draws on the example of BBC4, which functions as the BBC's "duty channel" (23) and carries primetime programming about environmental issues that does not appear in the wildlife blue chip products made for BBC1.

14. See the organization's corporate statement: corporate.discovery.com.

15. Chris (79–121) explains the rise of cable wildlife television and, in part, attributes its competiveness as a product in the marketplace to increasing attention since the 1990s to representations of animal sex.

16. Subjectification, the means by which humans are socially and psychically positioned to take up individual subjectivities, is a complicated proposition in relation to animals—while they may be subjected to human systems it is unclear how many species internalize this subjection. Due to my focus on cinema, I am primarily concerned with what the apparatus of cinema can produce and for this reason I steer away from analyzing animal subjectivity, except in the instances where it is postulated by the structures of the moving image text and its reception.

17. Matthew Brower's book, *Developing Animals: Wildlife and Early American Photography*, provides an important intervention into these debates. Brower critiques Berger's claims as defining images of animals by what they "can reveal about human culture and interests" (xviii) and thus they become passive objects for the projection of meaning, rather than actors with a role to play in the production of images (xviii). Drawing on Foucault's notion of genealogy, Brower advocates moving beyond considering why we look at animals, or the meaning of the photograph, to analyzing how they function, given a particular set of contingencies (xxv). This position essentially mirrors that taken in this book, albeit realized through tools more concerned with the moving image and the senses.

18. See John Rundell's essay, "Modernity, Humans and Animals—Tensions in the Field of the Technical-Industrial Imaginary," for a nuanced theorization of this history as well as the place of animals in modernity.

19. Burt names a number of these organizations: "the Society for the Prevention of Cruelty to Animals, the Vegetarian Society, the Our Dumb Friends' League, the British Union for the Abolition of Vivisection, the Humane Slaughter Association, the Anti-Plumage League which was transformed into the Society for the Protection of Birds" ("John Berger's," 212).

20. Jonathan Burt begins this work in his investigation of cinema, animals, and the work of Henri Bergson and Jacques Derrida. Notably, in this essay Burt turns to a philosophical frame, rather than understanding the moving image through film theoretical approaches. For Burt, the mutability of the cinematic image is important, but it is on a par with animal/human relations or the interval, "the distance between two beings looking at each other or coexisting within the same sphere of existence ("Morbidity and Vitalism," 169). Moreover, he identifies two types of bond across the human–animal divide:

> The first is *life*, described at one point by Bergson as the insertion of indetermination into matter, and which binds both human and animal as entities representing moments of the actualisation of "elan vital." [. . .] The second is the *livingness* of bodies, where I define livingness as the mode of active coexistence whereby an individual's ability to live (or die) depends on the nature of its interaction with others. ("Morbidity and Vitalism," 169)

This is crucial for cinema, the relation between audiences and animals onscreen and between species in the world of the film. Film allows for an emphasis on the temporal dimensions of interspecies relations: "the importance of the gap—the time of the interval between action and reaction in perception—reminds us of the need to take account of relations as unfolding, as signifying constantly changing distributions of responses, powers, and actions across the spaces between human and animal" ("Morbidity and Vitalism," 172).

21. See Miriam Hansen's discussion of Kracauer's Marseille notebooks of 1940 for a fuller discussion about how such an address to the spectator attends to

an alienated historical reality and one that debunks humanist sentiment and also challenges the bourgeois subject, one who is, due to their affluence, distanced from the material reality of life ("With Skin and Hair," 450).

22. See Ian Aitken's essay "Distraction and Redemption: Kracauer, Surrealism and Phenomenology" (127), for an elaboration of the Husserlian influences on Kracauer's theory of film. Kracauer is often understood as a film realist rather than formalist, yet I am more interested in how his work fits into a legacy of phenomenological thinking in ways that disturb distinctions between the two.

23. Other work that contributes to this arena of film studies includes Vivian Sobchack's *Carnal Thoughts: Embodiment and Moving Image Culture* (2004), Malin Walberg's *Documentary Time: Film and Phenomenology* (2008), Thomas Elsaesser and Malte Hagener's *Film Theory: An Introduction Through the Senses* (2010), Eugenie Brinkema's *The Forms of the Affects* (2014), and Jennifer Barker's *The Tactile Eye: Touch and the Cinematic Experience* (2009). Alexa Weik von Mossner's edited collection, *Moving Environments: Affect, Emotion, Ecology, and Film*, explores affect and the specific intersection between ecology and film.

Chapter 2. Labor, Agriculture, and Long Take Cinema: Working on the Surface of the Earth

1. See Cynthia Chris' book *Watching Wildlife* for an elaboration of this genre.

2. In her book, *Experimental Ethnography: The Work of Film in the Age of Video*, Catherine Russell persuasively makes the case for this blurring of boundaries in relation to experimental ethnography.

3. I borrow this phrase from Scott MacDonald who views the task of a predominately avant-garde eco-cinema as a "retraining of perception, as a way of offering an alternative to conventional media spectatorship, or [. . .] as a way of providing something like a garden—an 'Edenic' respite from conventional consumerism—within the machine of modern life, as modern life is embodied by the apparatus of media" ("Toward," 109).

4. See Sarah Pink's *The Future of Visual Anthropology: Engaging the Senses* for further work in this area.

5. This turn, for Kirksey and Helmreich (545–548), however, directly references an acknowledgment of the situatedness of humans, or more specifically, anthropos, in the Anthropocene. It signals a recognition emerging about the role of humans in triggering environmental crisis. This awareness is the basis for an equally ecological response, with multispecies ethnography attending to the connectivities between and within species communities. See Jaimie Lorimer ("Moving Image Methodologies") for a perceptive analysis of multispecies considerations in moving image methodologies in geography.

6. Husserl poses the notion of a transcendental subjectivity, and thus argues for a commonly shared perception that assumes that similar beings will experience the world in similar ways: "The lifeworld does have, in all its relative features, a

general structure. This general structure, to which everything that exists relatively is bound, is not itself relative. We can attend to it is its generality and, with sufficient care, fix it for once and for all in a way equally accessible for all" (139, italics in the original). Husserl's phenomenology poses such an objective structure that is valid for perceiving subjects while marrying this with an emphasis on subjective bodily experience and sense perception. In this respect, grasping the nature of life structures, things, and concepts in an intersubjective activity. While Husserl's notion leaves open the possibility for any being that has the capacity for intentional consciousness to be included in this intersubjectivity, in this chapter I am concerned only with the human lifeworld.

7. In this, my approach departs from that of Jennifer Ladino who poses a critique of the "speciesed camera" ("Working with Animals," 130), a mode of vision that privileges human perception. For Ladino, *Sweetgrass* presents the possibility of subverting this gaze (through a Haraway-inspired move) in ways that entail a more ethical "sharing of words" ("Working with Animals," 131). I follow, instead, the potential that is offered by pursuing the anthropomorphism of film worlds, attending to cinema's historical antecedents and its role as a technological extension of the human gaze.

8. In his well-known article in Danish film journal, *16:9*, Matthew Flanagan (http://www.16-9.dk/2008-11/side11_inenglish.htm) considers the structure and sensibility of the long take within the context of an aesthetic recently identified as "slow cinema." Elena Gorfinkel's observations (313) build on this approach. Rather than finding parallels with this wider movement, this chapter is more concerned with accounting for the specificity of a contemporary agrarian cinema, one that references documentary traditions of labor and ethnographic cinema.

9. The pair is known internationally for the award-winning trilogy, *Eye of the Day* (2001), *Shape of the Moon* (2004), and *Position Among the Stars* (2010), which is shot in a similar "long take" style to *Raw Herring*.

10. These images are presumably shot with a GoPro camera, well known for being waterproof but also for anamorphically distorting the proportion of the image slightly and accentuating contrasts of light and dark.

11. See Brian Winston (37) for one such critique.

12. See Dickey-Collas et al. for an account of the causes and management of fluctuating herring stocks.

13. While these films bear the stamp of the Sensory Ethnography Lab, they have, for the most part, not featured in ethnographic film festivals. The most visible forum for the films' circulation has been art institutions, with *Leviathan* especially featuring in key exhibitions at the Whitney and the Tate Modern.

14. See Scott MacDonald (*American Ethnographic*), Anna Grimshaw, Jennifer Ladino "Working with Animals"), and Robert Koehler (*Sweetgrass*).

15. There are many similarities between *Sweetgrass* and *Grass: A Nation's Battle for Life*, made, as I have noted, during the silent period. Not only does "grass" feature in the title of both, the earlier film follows the seasonal migration of the Bakhtiari, a large nomadic tribe in Iran who must move thousands of livestock

across mountains for summer grazing. The film aligns with the ethnographic preference of the time to depict racialized traditionalism, isolated from modernity. Thus, there is much to suggest that with *Sweetgrass* the filmmakers seek to draw attention to the connections between these documentaries.

16. Bazin had a keen interest in animals. As Sueng-Hoon Jeong and Dudley Andrew note "Although inheriting western metaphysics, including the existentialism and phenomenology that were rife in his day, he was also, since boyhood, a fanatical naturalist who lived among animals and studies their behavior. Bazin felt the cinema capable of staring at the otherness of animals with a preternatural eye" (3).

17. Animals abound in Bazin's essay "The Virtues and Limitations of Montage," where he explores the possibilities of anthropomorphism.

18. This is suggested by Castaing-Taylor when in an interview he states that rather than exploring the politics of land use, "We ended up trying to be more phenomenological, you could say: evoking the lifeworld of the sheepherders as best we could, and to let that speak for itself, without any overt editorialising on our part. But not just the sheepherders—also the sheep, and especially the place itself. It's out of fashion to see nature as anything other than some secondary cultural construction, but we're all part of it, as much as city folks suppose otherwise, and throughout history humans and animals have commingled in ways that have deeply affected the kinds of beings we've become" (PBS).

19. Scott MacDonald notes a number of such traces of modernization in the film. Further, he argues that Barbash and Castaing-Taylor consciously contest the conceit that has characterized ethnographic filmmaking in the tradition of Flaherty, Marshall, and Gardner—that cultures can be represented in isolation from the corrupting forces of modernization. Instead, for MacDonald "the quest to represent this kind of cultural "purity" is pointless, because culture by its very nature is always in transition, and every particular cultural practice is regularly confronted by, even formed by, influences from outside itself" (*American Ethnographic*, 322).

20. Castaing-Taylor describes these factors in an interview with the Public Broadcasting Service (PBS).

21. Polgovsky has demonstrated a consistent approach to documentary. He had previously directed *Tropico de Cancer* (2004), a film that shares much with *Los Herederos* as it depicts poor families living near the Mexican town of San Luis Potosi who make a living by selling animals they have hunted or trapped by the highway. In comparison, his later documentary, *Mitote* (2012), focuses on Mexico City, exploring the collision of new and ancient tradition and ritual.

22. This is apparent in one instance of the reception of the film. As Koehler describes "Margarita Zavala, the wife of Mexican President Felipe Calderon, attended its world premiere at the 2008 Morelia film festival, and as the lights came up, all eyes accusingly stared at her" ("Agrarian," 14).

23. Here Chrulew makes reference to Hardt and Negri's discussion of the multitude and the proletariat. More broadly they take up Foucault's work to pose a global system of power, or "Empire." For Chrulew, their notion of the multitude and the common lend themselves to the elaboration of multispecies questions: "Non-

human animals also form part of the cooperative and communicative interspecies multitude. The affective labour of biopolitical production allows us to understand animal productivity in continuity with human labour, as opposed to the traditional Marxist exclusion. Ecological thought demands the recognition that the whole of the natural world produces the common" ("Animals in Biopolitical," 63).

Chapter 3. Meat, Animals, and Paradigms of Embodiment: Documentary Identification and the Problem of Food

1. I include *Leviathan* (2013) and *Raw Herring* (2013) in this grouping, films I discussed in the previous chapter. While their observational style constitutes them as more expressive that explicitly argumentative, they nevertheless depict the industrial processing of fish.

2. Examples of this thematic thread include *The Corporation* (2004), *Supersize Me* (2004), *The Yes Men* (2003), *Enron, The Smartest Guys in the Room* (2005), *Gasland* (2010), and the films of Michael Moore.

3. Notably, the "eco" prefix in this formulation references a broad anti-corporate ethos in the films' approach rather than a specific environmental critique. In one of the few studies to discuss the grouping of food documentary, Murray and Heumann locate different films within broader formal traditions of documentary and evaluate films such as *We Feed the World* (2005), *King Corn*, and *Our Daily Bread* in terms of how pastoral nostalgia figures into the cogency of their rhetorical address ("Contemporary Eco-Food"). In their article "Documentary Film and Ethical Foodscapes: Three Takes on Caribbean Sugar," Pamela Richardson-Ngwenya and Ben Richardson similarly focus on the efficacy of documentary in representing food ethics. Laura Lindenfeld ("Digging Down") also briefly elaborates on the radical potential of food films. None turn their attention specifically to animals and food.

4. See Paula Rabinowitz's work for one account of this tradition (16–34).

5. Such films focus on instructing audiences about issues such as nutrition and agricultural processes. Their public service agenda can be identified in a number of contemporary food documentaries, but importantly they do not share the more contemporary focus on politicizing consumers and posing ideological critique of the food system.

6. Shukin notes that the moving lines in vertical abattoirs had been operating in Cincinnati and Chicago since 1850, preceding Ford's automotive assembly line and influencing his production. Yet rather than assembly, Shukin describes the abattoirs as the "ulterior logistics of animal disassembly" (87).

7. In this respect, few documentaries are concerned with problematizing the killing and eating of animals on a local or mass scale. Exceptions to this are *Animals* (2003) and *A Cow at My Table* (1998).

8. Noting the special status of meat and the slaughter of livestock in contemporary food documentary, Michael Newbury observes the importance of animal slaughter in his discussion of *Food, Inc.* and *Supersize Me* (2004), arguing that these

films are part of a wider popular narrative of crisis and imminent industrial food apocalypse. He locates the treatment and slaughter of livestock at the center of these narratives of panic as they most intensely represent the "the horrors of agribusiness" (93) and the "horror of modern eating" (112). Newbury identifies the metaphorical potential of slaughter and its product, meat, observing its associations with death, crisis, and corruption.

9. Notably, the release of *Darwin's Nightmare* was accompanied by a storm of controversy that revolved around the truth claims of the film. Helen Hughes summarizes and evaluates the different perspectives on the film in her article on the film ("Scrutiny and Documentary").

10. This film owes a debt to *cinéma vérité* and filmmakers such as Fredric Wiseman (his films *Meat*, and even *Primate*, in particular). Yet *Our Daily Bread* offers a coldly lyrical perspective on the avant-garde observational tradition, even eschewing the humanism of overheard speech that observational film usually features on the sound track. The film resembles Wiseman's work in its critique of social institutions and systems that organize social existence.

11. *Food, Inc.* was released in cinemas and achieved more than 4½ million U.S. dollars at the box office, placing it among the most commercial successful documentaries of recent years. It was nominated for an Academy Award in 2009 but lost to *The Cove* (2009), another film concerned with, in part, food and issues of consumption.

12. For example, French audiences mobilized for boycotts of Nile perch in the wake of the release of *Darwin's Nightmare*. A version of the law Barbara Kowalcyk was working to have passed as shown in *Food, Inc.*, known Kevin's Law, was passed by U.S. congress as the Food Safety Modernization Act in 2011. In a different example of activity following the release of a film, the directors of *The Moo Man* initiated a successful Kickstarter campaign, making it the first British film to be released theatrically via crowdfunding. Moreover, the websites of most food documentaries detail specific organizations, issues, and links that facilitate an engagement in food activism.

13. *American Meat*, a documentary that focuses on the work of activist farmer, Joel Salatin (who appears in *Farmageddon* and *Food, Inc.*), is notable as a film that encourages both ethical consumption and the uptake of alternative farming practices.

14. For Laura Lindenfeld, films such as *Food, Inc.* demonstrate an anthropocentric framework "that prioritises human gain and benefit through the dominion over nature" ("Can Documentary," 383) and fail to adequately address environmental concerns.

15. Abbott is the co-director of another key film in the documentary renaissance, *The Corporation*.

Chapter 4. Arctic Futures and Extinction: Loss, the Archive, and (Wildlife) Film

1. Paleoanthropologists Richard Leakey and Roger Lewin project that one half of the animal and plant species existing today will have vanished in the next

one hundred years (233). While a background level of extinction is part of the balance of natural evolutionary processes, species loss has intensified in the current epoch. In 2009 biologists compiling the "Red List" of threatened species report that evidence shows nearly one quarter (22 percent) of the world's mammal species, nearly one-third (31 percent) of amphibians and more than one in eight birds (13.6 percent) are globally threatened or have become extinct (Hilton-Taylor et al., 18). In some cases the lack of reliable data means that the number may be far higher. The reasons for this decline range from habitat destruction, invasive species, pollution, human population growth, to overharvesting. The current rate of species loss, moreover, is causing an unprecedented loss of biodiversity.

2. See the *Arctic Climate Impact Assessment* (2004) for more detail of this.

3. Chrulew's reference is informed by Rose's essay "What if the Angel of History Were a Dog" in which she describes "double death" as "the amplification of death, so that the balance between life and death is overrun, and death starts piling up corpses in the land of the living" ("What if," 75).

4. Ricardo De Vos couches this in relation to the interventionist, interactive, practices of science: "While scientific discourse constructed upon the discovery, recording, collection, observation, testing, dissection and hypothesising of samples has enabled our current conceptions of extinction through the taxonomic classification of all known animals and plants, it is ironic that these very practices have also contributed to the extinction of so many plants and animals" (185).

5. Following the death of this animal in 1936, there have been no verified sightings of the thylacine, a wolf-like marsupial with a distinctive striped body. It was finally declared extinct in the 1980s. It is Australia's most conspicuous symbol of animal extinction, with its disappearance often blamed on human development and an apathetic approach to preservation. See Robert Paddle for a fuller investigation of the thylacine's extinction.

6. Specifically, pointing to Jean-Luc Godard and the phrase that cinema is "truth 24 times a second" Mulvey recasts this as "death 24 times a second" (15) expanding that if the photograph freezes reality, it creates a transition from inanimate image to animate cinema rather than Godard's inverse notion that begins with the animation of life and thus truth, to inanimate still image that is featured 24 times a second.

7. See David L. Roberts and Andrew R. Solow (245) for an assessment of the date of extinction. They estimate it was thirty years after previous estimations.

8. Flagship species should be understood as distinct from "keystone" and "umbrella" species, those that play a more vital ecological, rather than populist, role and are afforded enhanced conservation status due to the "ecological roles they perform" (Lorimer "Nonhuman Charisma," 923).

9. Although iconic species collapse the politicization of ecologies into a narrow and consumable optic, they are a powerful tool for fundraising. Under the umbrella of the "panda brand" the WWF raises money and campaigns not only for the species but also for all global biodiversity and, by extension, for policies to ameliorate climate change, reduce deforestation, and prevent water pollution (see wwf.org). Resources amassed from the charisma of the panda trickle-down all over the world.

10. Fatimah Tobing Rony presents further detail about this sphere of filmmaking.

11. Luca Comerio's 57-minute film, titled *From the Pole to the Equator* was released in 1929 and shot between 1898 and the early 1920s. Comerio's footage, including the hunting of Arctic animals, appears in Yervant Gianikian and Angela Ricci-Lucchi's 1986 feature length remix of Comerio's archive, also titled *From the Pole to the Equator*.

12. After World War II there was a renewed interest in ethnographic film set in the Arctic (for example *Eskimo Hunters of Northwest Alaska*, 1949, and *Face of the High Arctic*, 1959), and the genre of the travel film offered a new frame for images of Arctic life and landscape (*Alaskan Adventure*, 1959, *Arctic Thrills*, 1927/1956). There was also a new interest in wildlife on film, one that had not been seen since the adventure films of the 1920s. This revival was lead, as Cynthia Chris writes (28–41), by Disney's True-Life Adventures. A pinnacle of this genre, *White Wilderness* (1958) brought images of Arctic wildlife to a new audience.

13. The extent of this dissimulation is demonstrated by the fact that, as Ginsburg describes, many Inuit served as technicians during the course of the production of the film (92).

14. Sir William Mackenzie, the Canadian railroad entrepreneur and Flaherty's employer when he was a young man offered pivotal advice as Flaherty prepared for his third expedition to the Arctic in 1913, asking: "you're going into interesting country—strange people—and animals and all that—why don't you include in your outfit a camera for making film?" (Barnouw, 33).

15. Notably, Flaherty had wanted to capture the caribou migration when he was shooting *Nanook* but was thwarted because he was shooting in the wrong location (Mitman, 41).

16. The structuring presence of the journey mirrors the impetus of *Sweetgrass* in many respects. However, while *Sweetgrass* is concerned with shepherding and farm animals, *Being Caribou* is about wild animals and following, expressing the materiality *and* the agency of animals.

17. Notably, Hansen describes Kracauer's interest in " 'the flow of life' as the locus of opacity and indeterminacy—not just a multiplicity of and changeability of meanings but the possibility of a basic indifference to sense and legibility" ("Introduction," xxx). This open-ended approach to "life" in cinema was integral to his approach to film realism within which a move away from intention and humanism was also a move away from and part of his critique of the bourgeois subject.

18. As Hansen notes, for Kracauer, "some types of narrative are more apt than others to mobilize the medium's purchase on material contingency, to maintain an awareness of the tensions involved in their own construction" ("Introduction," xxxii). In this vein, I pose *Being Caribou* with its aesthetic of following, as working towards this type of documentary narrative.

19. Bousé offers useful criteria for defining blue chip films, including the depiction of "megafauna," visual splendor, dramatic narrative and the absence of history and politics ("Are Wildlife," 134). The move toward what Molloy refers

to as "ecological entertainment," which includes commentary about environmental degradation in the film, indicates a shift in this subgenre since Bousé was writing in 1998. Morgan Richards offers an account of the shift from blue chip to "green chip" wildlife film in a British context since 2000 ("Greening Wildlife").

20. *Arctic Tale* only recorded a modest $2 million on theatrical release, a sum that is nevertheless sizable for a documentary. Producers note that the film was predicted to achieve far fewer returns than *March of the Penguins*, but they perceived the value of the film to lie in its potential for raising funds for and awareness about the environment. In an article in the *Washington Post*, a marketing executive for Paramount Classics, the distributor for *Arctic Tale*, states: "it's important for us to put our money where our mouth is. We feel it's important people feel that just by going to the movie, they've done something. They've taken a step in the right direction" (Thomson). The film followed the same model of distribution used with *An Inconvenient Truth*, with 5 percent of the film's gross returns earmarked for a fund to benefit four pro-wildlife organizations.

21. *Earth* was produced by BBC Worldwide and Greenlight Media. The film was released in Europe in 2007 and in the United States in 2009 as the first feature to be distributed under the Disneynature brand established in 2008. Patrick Stewart narrated the U.K. version and James Earl Jones replaced him for U.S. distribution. Much of the footage shot for *Earth* also appears in the BBC/Discovery television series narrated by David Attenborough, *Planet Earth* (2006), with the Arctic footage featuring in the episode titled *Ice Worlds*.

22. See Morgan Richards for a discussion of the problem of climate science in BBC productions and a historical context for the British approach to scientism and natural history programming ("Greening Wildlife").

23. Throughout the 1950s, Disney's True-Life Adventure series offered a renaissance to the wildlife genre that had existed in the silent period, bringing renewed popularity to nature on the big screen. Disney's series relied on strong cinematography and a premise that "nature" dictated the drama that was both visual and described in narration. Chris describes the structure of the drama in these films as concerned with animals' struggle for existence in the face of harsh and/or beautiful landscapes. Notably, even in the 1950s, the Disney films were ridiculed by critics for their use of melodramatic codes, which were thought to impinge on the "documentary ethos" (Chris 35).

24. As I described in chapter 1, wildlife film and television has an ambiguous relationship with the category "documentary." Bousé observes that in the film industry and in television schedules documentary is the preferred category for wildlife film. Yet accounts of film history, and in film and media studies more widely, wildlife film is, beyond some notable exceptions, seldom categorized as documentary ("Are Wildlife," 116). Wildlife, thus, exists on the margins in studies of documentary.

25. See Woodson for a fuller analysis of this ideological device in the film (428–432).

26. Although images of polar bears continue to proliferate, and it is thus constantly re-created in new moving image forms, films such as *Arctic Tale* contribute

to the expression of the flagship animal as a caricature, already defined by loss and the potential absence of extinction. Due to this definition, it is already well featured in the archive as an endangered species and participates in a vicious loop—a well-archived example of animal life is easily recruited into narratives of environmental decline. The thylacine offers an instructive example of this. As it approached extinction, its image proliferated in the archive. Carol Freeman identifies this in the late twentieth and early twenty-first century as "dozens of logos and emblems in Tasmania use the figure of the thylacine" (235). Its likeness is now popularized and recognizable, chronicled and embalmed into a predictable form, reworked and taken up across a range of contexts to symbolize cultural identity.

27. Moreover, charisma, for Lorimer, presents a targeted and prudent environmental ethics: "In contrast to the panoptic, normative, and utilitarian ethics of the official discourse of biodiversity conservation, which exhorts us to save everything, everywhere, to preserve our life-support system, an environmental ethics of nonhuman charisma is relational, ethological, and affective" ("Nonhuman Charisma," 928).

Chapter 5. Antarctica, Science, and Exploration: Encounters at the End of the World

1. From behind the camera Ponting also experienced the technical difficulties of filming in the extreme cold and with unpredictable animals. As Daniel Lynch writes, the work itself was life threatening and he constantly risked frostbite, lost a part of his tongue, which froze when using it to assist with rethreading the camera and was almost taken by killer whales who approached under a sheet of thin ice (292).

2. See the work of John Pickstone, *Ways of Knowing: A New History of Science, Technology and Medicine*, for an account of how different ways of knowing developed through the history of science, with observation and description an early method in this history.

3. Together they made the one-minute film, *Cheese Mites* (1903), an early landmark science film shot through a microscope.

4. Yet, natural history filmmakers were perceived through their classed associations with "artisans" rather than professionals. Excluded from the elite biological sciences of the time, natural history of this kind was denigrated, aligned with popular science and yet also seen as an avenue for professional biologists to extend their influence over public understandings of nature (Boon 16).

5. Leane and Nichol also describe Frank Hurley's film of Ernest Shackleton's 1914–1917 expedition, noting that on failing to secure images of animals on his first trip, he returned to the island of South Georgia to get footage, specifically, of penguins. He had seen Ponting's illustrated lectures and was so impressed by the animal theatrics he thought it was crucial to include similar footage to ensure the successful reception of the film (137).

6. While in his discussion of celebrity and the environment Dan Brockington includes Attenborough in a formulation that marries celebrity and conservation culture, I choose to locate Attenborough more squarely in relation to popular science, acknowledging his long history of television work that only explicitly explored the politics of environmentalism since 2000.

7. See Helen Wheatley for a discussion of the ways in which wildlife film to international distribution and the ease with which voiceovers are replaced to increase the appeal for local audiences (328–330). See Morgan Richards for a further discussion about BBC Initiative to produce wildlife content that might be marketable internationally, particularly to the United States ("Global Nature").

8. Simon Cottle ties the environmental conservatism of natural history television with the requirement for international distribution: "Entertainment-based channels and distributors seeking to maximize audiences are generally disposed to avoid contentious, audience splitting issues and a general avoidance of the 'gloom and doom' series (such as those purportedly thought to have turned away audiences in the 1970s) acts as a further barrier to the production of environmentally engaged programmes" (97). Writing in 2004, he notes the shift, albeit slight, toward more environmentally political programs, such as *State of the Planet*.

9. See Cottle for a description of the conscious move, on the part of the BBC, to include human activity in the natural history genre as a way to reinvigorate the form (94–95).

10. In a 2002 response to George Monbiot, who criticized Attenborough for not attending to environmental crisis in every production (*State of the Planet*, 2000, was the first of his series to address ecological politics), he outlined his core alignment with zoology: "There is a science called zoology. People study it at universities because they are deeply interested in the nature of other animals, the way they live and the processes of evolution that have brought them into existence. The present BBC 1 series, *The Life of Mammals*, is I hope catering for the same interest among viewers" ("Planet of Fakes"). Monbiot offers a further critique/response to *Frozen Planet* in 2011.

11. Wheatley identifies that with the increasing focus on spectacle, the proportion of screen time that features voiceover narration has lessened in the case of blue chip examples (334). This might be understood as a move toward the cinematic, and away from the televisual, which emphasizes listening as much as gazing.

12. For further information about the importance of this footage and how it was obtained, see an article by the producer of this episode, Dan Rees.

13. Moreover, Eric Ames recent book, *Ferocious Reality: Documentary According to Werner Herzog*, convincingly locates Herzog's work within the terms and codes of documentary.

14. Praeger discusses the complex relation between romanticism, Herzog and his films at greater length (11–16).

15. Herzog's goal to produce a vastly different film to these predecessors is certainly fulfilled, despite the fact that the most discussed scene in the film focuses on a lone penguin, as I describe later.

16. Just as Herzog scripts some of the interview dialogue in the film, it is not difficult to believe he encouraged the scientist to present himself in this way for filming.

17. For Ames, this sequence offers an implicit commentary on *March of the Penguins* and the debates that followed its release, especially criticisms of the normative family values expressed in the film. Ames writes that the lone, disoriented penguin indicates solitude and death, which are set in opposition to the "heroic and sentimental journey of the family" (260) in the earlier film.

18. Significantly, Grosz also discusses art and artfulness through Darwinian theory, tying it to sexual selection and locating it as part of human and nonhuman life: "life is artistic in the biological forms it induces, in the variations in patterns of living it generates and, above all, in the forces of sexual intensification, as highly variable as these are, it proliferates" (173).

Chapter 6. The Nonfiction of YouTube and "Naturecams": Posthumanism and Reflections on Agency

1. In posing this taxonomy, I draw on Craig Hight's mapping of the changing mutations between the digital and documentary media (3–7).

2. Primary examples discussed by Elsaesser and Hagener include *Waltz with Bashir* and *Waking Life*, films that not only employ animation techniques, but also convey a dreamlike quality, staging the drama between the terms of agency and the unconscious.

3. Rose's formulation also incorporates contemporary discoveries in science that have led to a recognition that it may not be possible for humans to comprehend the complexity of ecosystems; with the assertion that "the whole is greater than its parts" (*Wild Dog Dreaming*, 46) some scientists have signaled a radical rethinking of past certitude about the cosmos and life as it exists on Earth.

4. Treadwell would not have been able to document his life with the bears without the mobility and affordability of this video equipment. Larger electronic cameras of a previous era, let alone film cameras would not have proved as mobile or durable.

Chapter 7. In Conclusion: Documentary, Science, and the Umwelt

1. Jakob von Uexküll (1864–1944) was writing primarily during the first half of the twentieth century. His work on the environments of animals has influenced many well-known philosophers including Martin Heidegger, Jacques Lacan, Maurice Merleau-Ponty, Gilles Deleuze, and Giogio Agamben. Brett Buchanan explores this legacy in his book *Onto-Ethologies: The Animal Environments of Uexküll, Heidegger, Merleau-Ponty and Deleuze.*

2. For further discussion of this point, particularly in relation to Charles Darwin, see Grosz (176).

Works Cited

Adams, William M. *Against Extinction: The Story of Conservation*. London: Earth-scan, 2004.

Aitken, Ian. "Distraction and Redemption: Kracauer, Surrealism and Phenomenology." *Screen* 39.2 (1998): 124–140.

Ames, Eric. *Ferocious Reality: Documentary According to Werner Herzog*. Minneapolis: University of Minnesota Press, 2012.

Arctic Climate Impact Assessment. *Impacts of a Warming Arctic: Arctic Climate Impact Assessment*. Arctic Council. New York: Cambridge University Press, 2004.

Austin, Thomas. *Watching the World: Screen Documentary and Audiences*. Manchester: Manchester University Press, 2007.

Banting, Pamela. "The Ontology and Epistemology of Walking: Animality in Karsten Heuer's Being Caribou: Five Months on Foot with an Arctic Herd." *Greening the Maple: Canadian Ecocriticism in Context*. Ella Soper and Nicholas Bradley (eds). Calgary: University of Calgary Press, 2013.

Barker, Jennifer M. *The Tactile Eye: Touch and the Cinematic Experience*. Los Angeles: University of California Press, 2009.

———. "Chew On This: Disgust, Delay, and the Documentary Image in *Food, Inc.*" *Film-Philosophy* 15.2 (2011): 70–89.

Barnett, Clive, Paul Cloke, Nick Clarke, and Alice Malpass. *Globalizing Responsibility: The Political Rationalities of Ethical Consumption*. West Sussex: Wiley-Blackwell, 2011.

Barnouw, Erik. *Documentary: A History of the Non-Fiction Film*. Oxford: Oxford University Press, 1993.

Bazin, André. *Qu'est-ce Que le Cinéma?* Paris: Éditions du Cerf, 1958–1962.

Bengtson, Sven-Axel. "The Great Auk (Pinguinus Impennis): Anecdotal Evidence and Conjectures." *The Auk: A Quarterly Journal of Ornothology* 101.1 (1984): 1–12.

Bennett, Jane. *Vibrant Matter: A Political Ecology of Things*. Durham: Duke University Press, 2009.

Benson, Thomas W. "The Rhetorical Structure of Frederick Wiseman's *Primate*." *Critical Questions: Invention, Creativity, and the Criticism of Discourse and*

Media. William L. Nothstine, Carole Blair, and Gary Copeland (eds.). New York: St. Martin's Press, 1994. 189–205.

Berger, John. "Why look at Animals." *About Looking*. New York: Pantheon Books, 1980. 3–28.

Blewitt, John. *Media, Ecology and Conservation: Using the Media to Protect the World's Wildlife and Ecosystems*. Totnes: Green Books, 2010.

Bogle, Ariel. "The Sky's the Limit: Why We Cheer When Birds Attack Drones." *Slate*, October 28, 2014. Web. February 16, 2015.

Boon, Timothy. *Films of Fact: A History of Science in Documentary Films and Television*. London: Wallflower Press, 2008.

Bousé, Derek. "Are Wildlife Films Really 'Nature Documentaries'?" *Critical Studies in Mass Communication* 15 (1998): 116–140.

———. *Wildlife Films*. Philadelphia: University of Pennsylvania Press, 2000.

Brereton, Pat. *Hollywood Utopia: Ecology in American Cinema*. Bristol: Intellect, 2005.

Brinkema, Eugenie. *The Forms of the Affects*. Durham: Duke University Press, 2014.

Brockington, Dan. *Celebrity and the Environment: Fame, Wealth and Power in Conservation*. London: Zed Books, 2009.

Brower, Matthew. *Developing Animals: Wildlife and Early American Photography*. Minneapolis: University of Minnesota Press, 2011.

Buchanan, Brett. *Onto-Ethologies: The Animal Environments of Uexküll, Heidegger, Merleau-Ponty, and Deleuze*. Albany: State University of New York Press, 2008.

Buchanan, Brett, Jeffrey Bussolini, and Matthew Chrulew. "General Introduction: Philosophical Ethology." *Angelaki: Journal of the Theoretical Humanities* 19.3 (2014): 1–3.

Burke, Edmund. *A Philosophical Enquiry into the Origin of Our Ideas of the Sublime and Beautiful*. London: Routledge and Kegan Paul, 1958.

Burt, Jonathan. *Animals in Film. Locations*. London: Reaktion Books, 2002.

———. "John Berger's 'Why Look at Animals?': A Close Reading," *Worldviews* 9 (2005): 203–218.

———. "Review: A Day in the Life of a Massachusetts Slaughterhouse." *Society & Animals* 13:4 (2005): 347–354.

———. "Morbidity and Vitalism: Derrida, Bergson, Deleuze, and Animal Film Imagery." *Configurations* 1–2.14 (2006): 157–179.

Calarco, Matthew. *The Question of the Animal: From Heidegger to Derrida*. New York: Columbia University Press, 2008.

Chris, Cynthia. *Watching Wildlife*. Minneapolis: University of Minnesota Press, 2006.

Chrulew, Matthew. "Managing Love and Death at the Zoo: The Biopolitics of Endangered Species Preservation." *Australian Humanities Review* 50 (2011). www.australianhumanitiesreview.org/archive/Issue-May-2011/chrulew. html#bio

———. "Animals in Biopolitical Theory: Between Agamben and Negri." *New Formations* 76 (2012): 53–67.

Colebrook, Claire. *Death of the PostHuman: Essays on Extinction, Vol. 1*. Ann Arbor: Open Humanities Press, 2014.

Corner, John. "Documenting the Political." *Studies in Documentary* Film 3:2 (2009): 113–129.

Corrigan, Timothy. *The Essay Film: From Montaigne, After Marker*. Oxford: Oxford University Press, 2011.

———. "The Pedestrian Ecstasies of Werner Herzog." *A Companion to Werner Herzog*. Brad Prager (ed.). West Sussex: Wiley-Blackwell, 2012. 80–98.

Cottle, Simon. "Producing Nature (s): On the Changing Production Ecology of Natural History TV." *Media, Culture & Society* 26.1 (2004): 81–101.

Cowie, Elizabeth. *Recording Reality, Desiring the Real*. Minneapolis: University of Minnesota Press, 2011.

Cronin, Paul (ed.). *Herzog on Herzog*. London: Faber & Faber, 2002.

Csordas, Thomas. "Embodiment and Cultural Phenomenology." *Perspectives on Embodiment: The Intersections of Nature and Culture* (1999): 143–162.

Cubitt, Sean. *EcoMedia*. Amsterdam: Rodopi, 2005.

———, Salma Monani, and Stephen Rust (eds.). *Ecocinema Theory and Practice*. New York: Routledge, 2012.

Daney, Serge. "The Screen of Fantasy (Bazin and Animals)." Trans. Mark A. Cohen. *Rites of Realism: Essays on Corporeal Film*. Ivone Margulies (ed.). Durham: Duke University Press, 2003. 32–41.

Darwin, Charles. *The Origin of Species by Means of Natural Selection: Or, The Preservation of Favored Races in the Struggle for Life*. 6th ed. London: John Murray, 1880.

———. *The Descent of Man (Part One)*. Pref. Major Leonard Darwin. London: Watts & Co., 1930.

Daston, Lorraine, and Gregg Mitman. "Introduction: The How and Why of Thinking with Animals." *Thinking with Animals: New Perspectives on Anthropomorphism*. Lorraine Daston and Gregg Mitman (eds.). New York: Columbia University Press. 1–14.

Derrida, Jacques. *Archive Fever: A Freudian Impression*. Chicago: University of Chicago Press, 1996.

———. "The Animal That Therefore I Am (More to Follow)." Trans. Gary Wills. *Critical Inquiry* 28.2 (2002): 369–418.

De Vos, Ricardo. "Extinction Stories: Performing Absence(s)." *Knowing Animals*. Laurence Simmons and Philip Armstrong (eds.). Leiden: Brill, 2007. 183–195.

Dickey-Collas, Mark, et al. "Lessons Learned from Stock Collapse and Recovery of North Sea Herring: A Review." *ICES Journal of Marine Science: Journal du Conseil* 67.9 (2010): 1875–1886.

Discovery Communications. Corporate Discovery, 2015. Web. November 12, 2015.

Ebert, Roger. "Grizzly Man." *RogerEbert.Com*. August 11, 2005. Web. January 24, 2015.

Elsaesser, Thomas, and Malte Hagener. *Film Theory: An Introduction Through the Senses*. London: Routledge, 2010.

Flanagan, Matthew. "Towards an Aesthetic of Slow in Contemporary Cinema." *16:9* 29 (2008). Web.

Foucault, Michel. *The Will to Knowledge*. Trans. Robert Hurley. 3 vols. *Vol. 1, The History of Sexuality*. London: Penguin Books, 1998.

Friedberg, Anne. *The Virtual Window: From Alberti to Microsoft*. Cambridge: MIT Press, 2006.

Fudge, Erica. "A Left-Handed Blow: Writing the History of Animals." *Representing Animals*. Nigel Rothfels (ed.). Bloomington: Indiana University Press, 2002. 3–18.

Gaines, Jane. "The Production of Outrage: The Iraq War and the Radical Documentary Tradition." *Framework* 48.2 (2007): 36–55.

Ginsburg, Faye. "Indigenous Media: Faustian Contract or Global Village?" *Cultural Anthropology* 6.1 (1991): 92–112.

Gorfinkel, Elena. "Weariness, Waiting: Enduration and Art Cinema's Tired Bodies." *Discourse: Journal for Theoretical Studies in Media and Culture* 34.2–3 (2012): 311–347.

Grant, Barry Keith. *Voyages of Discovery: The Cinema of Fredrick Wiseman*. Urbana: University of Illinois Press, 1992.

Greenpeace USA. "Marmot Licks GoPro." Online video clip. YouTube. YouTube, August 9, 2014. Web. September 9, 2015.

Grimshaw, Anna. "The Bellweather Ewe: Recent Developments in Ethnographic Filmmaking and the Aesthetics of Anthropological Enquiry." *Cultural Anthropology* 26:2 (2011): 247–262.

Grosz, Elizabeth. *Becoming Undone: Darwinian Reflections on Life, Politics, and Art*. Durham: Duke University Press, 2011.

Hansen, Miriam. "'With Skin and Hair': Kracauer's Theory of Film, Marseille 1940." *Critical Inquiry* 19 (1993): 437–469.

———. "Introduction." *Theory of Film: The Redemption of Physical Reality*. Siegfried Kracauer. Princeton: Princeton University Press, 1997. vii–xlv.

Haraway, Donna. *When Species Meet*. Minneapolis: University of Minnesota Press, 2008.

Hardt, Michael, and Antonio Negri. *Multitude: War and democracy in the Age of Empire*. London: Penguin, 2005.

Heise, Ursula K. "Lost Dogs, Last Birds, and Listed Species: Cultures of Extinction." *Configurations* 18.1–2 (2010): 49–62.

Higgins, Lynn A. "Documentary in an Age of Terror." *South Central Review* 22:2 (2005): 20–38.

Hight, Craig. "The Field of Digital Documentary: A Challenge to Documentary Theorists." *Studies in Documentary Film* 2.1 (2008): 3–7.

Hilton, Matthew. "The Legacy of Luxury: Moralities of Consumption Since the 18th Century." *Journal of Consumer Culture* 4 (2004): 101–123.

Hilton-Taylor, Craig, et al. "State of the World's Species." *Wildlife in a Changing World–An Analysis of the 2008 IUCN Red List of Threatened Species*. Vié, Jean-Christophe, Craig Hilton-Taylor, and Simon N. Stuart (eds.). Gland, Switzerland: IUCN, 2009. 15–42.

Hinchliffe, Steve. "Reconstituting Nature Conservation: Towards a Careful Political Ecology." *Geoforum* 39 (2008): 88–97.

Horak, Jan-Christopher. "Wildlife Documentaries: From Classical Forms to Reality TV." *Film History* 18.4 (2006): 459–475.

Hughes, Helen. "Scrutiny and Documentary: Hubert Sauper's *Darwin's Nightmare*." *Screen* 53:3 (2012): 246–265.

———. *Green Documentary: Environmental Documentary in the 21st Century*. Bristol: Intellect Books, 2014.

Husserl, Edmund. *The Crisis of European Sciences and Transcendental Phenomenology: An Introduction to Phenomenological Philosophy*. Trans. David Carr. Evanston: Northern University Press, 1970.

Ingram, David. *Green Screen: Environmentalism and Hollywood Cinema*. Exeter: University of Exeter Press, 2000.

Ivakhiv, Adrian J. *Ecologies of the Moving Image: Cinema, Affect, Nature*. Waterloo: Wilfrid Laurier University Press, 2013.

Jeffries, Michael. "BBC Natural History Versus Science Paradigms." *Science As Culture* 12.4 (2003): 527–545.

Jeong, Seung Hoon, and Dudley Andrew. "Grizzly Ghost: Herzog, Bazin and the Cinematic Animal." *Screen* 49.1 (2008): 1–12.

Kirksey, S. Eben, and Stefan Helmreich. "The Emergence of Multispecies Ethnography." *Cultural Anthropology* 25.4 (2010): 545–576.

Koehler, Robert. "Agrarian Utopias/Dystopias: The New Nonfiction." *Cinema Scope* 40 (2009): 12–15.

———. "*Sweetgrass* and the Future of Nonfiction Cinema." Public Broadcasting Service. *POV: Documentaries with a Point of View* July 5, 2011. Web. February 20, 2014.

Kracauer, Siegfried. *Theory of Film: The Redemption of Physical Reality*. Princeton: Princeton University Press, 1997.

Ladino, Jennifer K. "For the Love of Nature: Documenting Life, Death and Animality in *Grizzly Man* and *March of the Penguins*." *Interdisciplinary Studies in Literature and the Environment* 16.1 (2009): 53–90.

———. "Working with Animals: Regarding Companion Species in Documentary Film." *Ecocinema Theory and Practice*. Sean Cubitt, Salma Monani, Stephen Rust (eds.). New York: Routledge, 2012.

Lage, Sandrine. "Is Documentary the Privileged Genre of Eco-Cinema?" *Dox: European Documentary Magazine*. September 2, 2014. Web.

Leakey, Richard E., and Roger Lewin. *The Sixth Extinction: Patterns of Life and the Future of Humankind*. New York: Doubleday, 1995.

Leane, Elizabeth, and Stephen Nicol. "Filming the Frozen South: Animals in Early Antarctic Exploration Films." *Screening Nature: Cinema Beyond the Human*. Anat Pick and Guinevere Narraway (eds.). New York: Berghahn Books, 2013. 127–142.

Leitner, Florian. "On Robots and Turtles: A Posthuman Perspective on Camera and Image Movment after Michael Snow's *La Région Centrale*." *Discourse* 35.2 (2013): 263–277.

Lindenfeld, Laura. "Can Documentary Food Films Like Food Inc. Achieve their Promise?" *Environmental Communication* 4:3 (2010): 378–386.

———. "Digging Down to the Roots On the Radical Potential of Documentary Food Films." *Radical History Review* 110 (2011): 155–160.

Lippit, Akira Mizuta. *Electric Animal: Toward a Rhetoric of Wildlife*. Minneapolis: University of Minnesota Press, 2000.

Lorimer, Jamie. "Nonhuman Charisma." *Environment and Planning D: Society and Space* 25 (2007): 911–932.

———. "Moving Image Methodologies for More-than-Human Geographies." *Cultural Geographies* 17.2 (2010): 237–258.

Lynch, Dennis. "The Worst Location in the World: Herbert G. Ponting in the Antarctic, 1910–1912." *Film History* 3 (1989): 291–306.

MacDonald, Scott. *The Garden in the Machine: A Field Guide to Independent Films About Place*. Berkeley: University of California Press, 2001.

———. "Toward an Eco-cinema." *Interdisciplinary Studies in Literature and Environment* 11.2 (2004): 107–132.

———. *American Ethnographic Film and Personal Documentary: The Cambridge Turn*. Berkeley: University of California Press, 2013.

Mitman, Gregg. *Reel Nature: America's Romance with Wildlife on Film*. 2nd ed. Cambridge, MA: Harvard University Press, 2009.

Molloy, Claire. *Popular Media and Animals*. New York: Palgrave Macmillan, 2011.

———. "Nature Writes the Screenplays: Commercial Wildlife Films and Ecological Entertainment." Rust, Stephen, Salma Monani, and Sean Cubitt (eds.). *Ecocinema Theory and Practice*. London: Routledge, 2013. 169–188.

Monbiot, George. "Planet of Fakes." *Guardian*, December 17, 2002.

Mulvey, Laura. *Death 24x a Second: Stillness and the Moving Image*. London: Reaktion Books, 2006.

Murray, Robin L., and Joseph K. Heumann. *Ecology and Popular Film: Cinema on the Edge*. Albany: State University of New York Press, 2009.

———. "Contemporary Eco-Food Films: The Documentary Tradition." *Studies in Documentary Film* 6.1 (2012): 43–59.

———. *Film and Everyday Eco-disasters*. Lincoln: University of Nebraska Press, 2014.

Newbury, Michael. "Fast Zombie/Slow Zombie: Food Writing, Horror Movies, and Agribusiness Apocalypse." *American Literary History* 24: 1 (2012): 87–114.

Nichols, Bill. *Representing Reality*. Bloomington: Indiana University Press, 1991.

Paddle, Robert. *The Last Tasmanian Tiger: The History and Extinction of the Thylacine*. Cambridge: Cambridge University Press, 2000.

Petterson, Palle B. *Cameras Into the Wild: A History of early Wildlife and Expedition Filmmaking, 1925–1928*. Jefferson: Mcfarlane, 2011.

Peucker, Brigitte. "Herzog and Auteurism." *A Companion to Werner Herzog*. Brad Prager (ed.). West Sussex: Wiley-Blackwell, 2012. 35–57.

Pick, Anat. "*Ecovisions: Seeing Animals in Recent Ethnographic Film*." Vertigo 3.4 (2007): 33–37.

———. *Creaturely Poetics: Animality and Vulnerability in Literature and Film*. New York: Columbia University Press, 2011.

———. "Three Worlds: Dwelling and Worldhood on Screen." *Screening Nature: Cinema Beyond the Human*. Anat Pick and Guinevere Narraway (eds.). New York: Berghahn Books, 2013. 21–36.

———, and Guinevere Narraway (eds.). *Screening Nature: Cinema Beyond the Human*. New York: Berghahn Books, 2013.

Pickstone, John V. *Ways of Knowing: A New History of Science, Technology and Medicine*. Chicago: University of Chicago Press, 2000.

Pink, Sarah. *The Future of Visual Anthropology: Engaging the Senses*. London: Routledge, 2006.

Ponsoldt, James. "Interview: *Position Among the Stars*—Director Leonard Retel Helmrich." *Filmmaker Magazine* January 31, 2011. Web. March 1, 2014.

Prager, Brad. *The Cinema of Werner Herzog: Aesthetic Ecstasy and Truth*. London: Wallflower Press, 2007.

Public Broadcasting Service (PBS). "Interview with Ilisa Barbash and Lucien Casting-Taylor." *POV: Documentaries with a Point of View* July 5, 2011. Web. February 20, 2014.

Pyne, Stephen J. *The Ice: A Journey to Antarctica, Cycle of Fire*. Iowa City: University of Iowa Press, 1986.

Rabinowitz, Paula. "Sentimental Contracts: Dreams and Documents of American Labour." *Feminism and Documentary*. Janet Walker and Diane Waldman (eds.). Minneapolis: University of Minnesota Press, 1999. 43–63.

Rees, Dan. "Frozen Planet: Capturing the Wilkins Ice Shelf in Full Collapse." *Guardian* December 8, 2011. www.theguardian.com/environment/2011/dec/07/frozen-planet-ice-shelf-collapse

Rich, Ruby B. "Documentary Disciplines: An Introduction." *Cinema Journal* 46.1 (2006): 108–115.

Richards, Morgan. "Global Nature, Global Brand: BBC Earth and David Attenborough's Landmark Wildlife Series." *Media International Australia* 146 (2013a): 143–154.

———. "Greening Wildlife Documentary." *Environmental Conflict and the Media*. Libby Lester and Brett Hutchins (eds.) New York: Peter Lang, 2013b. 171–185.

Richardson-Ngwenya, Pamela, and Ben Richardson. "Documentary Film and Ethical Foodscapes: Three Takes on Caribbean Sugar." *Cultural Geographies* 20 (2013): 339–356.

Roberts, David L., and Andrew R. Solow. "Flightless Birds: When did the Dodo Become Extinct?" *Nature* 426 (2003): 245.

Rodowick, D.N. *The Virtual Life of Film*. Cambridge: Harvard University Press, 2009.

Roe, Emma. "Things Becoming Food and the Embodied, Material Practices of an Organic Food Consumer." *Sociologia Ruralis* 46. 2 (2006): 104–121.

Rony, Fatimah Tobing. *The Third Eye: Race, Cinema, and Ethnographic Spectacle*. Durham: Duke University Press, 1996.

Rose, Deborah Bird. "What if the Angel of History Were a Dog?" *Cultural Studies Review* 12.1 (2006): 67–78.

———. *Wild Dog Dreaming: Love and Extinction*. Charlottesville: University of Virginia Press, 2011.

Rundell, John. "Modernity, Humans and Animals—Tensions in the Field of the Technical-Industrial Imaginary." *New Formations* 76 (2012): 8–20.

Russell, Catherine. *Experimental Ethnography: The Work of Film in the Age of Video*. Durham: Duke University Press, 1999.

Schmidt, Christopher. "Hawk vs. Drone! (Hawk Attacks Quadcopter)." Online video clip. YouTube. YouTube, October 8, 2014. Web. September 9, 2015.

Sellbach, Undine. "The Traumatic Effort to Understand: Werner Herzog's *Grizzly Man*." *Considering Animals Contemporary Studies in Human-Animal Relations*. Carol Freeman, Elizabeth Leane, and Yvette Watt (eds.). Farnham: Ashgate, 2011.

Shaviro, Steven. *The Cinematic Body*. Minneapolis: University of Minnesota Press, 1993.

———. *The Universe of Things: On Speculative Realism*. Minneapolis: University of Minnesota Press, 2014.

Shoard, Catherine. "The Eco-Documentary: An Endangered Species?" *Guardian*. October 16, 2009.

Shukin, Nicole. *Animal Capital: Rendering Life in Biopolitical Times*. Minneapolis: University of Minnesota Press, 2009.

Siskind. Mariano. "Captain Cook and the Discovery of Antarctica's Modern Specificity: Towards a Critique of Globalization." *Comparative Literature Studies* 42.1 (2005): 1–23.

Sobchack, Vivian. "Inscribing Ethical Space: Ten propositions on Death, Representation, and Documentary." *Quarterly Review of Film Studies* 9.4 (1984): 283–300.

———. "Introduction." *Meta Morphing: Visual Transformation and the Culture of Quick-change*. Vivian Sobchack (ed.). Minneapolis: University of Minnesota Press, 2000. xi–xxiii.

———. *Carnal Thoughts: Embodiment and Moving Image Culture*. Berkeley: University of California Press, 2004.

Steingröver, Reinhild. "Encountering Werner Herzog at the End of the World." *A Companion to Werner Herzog*. Brad Prager (ed.). West Sussex: Wiley-Blackwell, 2012. 466–483.

Stern, Lesley. "Paths That Wind Through the Thicket of Things." *Critical Inquiry* 28:1 (2001): 317–354.

Thomson, Desson. "March of the Cuddly-Wuddly Documentaries." *Washington Post*, July 29, 2007.

Uexküll, Jakob von. "A Stroll Through the Worlds of Animals and Men." *Instinctive Behaviour: The Development of a Modern Concept*. Claire Schiller (ed. and trans.). New York: International Universities Press, 1957.

———. "An Introduction to Umwelt." *Semiotica* 134.1/4 (2001): 107–110.

————. "The New Concept of Umwelt: A Link Between Science and the Humanities." 2001.

————. *A Foray into the Worlds of Animals And Humans: With a Theory Of Meaning*. Minneapolis: University of Minnesota Press, 2010.

Van Dooren, Thom. *Flight Ways: Life and Loss at the Edge of Extinction*. New York: Columbia University Press, 2014.

Von Mossner, Alexa Weik (ed.). *Moving Environments: Affect, Emotion, Ecology, and Film*. Waterloo, Ontario: Wilfrid Laurier University Press, 2014.

Wahlberg, Malin. *Documentary Time: Film and Phenomenology*. Minneapolis: University of Minnesota Press, 2008.

Walker, Janet. "Eavesdropping in *The Cove*: Interspecies Ethics, Public and Private Space, and Trauma Under Water." *Studies in Documentary Film* 7.3 (2013): 209–232.

Waugh, Thomas (ed.). *Show Us Life: Toward a History and Aesthetics of the Committed Documentary*. Metuchen: Scarecrow Press, 1984.

Weil, Kari. "A Report on the Animal Turn." *Differences* 21.2 (2010): 1–23.

Weiss, Gail. *Body Images: Embodiment as Intercorporeality*. London: Routledge, 1999.

Welling, Bart H. "On the 'Inexplicable Magic of Cinema': Critical Anthropomorphism, Emotion, and the Wildness of Wildlife Films." *Moving Environments: Affect, Emotion, Ecology and Film*. Alexa Weik von Mossner (ed.). Waterloo, Ontario: Wilfrid Laurier University Press, 2014. 81–101.

Wheatley, Helen. "The Limits Of Television? Natural History Programming and the Transformation of Public Service Broadcasting." *European Journal of Cultural Studies* 7.3 (2004): 325–339.

Wilkins, Jennifer L. "Eating Right Here: Moving from Consumer to Food Citizen." *Agriculture and Human Values* 22 (2005): 269–273.

Williams, Deane. "*Industrial Britain*." *Encyclopedia of the Documentary Film*. Ian Aitken (ed.). London: Routledge, 2006. 622–624.

Willoquet-Maricondi, Paula (ed.). *Framing* the *World*: *Explorations* in *Ecocriticism* and *Film*. Charlottesville: University of Virginia Press, 2010.

Winston, Brian. *Claiming the Real: The Documentary Film Revisited*. London: BFI Publishing, 1995.

Woodson, Mary Beth. "Two Trips Across One Globe: *Earth* and *Planet Earth*." *Society and Animals* 18.4 (2010): 428–432.

Wolfe, Cary. *What Is Posthumanism?* Minneapolis: University of Minnesota Press, 2010.

Yusoff, Kathryn. "Biopolitical Economies and the Political Aesthetics of Climate Change." *Theory, Culture & Society* 27.2–3 (2010): 73–99.

————. "Aesthetics of Loss: Biodiversity, Banal Violence and Biotic Subjects." *Transactions of the Institute of British Geographers* 37.4 (2012): 578–592.

Filmography

90 Degrees South (90° South), Dir. Herbert Ponting, Antarctic Film Trust/New Era Films, 1933.

A Cow at My Table, Dir. Jennifer Abbott, Flying Eye Productions, 1998.

A Day in the Life of a Massachusetts Slaughterhouse, PETA, 1998.

African Animals, Dir. Cherry Kearton, 1909.

African Cats, Dir. Alastair Fothergill and Keith Scholey, Walt Disney Studios, 2011.

Alaskan Adventure, United World Films, 1959.

American Dream, Dir. Barbara Kopple, Cabin Creek/Catholic Communication Campaign/Channel Four Films, 1990.

American Meat, Dir. Graham Meriwether, The Orchard, 2013.

An Inconvenient Truth, Dir. Davis Guggenheim, Lawrence Bender Productions/Participant Media, 2006.

Animals, Dir. Arik Alon, Jaffa Films, 2003.

Arctic Tale, Dir. Adam Ravetch and Sarah Robertson, Visionbox Pictures/National Geographic Films/Starbucks Entertainment, 2007.

Arctic Thrills, Castle Films, 1927/1956.

Bacon, The Film (Bacon, le film), Dir. Hugo Latulippe, National Film Board of Canada, 2002.

Bears, Dir. Alastair Fothergill and Keith Scholey, Disneynature, 2014.

Beef, Inc., Dir. Carmen Garcia, National Film Board of Canada, 1999.

Being Caribou, Dir. Leanne Allison, National Film Board of Canada, 2004.

Bestiaire, Dir. Denis Côté, Metafilms/Le Fresnoy Studio National des Arts Contemporains, 2012.

Blackfish, Dir. Gabriela Cowperthwaite, Manny O Productions, 2013.

Bowling for Columbine, Dir. Michael Moore, Dog Eat Dog Films/Alliance Atlantis/Iconolatry Productions, 2002.

Chang: A Drama of the Wilderness, Dir. Merian C. Cooper and Ernest Schoedsack, Famous Players-Lasky Corporation/Paramount Pictures, 1927.

Cheese Mites, Dir. Charles Urban and Francis Martin Duncan, Charles Urban Trading Company, 1903.

Chimpanzee, Dir. Alastair Fothergill and Mark Linfield, Great Ape Productions, 2012.

Crittercam (television), Cre.Greg Marshall, National Geographic Television, 2004.

Darwin's Nightmare, Dir. Hubert Sauper, Mille et Une Productions/Coop 99/Saga Film, 2004.

Drifters, Dir. John Grierson, Empire Marketing Board/New Era Films, 1929.

Earth, Dir. Alastair Fothergill and Mark Linfield, Disneynature/BBC/Greenlight Media AG/Discovery Channel, 2007/2009.

Electrocuting an Elephant, Prod. Thomas Edison, Edison Manufacturing Company, 1903.

Elsewhere, Dir. Nikolaus Geyrhalter, Nikolaus Geyrhalter Filmproduktion GmbH, 2000.

Encounters at the End of the World, Dir. Werner Herzog, Creative Differences Productions/Discovery Channel, 2007.

End of the Line, Dir. Rupert Murray, Arcane Pictures/Clam Productions/Dartmouth Films, 2007.

Enron, The Smartest Guys in the Room, Dir. Alex Gibney, 2929 Entertainment/ HDNet Films, 2005.

Eskimo Hunters of Northwest Alaska, Dir. W. Kay Norton, Loius de Richemont Associates, 1949.

Être et Avoir (To be and to have), Dir. Nicholas Philibert, Maïa Films/Arte France Cinéma/Les Films d'Ici, 2002.

Eye of the Day (De stand vand de zon), Dir. Leonard Retel Helmrich, Scarabee Filmproducties Nederland, 2001.

Face of the High Arctic, Dir. Dalton Muir, National Film Board of Canada, 1959.

Fahrenheit 9/11, Dir. Michael Moore, Dog Eat Dog Films, 2004.

Farmageddon: The Truth About the Food and Dairy Industry, Dir. Kristin Canty, 2012.

Feeding the Doves, Dir. James H White, Edison Manufacturing Company, 1896.

Food, Inc., Dir. Robert Kenner, Participant Media/Dogwoof Pictures/River Road Entertainment, 2008.

Fresh, Dir. Ana Sofia Joanes, Ripple Effect Films, 2009.

From the Pole to the Equator, Dir. Luca Comerio, 1929.

From the Pole to the Equator, Dir. Yervant Gianikian and Angela Ricci-Lucchi, Gianikian-Ricci Lucchi/Zweites Deutsches Fernsehen (ZDF), 1986.

Frozen Planet (television), Nar. David Attenborough, BBC/Discovery Channel/ Antena 3 Televisión/ZDF/SKAI, 2011.

Gasland, Dir. Josh Fox, HBO Documentary Films/International WOW Company, 2010.

Grass: A Nation's Battle for Life, Dir. Merian C. Cooper and Ernest Schoedsack, Famous Players-Lasky Corporation/Paramount Pictures, 1925.

Green, Dir. Patrick Rouxel, 2009.

Grizzly Man, Dir. Werner Herzog, Real Big Production, 2005

Happy Feet, Dir. George Miller, Kingdom Feature Productions/Animal Logic/Kennedy Miller, 2006.

Heia Safari, Dir. Martin Rikli, Dr. Martin Rikli (Dresden), 1928.

I Do Not Know What It Is I Am Like, Dir. Bill Viola, 1986.

Industrial Britain, Dir. Robert Flaherty, John Grierson and Edgar Anstey, Empire Marketing Board, 1931.

King Corn, Dir. Aaron Woolf, ITVS/Mosaic Films, 2007.

King Kong, Dir. Merian C. Cooper and Ernest Schoedsack, RKO, 1933.

La Libertad, Dir Lisandro Alonso, 4L, 2001.

La Région Centrale, Dir. Michael Snow, 1971.

Le Peuple Migrateur (Winged Migration), Dir. Jacques Perrin, Jacques Cluzaud and Michel Debats, Canal+/Bac Films, 2001.

Le Sang des bêtes, Dir. Georges Franju, Forces et voix de la France, 1949.

Leviathan, Dir. Lucien Castaing-Taylor, Arrête ton Cinéma/Harvard Sensory Lab/ Le Bureau, 2013.

Los Herederos (The Inheritors), Dir. Eugenio Polgovsky, Tecolote Films/Visions Sud Est, 2008.

Louisiana Story, Dir. Robert Flaherty, Robert Flaherty Productions/Standard Oil, 1948.

Maharajah Burger, Dir. Thomas Balmès, Canal+/Quark Productions/TBC, 1997.

Man with a Movie Camera, Dir. Dziga Vertov, VUFKU, 1929.

March of the Penguins (La Marche de l'empereur), Dir. Luc Jacquet, National Geographic Films/Bonne Pioche/APC, 2005.

Meat, Dir. Fredric Wiseman, 1976.

Meat the Truth, Dir. Karen Soeters and Gertjan Zwanikken, Alalena, 2008.

Meet Your Meat, Dir. Bruce Friedrich, PETA, 2003.

Milk In The Land: Ballad of An American Drink, Dir. Ariana Gerstein and Monteith McCollum, Thirtymilesfromanywhere, 2007.

Mitote, Dir. Euhenio Polgovsky, Tecolote Films, 2012.

Mondo Cane, Dir. Gualtiero Jacopetti, Franco Prosperi and Paolo Cavara, Cineriz, 1962.

Monkey Kingdom, Dir. Alastair Fothergill and Mark Linfield, Disneynature/Silverback Films, 2015.

Mot ukjent land, Photo. Hjalmar Riiser-Larsen, Norvegua Film-Co., 1930.

Nanook of the North, Dir. Robert Flaherty, Les Frères Revillon/Pathé Exchange, 1922.

Native Lion Hunt, Dir. Cherry Kearton, 1909.

Night Mail, Dir. Harry Watt and Basil Wright, GPO Film Unit, 1936.

Oceans, Dir. Jacques Perrin and Jacques Cluzaud, Disneynature/Participant Media/Galatée Films/Pathé/Canal+, 2010.

Our Daily Bread, Dir. Nikolaus Geyrhalter, Nikolaus Geyrhalter Filmproduktion/ZDF/3Sat, 2005.

Pig Business, Dir. Tracy Worcester, Price of Progress Productions, 2009.

Planet Earth (television), Dir. Alastair Fothergill, Nar. David Attenborough, BBC/Discovery Channel, 2006.

Position Among the Stars, Dir. Leonard Retel Helmrich,Scarabee Filmproducties Nederland, 2010.

Primate, Dir. Fredric Wiseman, 1974.

Racetrack, Dir. Fredric Wiseman, 1984.

Raw Herring (Hollandse Nieuwe), Dir. Leonard Retel Helmrich and Hetty Naaijkens-Retel Helmrich, In-Soo Productions, 2013.

Rules of the Game, Dir. Jean Renoir, Nouvelles Éditions de Films, 1939.

Shape of the Moon, Dir. Leonard Retel Helmrich, Scarabee Filmproducties Nederland, 2004.

Sharkwater, Dir. Rob Stewart, Sharkwater Productions/Diatribe Pictures, 2006.

Simba: The King of Beasts, a Saga of the African Veldt, Dir. Martin and Osa Johnson, Martin Johnson Africa Expedition, 1928.

Sleep Furiously, Dir. Gideon Koppel, Bard Entertainments/Van Film, 2007.

South, Dir. Frank Hurley, Ralph Minden Film, 1919.

Spellbound, Dir. Jeffrey Blitz, Blitz/Welch, 2003.

State of the Planet (television), Dir. Kate Broome, Nar. David Attenborough, BBC/ Discovery Channel UK, 2000.

Supersize Me, Dir. Morgan Spurlock, Con, The/Kathbur Pictures, 2004.

Sweetgrass, Dir. Lucien Castaing-Taylor and Ilisa Barbash, Harvard Sensory Lab, 2009.

The Acrobatic Fly, Dir. Percy Smith, Charles Urban Trading Company, 1910.

The Animal Condition, Dir. Michael Dahlstrom, Code Talk Films, 2014.

The Blue Planet (television), Prod. Alastair Fothergill, Nar. David Attenborough, BBC/ARD, 2001.

The Burning Stable, Dir. James H White, Edison Manufacturing Company, 1896.

The Corporation, Dir. Mark Achbar and Jennifer Abbott, Big Picture Media, 2004.

The Cove, Dir. Louie Psihoyos, Diamond Docs/Skyfish Films, 2009.

The Great White Silence, Dir. Herbert Ponting, Gaumont British Picture, 1924.

The Last Ocean, Dir. Peter Young, Fisheye Films, 2012.

The Life of Mammals (television), Nar. David Attenborough, BBC/Discovery Channel UK, 2002.

The Love Life of an Octopus, Dir. Jean Painlevé, 1965.

The Moo Man, Dir. Andy Heathcote, Trufflepig Films/Bachelier Filmproduktion, 2012.

The Private Life of the Gannets, Dir. Julian Huxley, London Film Productions/Skibo Productions, 1934.

The Romance of the Far Fur Country, Hudson's Bay Company, 1920.

The Seahorse, Dir. Jean Painlevé, Cinégraphie Documentaire, 1934.

The Undying Story of Captain Scott, Photo. Herbert Ponting, Gaumont British Picture, 1914.

The Wedding of Palo, Dir. Friedrich Dalsheim, Palladium, 1934.

The Yes Men, Dir. Dan Ollmann, Sarah Price and Chris Smith, Yes Men Films, 2003.

To Live with Herds, Dir. David and Judith MacDougall, 1972.

Touching the Void, Dir. Kevin Macdonald, Darlow Smithson Productions/Channel 4/PBS, 2004.

Toy Story, Dir. John Lasseter, Pixar/Walt Disney Pictures, 1995.

Tropico de Cancer, Dir. Eugenio Polgovsky, Centro de Capacitación Cinematográfica, 2004.

Waking Life, Dir. Richard Linklater, Flat Black Films/Detour Filmproduction, 2001.

Waltz with Bashir, Dir. Ari Folman, Bridgit Folman Film Gang/Les Films d'Ici/ Razor Film Produktion GmbH, 2008.

We Feed the World, Dir. Erwin Wagenhofer, Allegro Film, 2005.

White Wilderness, Dir. James Algar, Walt Disney Pictures, 1958.

Zoo, Dir. Fredric Wiseman, Zipporah Films, 1993.

Index